Isaac Taylor

Etruscan researches

Isaac Taylor

Etruscan researches

ISBN/EAN: 9783741159282

Manufactured in Europe, USA, Canada, Australia, Japa

Cover: Foto ©Andreas Hilbeck / pixelio.de

Manufactured and distributed by brebook publishing software (www.brebook.com)

Isaac Taylor

Etruscan researches

ETRUSCAN RESEARCHES

BY

ISAAC TAYLOR, M.A.

VICAR OF HOLY TRINITY, TWICKENHAM
AUTHOR OF 'WORDS AND PLACES'

London
MACMILLAN AND CO.
1874

All rights reserved

PREFACE.

No one can be more conscious than myself of the shortcomings of this book. I will not, however, apologise for them, as I am sure that my readers will make full allowances for the difficulties and perils which beset the explorer of an unknown territory.

I have avoided technical language, and have endeavoured throughout to introduce such popular explanations as might make the book intelligible to any ordinary educated person. Readers who have no special fondness for philological investigations will probably content themselves with the perusal of the first six chapters and the last.

Exception will perhaps be taken to certain assumptions which I have made as to the ethnic affinities of the Picts, Egyptians, Lycians, and Sabines. I trust before long to be able to justify these assertions by the production of the requisite evidence.

I had hoped to have added an appendix, dealing with the laws which regulate phonetic changes in the several Ugric languages; but space and time have failed me. I must therefore content myself with referring to the two treatises which Dr. W. Schott has written on the subject.[1] I have confined myself rigorously to those phonetic equivalencies which he has succeeded in establishing.

I have to acknowledge special obligations to four preceding labourers. Fabretti's exhaustive collection of Etruscan inscriptions[2] has made the task of interpreting the Etruscan language tenfold easier than it would otherwise have been. It might almost be affirmed that the completion of this great work at once rendered inevitable, sooner or later, the recovery of the Etruscan language and the interpretation of the Etruscan records.

[1] *Ueber das Altai'sche oder Finnisch-Tatarische Sprachengeschlecht*, Berlin, 1849; *Versuch über die Tatarischen Sprachen*, Berlin, 1836.

[2] *Corpus Inscriptionum Italicarum.* Turin, 1867.

My obligations to Mr. George Dennis[1] are scarcely smaller in amount. No less essential have been the Grammars and Vocabularies of Siberian languages, and the digest of the mythology of the Kalevala, which we owe to Alexander Castrén.[2] Where Castrén failed me, I have made cautious use of the Asia Polyglotta of Klaproth, as well as of the monographs of Böhtlingk, Wiedemann, Schiefner, and other German and Russian scholars.

[1] *Cities and Cemeteries of Etruria.* 2 vols. London, 1848.
[2] *Nordische Reisen und Forschungen.* 11 vols. St. Petersburg, 1849-1862.

CONTENTS.

CHAPTER I. THE PROLOGUE.
Outline of the argument 1

CHAPTER II. TYRRHENIANS AND TURANIANS.
Historic and ethnologic starting points. Explanations of terms 10

CHAPTER III. ETHNOGRAPHIC NOTES ON THE ETRUSCAN PEOPLE.
The Turanian affinities of the Etruscans as indicated by their sepulchral usages, their magical practices, their law of inheritance, their physical and mental type, their artistic faculty, their isolation, and their form of government . . 30

CHAPTER IV. THE ETRUSCAN MYTHOLOGY.
The Ghost-world. The Guardian Spirits. The Heavenly Powers 66

CHAPTER V. THE ETRUSCAN NUMERALS.
The six digits on the Dice of Toscanella. Cardinals and ordinals. The radix. Kiemzuthrms . . 155

CHAPTER VI. EPITAPHS.
The five mortuary formulæ. Records of death, age, and burial 194

CHAPTER VII. WORDS DENOTING KINSHIP.
The Matronymic. Child, wife, and mother. The genealogies of the tombs 218

CONTENTS.

CHAPTER VIII. THE BILINGUAL INSCRIPTIONS.

The system of nomenclature. The Agnomen, the Cognomen, and the Prænomen. Latin translations of Etruscan names 249

CHAPTER IX. FORMS OF DEDICATION.

Inscriptions on lares and sepulchral gifts. Etruscan Grammar. Verbs, pronouns, and participles. Translations of inscriptions . . . 269

CHAPTER X. THE ANCIENT VOCABULARIES.

Admixture of Keltic words. True Etruscan words. The Turanian element in Latin . . . 312

CHAPTER XI. NAMES.

The national appellations. Names of rivers, mountains, and cities 337

CHAPTER XII. THE EPILOGUE.

Summary of arguments as to the affinities of the Etruscans. The evidence of language. Siberian traditions. The Trojan horse. The Myth of Romulus. The path of migration. Conclusion . 340

GLOSSARY OF ETRUSCAN WORDS . . . 379

INDEX 385

WOODCUTS.

1. Sacrifice of Trojan prisoners . . .	*Frontispiece*
2. Hut-urns . . .	44
3. The Aphuna Sarcophagus . . .	94
4. The Necromancy of Odysseus . . .	104
5. The Death of Clytemnestra . . .	119
6. The Trojan Horse . . .	367

ETRUSCAN RESEARCHES.

CHAPTER I.

THE PROLOGUE.

The Etruscans probably a Ugric People—Failure of former Attempts to Explain their Language—Application of the Ugric Key—Vocabulary—Numerals—Grammar—Mythology—Bearing of the Discovery on Roman History—And on Comparative Mythology.

A TIME of enforced abstention from the active duties of an absorbing and laborious profession has enabled me to resume certain ethnological studies which had been laid aside for a considerable period. These researches had for their object the elucidation of the obscure relationships which subsist between the pre-Keltic peoples, and the existing non-Aryan races of Europe.

While engaged on these investigations I was led

to the conclusion that the creed and customs of the Etruscans, and the existing monuments of their civilisation, more especially the sepulchral remains, indicated clearly that the Etruscan people must have belonged to the Ugric, or Tatar family of nations.

I arrived at this conclusion on grounds wholly independent of philology. But the ultimate and surest test of race is language. This test, if it could be applied, would either at once disprove, or would firmly establish, the correctness of the hypothesis.

We have no literary remains of the Etruscan speech, but ancient writers state that it was wholly different from Latin, that it was unlike any known language, and totally unintelligible to the Romans. This might suffice to raise a presumption as to its non-Aryan character.

Fortunately we possess ample monumental records written in the Etruscan language, but they have hitherto successfully defied all attempts at interpretation. Now that the Assyrian and Egyptian records have been read, these Etruscan inscriptions present the only considerable philological problem that still remains unsolved. But that it remains unsolved has not been for want of pains. A vast amount of ingenuity and of erudition has been wasted in attempts to explain the inscriptions by the aid of various Aryan, Semitic, and Turanian languages. Latin, Greek, Oscan, Hebrew, Phœnician, Arabic, Ethiopic, Chinese, Coptic, and Basque have all been tried in turn. Sir W. Betham believed the Etruscan to be a Keltic dialect. Dr. Donaldson and the Earl of Crawford have attempted to show that it is Gothic. Mr. Robert Ellis has expended much ingenuity and learning in the attempt to prove its Armenian affinities. Dr. Steub maintains that it is a Rhæto-Romansch speech.

It may be safely affirmed that none of these attempts have been regarded as satisfactory by any person except their authors.

I confess I was not sanguine enough to imagine that I should succeed in discovering the solution of the riddle which has baffled so many ingenious and erudite labourers. I thought it probable that I might succeed in showing that the nature of the Etruscan language was not absolutely inconsistent with my hypothesis as to the Ugric affinities of the nation, but I expected that this would be the utmost that could be effected, and that the full interpretation of the language would remain, as it has so long remained, the unsolved problem, the standing reproach of Philology.

It was, therefore, more out of curiosity than from any absolute expectation of success that I turned to the three or four Etruscan words of which the meaning may be regarded as reasonably certain, and attempted to test them by means of the Finno-Turkic languages, in order to ascertain if they were hopelessly non-Ugric in character. To my surprise and delight I found that my success was definite and instantaneous. The wards of the lock which had rusted for twenty centuries, and which had presented such obstinate resistance to all attempts to open it, yielded at once on the application of this key. Every key, except the right one, had already been tried in vain : when the right key was at length found, almost by accident, and inserted in the lock, there could be no question as to the precision of the fit. The languages of the Finno-Turkic family, those closely allied forms of speech which prevail throughout the region which lies between the Ural and the Altai, supplied the required sense for every genuine Etruscan word as to the significance of which there was any reasonable indication.

Proceeding with the investigation, it was, I confess, with some trepidation that I applied the key to the numerals, which rank, philologically, in the first class, as among the most unerring tests of linguistic affinity. The results of this investigation are recorded in the fifth chapter of this book. The argument from the numerals, standing by itself, seems to me nearly conclusive, but as a portion of a cumulative proof, its weight is much increased.

I then sought for some indications of Etruscan grammar, and I found that, like all the Ugric languages, the grammatical structure was agglutinative. I found also that the pronouns, the verb substantive, and the grammatical suffixes, as far as they could be recognised, were of the Finno-Turkic type, while in some important instances there was an absolute identity of form.

Comparative mythology is second only to comparative philology as a test of ethnological affinity.

THE PROLOGUE.

The names and natures of most of the Etruscan deities have long been known. Applying this, the only remaining test, I found that those divine beings who had been worshipped in Etruria for centuries before Roman History begins, in many cases bore the same names, and discharged the same offices, as the gods which are now worshipped by the pagan hunters and fishers—Ostiaks, Tunguses, and Samojeds—who roam by the shores of the Arctic Ocean. I found, moreover, that this Etruscan mythology corresponds in a remarkable manner with the mythological system which underlies the Kalevala, the ancient epic of the Finnic race.

It is obvious that the bearings of this discovery on the history of Roman civilisation must be immense. Niebuhr, foreseeing that the discovery would at some time be made, estimated so highly its importance that he said that he would willingly bestow half his fortune on the man who should find the clue.

Roman history is the history of an Aryan civilisation based upon a substratum of Turanian culture. The earliest structure which exists at Rome is constructed on an Etruscan model, and was probably built by Etruscan skill. At the earliest period at which Rome emerges into the light of authentic history we find her ruled by an Etruscan dynasty. The beginnings of her culture, her art, and her religion were, to a great extent, of Etruscan origin, and her social and her political institutions are not without traces of Etruscan influence.

For some centuries the history of Italy is the history of the gradual uprising to political power and social importance of the hitherto subject Aryan element—Latin, Umbrian, or Oscan—which at Rome first emancipated itself from Etruscan sovereignty, and then, gradually asserting its supremacy over all Etruria, succeeded finally in absorbing or superseding the arts, the laws, the language, and the nationality of the once dominant race.

The more obscure elements of Roman life—that portion of her civilisation which was certainly non-Hellenic, and probably even non-Aryan, may be assumed to be, if not directly Etruscan, at least to be due to that Finnic substratum of population which was the main support of the Etruscan ruling class.

Thus it is manifest that the discovery of the true character of the Etruscan people will entail the re-writing of much of the history of early Roman civilisation.

The results of this discovery as regards the Science of Comparative Mythology are scarcely less important than its bearings on early Roman history. The Roman mythology, so far as it differs from the Hellenic system, will now at last receive its interpretation, and take its place in the Science of Comparative Mythology. The Greek mythology has been successfully interpreted and explained by the aid of the Vedic Hymns. In the same way the non-Aryan portion of the Roman mythology will shew itself capable of explanation from the Kalevala, the great Finnic epic which answers to the Ramayana of the Hindoos or the Iliad of the Greeks. The Kalevala, moreover, throws light on those Ugric legends and beliefs which Virgil has incorporated into the sixth book of the Æneid. The legend of Numa is also presumably of Finnic origin, and the myth of Romulus suckled by the wolf must have been derived from Etruscan sources, since we find that the same myth has been disinterred from the tomes of Chinese historians, who relate it as the history of the founder and eponymus of that Turkic race of which the Etruscans were the earliest offshoot.

The possible bearings of this discovery have appeared to be so important that I have thought it well to put aside for a time my unfinished Chapters on the non-Aryan races of Europe—a book which it may probably take a considerable period to complete—in order at once to place before the world that portion of the work which relates to the Etruscans. I do this in the hope that Ugric scholars, more competent to the task than I can pretend to be, may elaborate the details of the work of which the rudiments are here put forward, and give the world the complete renderings of the hundreds—it might be said the thousands—of Etruscan inscriptions which we possess, the meaning of which has hitherto only been matter for wild and vague conjecture.

CHAPTER II.

TYRRHENIANS AND TURANIANS.

Sources of Information—Ancient Traditions as to the Origin of the Etruscans—The Lydian Tradition—Opinion of Dionysius—Its probable Value—Chronology—Extent of the Etruscan Realm—Mixed Character of the Population—The Ruling Race—Disappearance of their Language—The Subject Race—The Albanians—The Rhætians—The Thuschi—The Rasenna and the Tarsenna—Tyrrhenian and Turanian—Definitions of Ethnic Terms—Allophylian—Turanian—Ugric—Turkish—Turkic—Finn—Finnish—Funnic—Hungarian—Ugrian—Table of the Turanian Languages.

THE object of this book is to determine the affinities of the Etruscan people by means of the evidence which their own monuments supply. But before entering on this task it may be well to give a brief summary of the information which may be derived from external sources.

If the Etruscans possessed any literature of their own it has completely perished. No ancient book devoted to their history has come down to us.

Our knowledge is derived solely from their monuments, and from meagre and incidental notices in Greek and Roman writers.

At the time when Roman history begins, we find that a powerful and warlike race, far superior to the Latins in civilisation and in the arts of life, hemmed in the rising Roman dominion in the north.

The Greeks called them TURRHENOI, the Romans called them ETRUSCI, they called themselves the RASENNA. Who they were and whence they came has ever been regarded as one of the most doubtful and difficult problems in ethnology.

One conclusion only can be said to have been universally accepted both in ancient and in modern times. It is agreed on every hand that in all essential points, in language, in religion, in customs, and in appearance, the Etruscans were a race wholly different from the Latins.

There is also an absolute agreement of all ancient tradition to the effect that the Etruscans were not the original inhabitants of Etruria, but that they were an intrusive race of conquerors who arrived in Italy at some very remote period, and subjugated the aboriginal peoples—Siculians, Umbrians, or Pelasgians.

Herodotus reports that there was a tradition current among the Lydians which affirmed that the Etruscans were emigrants from Lydia. Strabo, Plutarch, Pliny, Virgil, Horace, Tacitus, and every other ancient writer on the subject, twenty-two in all, echo this tradition, which evidently represents the accepted opinion of the whole ancient world.

Dionysius of Halicarnassus is the only writer who is bold enough to dispute its truth. He does this on two grounds. His first argument is, that Xanthus, a competent Lydian historian, whose works are unfortunately lost, makes no mention of the emigration, of which, if it had been a fact, he must have been cognisant. In the second place, Dionysius, speaking, be it remembered, of his own day, at least a thousand years after the supposed migration, urges the argument that the Etruscans 'do not use the same language as the Lydians, nor do they worship the same gods, nor resemble them in their laws and customs.' He goes on to say that the Etruscan race 'is very ancient, and is not found to be like any other, either in speech or manners.'

We are able to appraise these arguments at their true value. The silence of Xanthus may probably be regarded as a conclusive proof that there was no actual migration from Lydia to Etruria. On the other hand, we cannot lightly set aside the concordance of ancient tradition which asserts that the Etruscans were an offshoot from the Lydian people. A scientific criticism will regard this tradition as the statement of an ethnological rather than of an historical fact. We may admit that the instinct of the ancient world was correct in recognising the Lydians and the Etruscans as kindred nations, belonging, both of them, to the same ethnic stock. According to the ancient unscientific mode of statement, this real ethnologic relationship would naturally be presented in the incorrect form of an actual and historical migration.

But even apart from this concurrence of ancient tradition, the striking similarity between the monumental remains of Etruria and those of Asia Minor lead us irresistibly to much the same conclusion. That the Lycians, who were the near neighbours and kinsfolk of the Lydians, belonged to the same family of nations as the Etruscans is also indicated by philological evidence, and by the prevalence among both nations of certain customs which are unknown among Aryan races, such customs as the tracing descent by the mother's side, and the addiction to the Ugric practice of sorcery. As regards the second argument of Dionysius, we see that he was wrong as to his facts; but it is easy to understand his statement, if we remember that in his time the rapid Hellenisation of the eastern corner of Asia Minor had almost effaced those points of agreement between Lydians and Etruscans which had so forcibly struck earlier observers, and which are so evident in the sepulchral remains of both nations.

It has been usually supposed that the Rasenna made their appearance in Italy some ten or twelve centuries before the Christian era. This would be about the time usually assigned to the Trojan war, and three or four centuries before the era of the foundation of Rome. For some six or seven centuries, the Etruscan power and territory continued steadily to increase, and ultimately stretched far south of the Tiber, Rome itself being included in the Etruscan dominion, and being ruled by an Etruscan dynasty.

The early history of Rome is to a great extent the history of the uprising of the Latin race, and its long struggle for Italian supremacy with its Etruscan foe. It took Rome some six centuries of conflict to break through the obstinate barrier of the Etruscan power. The final conquest of Etruria by Rome was effected in the year 281 B.C. The overthrow of the Etruscan nationality was probably due indirectly to the invasion of the Gauls, a calamity of which Etruria bore the first brunt, and from which she never fully recovered.

If our chronology be approximately correct the Etruscan civilisation existed in an independent form for about 800 or 1,000 years, which is a usual limit to the lifetime of a nation.

The Etruscan dominion, at the time of its greatest extension, when an Etruscan dynasty was ruling at Rome, stretched from Elba to the Adriatic, from the Rhætian Alps to the Gulf of Salerno; Chiavenna in the north and Capua in the south having been, both of them, Etruscan cities. This extended dominion was, however, a dominion of conquest, not of colonisation. The Rasennic people were collected mainly in the twelve great cities of Etruria proper, between the Arno and the Tiber. This region was the real seat of the Etruscan power, it is here that all the chief monuments of Etruscan art and civilisation have been found.

Irrespective of the ancient traditions, there are certain internal indications that the Rasenna were a race of conquering immigrants. The arguments of Niebuhr have made it evident that the population of Etruria was of a mixed character, consisting of two or more distinct elements. In support of this view we have the distinct statement of Livy, who tells us that the speech of the country districts of Etruria was not the same as the language of the towns. We gather, moreover, from the account of Dionysius that this rural population consisted of a race of serfs, πενέσται, employed in handicrafts and agriculture, who formed the bulk of the population, and constituted the main strength of the Etruscan armies. These serfs were doubtless the descendants of the conquered race. The Rasenna themselves formed probably but a small minority in the population of Etruria. They were an aristocracy of conquest, a race of ruling nobles who resided chiefly in the twelve cities of the Etruscan confederation, and mingled little, if at all, with the rural population. The tombs which have furnished us with such a mass of Etruscan inscriptions and works of art are found almost exclusively around the gates of these twelve Etruscan cities, and perhaps give us an exaggerated notion of the amount of the Rasennic element. The tombs are evidently the sepulchres of the wealthy, and the inscriptions which they contain are in the language of the Etruscan aristocracy; there are few tombs of the poorer class, and therefore there is little or no record of the language which was spoken by them.

At the present time we have in the Turkish empire a pretty exact parallel to the state of society which must have existed in ancient Etruria. The Turks, like their kinsmen the Turrhenna, constitute an aristocracy of conquest, a ruling class, dwelling almost exclusively in the great cities, and having no tendency to amalgamate with the subject-races.

Throughout Turkey, Syria, Egypt, Tunis, and Tripoli, the language of the court, of the law, of the bureaucracy, and of the aristocracy, is the Osmanli; various Greek, Sclavonic, Arabic, and Berber dialects being spoken by the artisans and the villagers, who constitute the great bulk of the population. If the Turkish empire were overthrown, the Turkish language would speedily fall into disuse, and the elements of the Turkish nationality would rapidly be absorbed.

These considerations may help to account for the rapid and complete disappearance of the Etruscan language from Etruria, and also for the fact that in the present speech of Tuscany few, if any, Etruscan elements can be detected. The inscriptions in the Etruscan tombs curiously disclose to us this change of language in the actual process of being effected. Again and again we find a family tomb, with its long series of Etruscan inscriptions. Then perhaps comes a single bilingual record, followed by one or two inscriptions of later date in Latin, exhibiting an Etruscan *nomen* and a Roman *prænomen*, and then the tomb is closed.

The predominance of languages of the Latin type must not, however, be regarded as any safe indication of the prevalence of Latin blood, either in Etruria or elsewhere. Latin was an intrusive language, derived from a single city, or at most from a very limited area, and which, owing chiefly to political causes, spread itself over vast regions occupied by populations of Finnic, Euskaric, Keltic, and Hellenic race.

It is impossible to determine with any precision the ethnic affinities of those aborigines who were conquered by the Rasennic invaders. The rapid prevalence of the Latin language, after the Roman conquest of Etruria had been effected, makes it probable that there was a considerable subject Aryan population, below which, according to all analogy, there was a Finnic substratum, belonging to the great Illyrian stock, to which probably the Ligures, Siculi, Marsi, and Sabines, all belonged. We shall find, as we proceed with our investigation, that there were extensive Finnic elements in the Etruscan language, and still more in the Etruscan mythology; and it may reasonably be conjectured that these may be attributed to a Finnic substratum of population.

It is probable that we should look to the Albanian language for any existing traces of the speech of these Finnic aborigines. The numerals, the auxiliary verb, the pronouns, and the general grammatical structure, prove that the Albanian language belongs to the Aryan class; but the Albanian vocabulary consists to a considerable extent of non-Aryan words, mostly of the Finnic type. In the following pages we shall find that the Albanian language occasionally enables us to throw light on the meaning of Etruscan words. It may also be noted that a portion of the modern Albanians still retain the name of Toscans.

It is also probable that some remnants of the speech of the conquering, as well as of the conquered race are still in existence. There is reason for believing that the Grisons, in eastern Switzerland, formed a portion of the Etruscan settlement. We gather from a statement of Livy that when the valley of the Po was overrun and occupied by the Gauls, a portion of the Etruscan population was driven northward, and took refuge among their kindred in the valleys of the Rhætian Alps. In these mountain fastnesses, if anywhere, we might expect to find in existence some vestiges of the Etruscan language and the Etruscan race. And, in fact, we do find in these remote valleys, not only ancient Etruscan monuments and inscriptions; but, as Dr. Steub has shown, there are hundreds of local names which are notably of the Etruscan type.

Livy informs us that the language spoken in Rhætia was a corrupt Etruscan dialect. The modern Rhæto-Romansch language is proved by its grammatical structure to belong to the Aryan family, and is essentially a debased form of Latin; but, as we shall see hereafter, it contains embedded in it a considerable number of Etruscan words. The very names RHÆTIA and GRISON may not improbably be corruptions of the name RASENNA.

It is also possible that a fragment of the Etruscan race may still exist in the Caucasus. Ptolemy mentions the TUSCI among the peoples of Asiatic Sarmatia. On the southern slopes of the Caucasus we still find a tribe called the THUSCHI, who speak a peculiar language, the grammatical structure of which, according to Schiefner, is of the Ugric type. It is possible that the affinity of the Thuschi and Etruscan languages may hereafter be demonstrated, for there are few known languages which do not possess representatives in the Caucasian Babel.

The Thuschi, like the Albanians and the Rhætians, are mountaineers. The mountain fastnesses in which these nations dwell have preserved their languages from the extinction which would otherwise have befallen them. But though the languages of mountaineers are ordinarily conserved with astonishing tenacity, they are more subject to phonetic corruption than the languages of tribes who enjoy a more extended intercourse. Hence, while we shall be able occasionally to illustrate an Etruscan word from these mountain dialects, we shall find that the Turkic tribes, from whom the Etruscans were an offshoot, have preserved the ancient Rasennic speech in a much purer and more recognisable form.

We are indebted to Dionysius of Halicarnassus for the important statement that the Etruscans called themselves the RASENNA. We have seen that they were not known by this name either to Greeks or Latins. They were known in Italy as TUSCI or ETRUSCI—names which, as Lepsius has shown, are evidently corruptions of the more ancient form TURSCI, which we find in the Eugubine Tables. The Greek writers universally call them either TURRHENOI or TURSENOI, the latter of which names manifestly links itself with the ancient Latin form TURSCI. Both the Greek and the Latin names may be regarded as ultimately identical, all the forms being probably derived from some original Etruscan name, which the analogy of the word Rasenna leads us to conjecture might be TURSENNA or TURRHENNA. We shall presently be in a position to investigate the etymology of these names, and it will be shown that the name RASENNA is a Ugric word meaning 'tribesmen,' or 'men of the nation,' while TURRHENNA or TURSENNA means 'Turk-men,' or 'Turco-man.'

From the *Shah-nameh*, the great Persian epic, we learn that the Aryan Persians called their nearest non-Aryan neighbours—the Turkic or Turcoman tribes to the north of them—by the name

TURAN, a word from which we derive the familiar ethnologic term TURANIAN. The Aryan Greeks, on the other hand, called the Turkic tribe of the Rasenna, the nearest non-Aryan race, by the name TURRHENOI.

The argument of this book is to prove that the Tyrrhenians of Italy were of kindred race with the Turanians of Turkestan. Is it too much to conjecture that the Greek form Turrhene may be identically the same word as the Persian form Turan?

A mere correspondence in sound between two ethnic names is a very unsafe foundation on which to base an ethnological theory. Such a similarity or identity of name as we find in this case may mean much, or it may mean little or nothing. But if, on other and surer grounds, we are led to infer an identity of race between two widely separated peoples, the fact of the absence of any correspondence between the ethnic names would be a strong negative argument which would require to be met. The change of name would have to be accounted for. If the Tyrrhenians were a Turanian or Turcoman horde which migrated into Italy from the frontier of Persia, we should reasonably expect to find that they carried with them the old name by which they were known in their former home. This seems to have been the case. Without relying on the identity of name, it may fairly be urged that a correspondence which we might expect to find is not lacking, and that one link is added to the chain of cumulative proof.

For the convenience of reference it may be well to define in this place the precise sense in which certain technical terms, relating to Turanian ethnology, are used throughout this book.

The word *Allophylian* is used as a comprehensive term, including all races of mankind except the Aryan and Semitic nations.

The word *Turanian*, though by no means free from objection, is used as the best known, and therefore as the most convenient term, to denote all those races of the Allophylian class which can be proved philologically to have had a genetic connection, and therefore to constitute a true linguistic family. It includes the Euskaric, Ugric, Caucasic, Egyptic, Dravidic, Malayic, and Tibetic races.

The word *Ugric* has been chosen as a general term to denote the Turanian tribes of the great Asiatic tableland, and their outlying congeners, and comprises the Finnic, Samojedic, Turkic (or Tataric), Mongolic, and Tungusic peoples. The word is not free from objection, as it is sometimes used in a more limited sense to denote what I have called Ugrians, namely the Magyars, and their congeners the Ostiaks and Woguls. The word Altaic, used by Castrén, would be a better term, and I should have used it in preference, had it not, unfortunately, been so unfamiliar to English readers. The word Finno-Turkic is a fairly accurate term, but it is too clumsy for constant use. The word Tataric might do, but it has been employed in so many senses by different writers that it is no longer suited for use as an accurate and precise ethnologic term.

The word Ugric, which I have chosen, means 'belonging to the highlands,' and it forms, therefore, an appropriate designation for the races whose home is the lofty plateau of central Asia. The root of the word appears in the names of the Uigurs, the Ugors, and other Finnic and Turkic tribes of highlanders, as well as in the name of the Ural mountain range.

The word *Turkish* is used to mean the Osmanli language, spoken at Constantinople.

The work *Turkic* is used to mean the family of languages of which the Turkish is the leading member, and it includes all the languages spoken by the Turkoman and Tatar nomads of northern Asia.

The word *Finn* (Quain or Suomi) is used to mean the language spoken by the Finns of Russian Finland.

The word *Finnish* (Tschud) denotes all the Ugric languages of the Baltic region, namely Finn, Esth, Karelian, Olonet, and Lapp.

The word *Finnic* has a still wider signification. It is taken as a generic term to comprehend all the languages of the Finnish type. There are four main subdivisions of the Finnic languages.

1. The Finnish or Tschudic languages of the Baltic region.
2. The Permian languages of the Ural.
3. The Bulgarian languages of the Wolga.
4. The Ugrian languages of the Danube and the Obi.

The term *Ugrian* includes the language of the Magyars of Hungary, and the Ostiak and Wogul dialects of Siberia. The Ugrians are therefore a small but typical subdivision of the Ugric nations.

The word *Hungarian* means the language spoken by the Magyars of Hungary.

The subjoined rough table is added, in the hope that it may make more clear the use of the technical terms employed. Much of the arrangement must be regarded as provisional and tentative. Our knowledge of the grammatical relations of the Turanian languages is, as yet, not sufficiently accurate to make it possible to construct anything like a perfect arrangement.

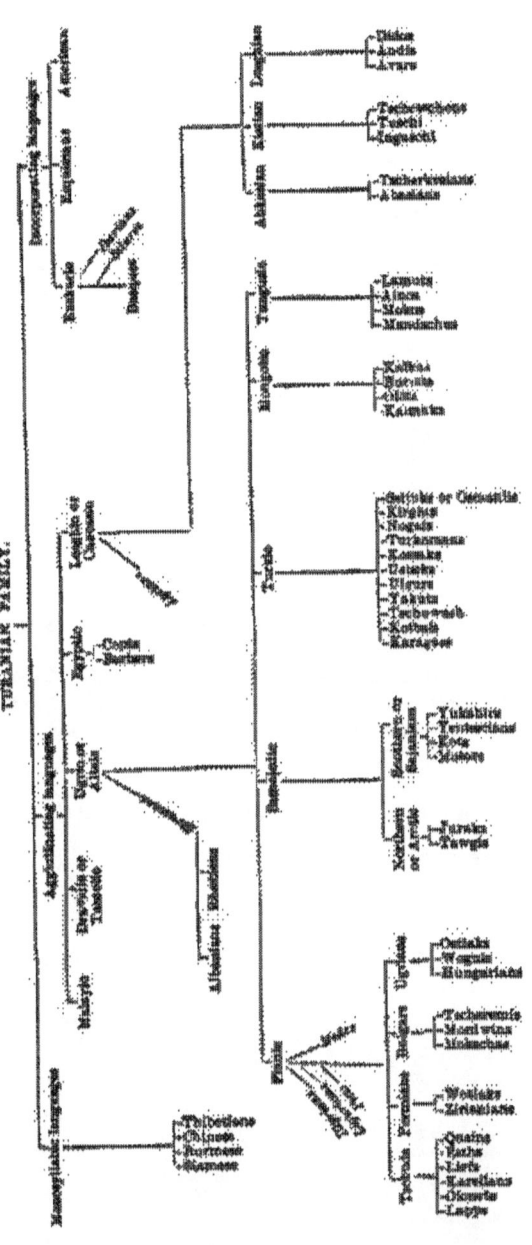

CHAPTER III.

ETHNOGRAPHIC NOTES ON THE ETRUSCAN PEOPLE.

The three Ethnologic Methods: Philology, Anthropology, and Psychology—Application of the last Method—Ethnologic Importance of the Constructive Arts—The Tomb-builders—Turanian Tombs express the Turanian Faith—Affinities of the Tomb-builders—The three civilised Races of Tomb-builders: Lycians, Egyptians, and Etruscans.

§ 1. *The Etruscan Tombs—The two Types—The Tumulus or Tent-tomb—The Stone Circle—Hut Urns—The Gallery—The Cave-tomb—Imitation of the House—Family Sepulture—The Funeral Feast—The Analogies of Egyptian and Lycian Tombs.*

§ 2. *The Etruscan Priesthood—Sorcery.*

§ 3. *The Law of Inheritance—Survivals indicating Tribal Polyandria—Exogamy—Inheritance through the Mother.*

§ 4. *Type of Body.*

§ 5. *Type of Mind.*

§ 6. *Etruscan Art—Love of Colour—Etruria and Tuscany.*

§ 7. *The Etruscan Isolation—Aryan Nations occupy continuous Areas—Isolation of the Ugric Nations: Mongolic, Turkic, Samojedic, and Finnic—Ugric Isolation accounted for—History of Ugric Migration—Migrations of Mongols, Tunguses, Avars, Cumanians, Seljuks, Huns, Bulgars, Alans, Magyars, Medes—The Isolation of the Etruscans makes it probable that they were Ugric Migrants—Parallels between the Etruscans, the Osmanli, and the Magyars—The Ugric Nature of the Etruscan Government.*

THERE are three chief methods of research which are open to the student of ethnology.

The first is the method of comparative philology —the most powerful, the most precise, and, within its proper limits, the most certain of all methods. But, valuable as the method is, it has its limitations and its dangers. It is almost as easy, and almost as frequent, for nations to change their language as to change their domicile. What have been supposed to be successive waves of population passing over a country, may, in reality, have been only successive waves of language. Thus within the last ten centuries, in Egypt and in Cornwall respectively, the Coptic speech has given place to Arabic, and the Keltic speech to English, without any corresponding changes of race.

The second ethnologic method is the method of comparative anthropology—the comparison of hair, colour, stature, crania. This most valuable method has also its limitations. In the case of extinct nationalities the materials of investigation are either not forthcoming, or their attribution is more or less doubtful, while the results of crossing and of changed conditions of life are most perplexing and misleading.

The third method is that which, for want of a better term, may be called the method of comparative psychology, or comparative phrenology.

The most human and distinctive thing about a man or a race is the mind. It is recognised that there exist, not only hereditary forms of speech and hereditary types of body, but, above all, hereditary types of mind. Mental peculiarities and distinctions are transmitted with more certainty and more persistency than either language or outward physical type.

The objection to the use of this powerful instrument of research lies mainly in the difficulty of applying it. It becomes necessary for the purposes of comparative ethnology to fix upon certain easily-ascertained outward indications of mental peculiarities.

Now it is found that in rude states of society the manners and customs of the people, the forms of government, the traditional laws which regulate the tenure of land and the descent of property, the limitions and usages of marriage, the modes of burial, together with folk lore, popular superstitions, nursery tales, signs, and, above all, religious beliefs and observances, are more permanent, more indestructible, and therefore of more value to the ethnologist than even the shape of the skull, the colour of the skin, or the form of speech.

But there is also another mode of detecting and comparing the mental peculiarities of nations which possesses great certainty, and which can be applied easily, and almost universally, to extinct races. The constructive arts are among the most valuable indications of ethnologic affinities. Temples, palaces, and tombs, may be regarded as the petrified aspirations, thoughts, and feelings of nations. They form a spontaneous and unconscious expression of hereditary mental peculiarities. They are of more available value because they are so permanent; they still remain as subjects for our study when language has been changed, when creeds have disappeared, when skulls have mouldered into dust, when the last traces of national existence have been effaced. How much should we know of ancient Assyria, of Lycia, or even of Egypt, if it had not been for their architectural monuments?

It is not so much the type, as the object and character of such remains, which is the sure sign of ethnic affinity. The Aryan and Semitic nations have been great builders; they have left us temples, theatres, basilicas, and palaces; they have made bridges, roads, sewers, but they have never been notable as tomb-builders. Their instinct has led them to concern themselves with the needs and domiciles of the living, rather than with the necessities and the resting-places of the dead.

But, scattered over the world, from Algiers to Kamtschatka, from the Orkneys to Ceylon, we find everywhere the conspicuous and unmistakable monuments of a great ancient tomb-building race. This race seems to form the ethnological substratum of the whole world; it is like the primary rock which underlies the whole series of subsequent formations. There can be no hesitation as to the existing stock to which these ancient non-Aryan tomb-builders belonged. The great Turanian race, which was the first to spread beyond the cradle of mankind, and of which the Chinese, the Mongols, the

Tatars, and the Finns are existing representatives, is pre-eminently the race of the tomb-builders.

The vast and numerous monuments which constitute the tombs of this race can always be recognized; they exhibit a most remarkable and most significant unity of design and purpose. These tombs are all developments of one hereditary type; they are all the expressions of one great hereditary belief, and they all serve the purposes of one great hereditary cultus. The type on which they are modelled is the house. The belief which they express is the fundamental truth which has been the great contribution of the Turanian race to the religious thought of the world—the belief in the deathlessness of souls. The cultus which they serve is the worship of the spirits of ancestors, which is the Turanian religion. The creed of the Turanians was Animism. They believed that everything, animate or inanimate, had its soul or spirit; that the spirits of the dead could still make use of the spirits of the weapons, ornaments, and utensils which they had used in life, and could be served by the spirits of their slaves, their horses, and their dogs, and needed for their support the spirits of those articles of food on which they had been used to feed. Hence when we open these ancient Turanian sepulchres we find that the resting-places for the dead have been constructed on the exact model of the abodes of the living—the dead have been carefully provided with the necessaries of life—the warrior is buried with his spear and his arrows, the woman with her utensils and her ornaments; by the side of the infant's skeleton we find the skeleton of the faithful house-dog—slaughtered in order that the soul of the brave and wise companion might safely guide the soul of the helpless little one on the long journey to the unknown land. In all respects the tomb is the counterpart of the house, with the sole difference that it is erected in a manner more durable and more costly.

The Turanian tombs are family tombs; the dead of a whole generation are deposited in the same chamber. We find, moreover, that careful provision is made for the recurring festival at which the surviving members of the family paid their annual devotion to the ancestral spirits.

These are the characteristic features of Turanian

sepulchres. As soon as this instrument of research is applied to the complicated problems of the ethnology of early races, order begins to evolve itself out of chaos. It becomes possible to track the footsteps of the tomb-builders across the continents, and to unite the scattered indications of the presence of the primæval peoples. In Siberia, Poland, Denmark, Sweden, Hanover, Britain, France, Spain, Algiers, India, we find tombs of one type, alike in all essential particulars. We have therefore the available monuments of the races who preceded the Aryans and Semites. Light begins to dawn on the relations of the primitive people whose stone implements fill our museums, who dwelt in the caves of Aquitaine, who built the Swiss Lake-dwellings, and whose sepulchres cover the Wiltshire downs, the Algerian plains, and the Siberian steppes.

It is manifest that the greater portion of these tomb-building peoples were in a very low stage of culture, little removed above the condition of mere savages.

But there have been three great civilized tomb-building races; one in Africa—the Egyptians; one in Asia—the Lydians and Lycians; and one in Europe—the Etruscans. The question arises, were these three cultured nations of the same race as the semi-savage Turanian tribes who form the pre-Aryan substratum of Western Europe, and who constitute the existing population of Northern Asia?

This question must, I think, be answered in the affirmative. The case of the Etruscans is dealt with in the following pages. The case of the Lycians stands or falls with that of the Etruscans; for it is difficult, if not impossible, to resist the consensus of ancient tradition which affirms that the Lycians, Lydians, Carians, and other closely related non-Hellenic races of Asia Minor, were of the same stock as the Etruscans. But even without this evidence a comparison of the Etruscan with the Lycian tombs would suffice to establish the fact that they cannot be altogether of independent origin. Some of the more striking similarities in structure will presently be noticed, as well as the curious correspondences between the two nations in certain non-Aryan customs. I believe, moreover, that I shall be able to prove that the language of the Lycian inscriptions belongs to the same stock as the language of the Etruscans. If this can be done the question will be finally set at rest.

Only one race of civilized tomb-builders—the Ancient Egyptians—will remain to be dealt with. Much evidence as to the essential identity of the ancient Egyptian speech with the Ugric languages has been adduced by Klaproth. It is, I think, sufficient to raise a very strong presumption, if not to amount to absolute proof. There is moreover much evidence which Klaproth has overlooked. This evidence is far too bulky to be brought forward in this volume; but I trust at some future time to have an opportunity of producing it, and of showing also that the mythologic system, and some other beliefs and customs of the Egyptians, are essentially those which are characteristic of the Turanian race. In the course of these pages, however, many facts will incidentally be noticed, tending to prove that the Etruscans and the Egyptians were of kindred race, distant branches of the same stock, just as English and Hindoos both belong to the great Aryan family.

We may now proceed to notice the general considerations which connect the Etruscans with the Turanian stock, and more especially with that portion of it which is called Ugric or Altaic—the tribes of Finns, Tatars, Mongols, Samojeds and Tunguses, who people the inhospitable regions of Northern Asia.

I shall now discuss in order—the character of the tombs of the Etruscans, the peculiarities of their priesthood, their law of inheritance, their physical type of body, their type of mind, the character of their art, their peculiarities as migrants and conquerors, and their religious beliefs. The discussion of their language will occupy the remainder of the book.

§ 1.—THE ETRUSCAN TOMBS.

With his usual acuteness Mr. James Fergusson has observed that if there were any doubt as to the Turanian affinities of the Etruscans, that doubt would be set at rest by the fact that all the knowledge which we possess respecting them is derived from their tombs.

We have already seen that the Turanians have

been, conspicuously, the tomb-builders of the world. No Semitic or Aryan nations have ever been notable tomb-builders, whereas every Turanian race, without exception, has marked its presence on the soil by the tombs which it has left behind.

This the Etruscans have done most notably. Hundreds of tombs cluster at the gates of every ancient Etruscan city. It is still more worthy of notice that though these tombs prove the Etruscans to have been most skilful builders, there is not a vestige left of a single Etruscan temple, or of a single Etruscan palace. Their constructive powers, and the resources of their decorative arts, were lavished on their tombs. The whole construction of these tombs is the abiding expression of the belief of the Etruscans as to the condition of the dead. The needs of the dead were essentially the same as the needs of the living. Therefore the Etruscan tombs are reproductions of the house.

The Etruscan tombs are of two types:

1. Chambered tumuli, or tent-tombs.
2. Rock-cut chambers, or cave-tombs.

Both of these types are, strictly speaking,

survivals, that is, traditional imitations, of the two ancient types of the house.

The ancient Turanian peoples dwelt either in caves or in tents. The modern Siberian *Yurt*, or permanent house, bears traces of both of these forms of habitation. The structure, though partly below the surface of the earth, is modelled on the plan of the tent—it is a permanent semi-subterranean winter tent.

When a man died, he was left, with all his possessions, in his tent. To keep the body from the wolves the tent was covered with a mound of earth or stones, preserving the original pyramidal form. This is doubtless the origin of the sepulchral tumulus. That the model of the tumulus was the tent is, moreover, indicated by a very curious and widely-spread survival. The tent was necessarily surrounded, as is still the case in Greenland and Siberia, with a circle of heavy stones, which were needed to keep down by their weight the skins of which the tent was composed. Long after the origin of the sepulchral tumulus had been forgotten, long after the tumulus-builders had ceased to dwell in tents, this circle of stones continued to be erected around the base of the funeral mound. This curious survival is seen in the stone circles which commonly surround the ancient British tumuli; and even when the tumulus had given place to the ordinary grave, the stone circle remains, as at Stonehenge, and bears witness to the primæval method of interment. It is the very uselessness of the stone circle which so conclusively proves it to be a survival of something which was once a needful portion of the structure.

In the Etruscan tumuli the stone circle is not absent, but it has been developed into a *podium*, or low encircling wall of masonry.

Perhaps the most singular and striking proof that the tumulus is only a survival of the tent is supplied by the small cinerary urns which have been found at Albano (close to Tusculum), two of which are in the British Museum.[1] They are evidently of immense antiquity, and are probably older than any other sepulchral remains of Italy. These 'hut-urns,' as they are called, are formed of

[1] Dennis, *Etruria*, vol. ii. pp. 61, 495.

rude and clumsy pottery, and are only a few inches in height. They are most distinctly intended to be imitations of tents or huts, framed with boughs and covered over with skins. Some of them are almost exact reproductions in pottery of the Tatar tent as now in use on the Siberian steppes. These 'hut-urns' prove that even when the body had been burnt, and when therefore no tumulus could be

HUT-URNS.

required, it was still deemed suitable that the ashes should inhabit a conventional tent. Is it unreasonable to attribute these 'hut-urns' to the period of the first arrival of the Rasenna in Italy, when the memory of their Siberian tent-life was still recent? It may be noted that at Savona there is a tomb formed out of a detached mass of rock which has been fashioned into the imitation of a skin-covered tent, the rounded roof being distinctly hoop-ribbed.[1]

The Etruscan tumular sepulchres, which are very numerous around the sites of Veii, Cære, Tarquinii, and other Etruscan cities, contain, as a rule, one or more central chambers, which are approached by a long vaulted passage of masonry, just large enough for a man to crawl through. The chambers are usually more or less below the natural surface of the ground, just as is the case with the Siberian Yurts. The long entrance passage, usually some ten or twelve feet long, but occasionally sixty or even one hundred feet in length, is a distinct survival of the low entrance passage some ten feet in length, through which the Laplanders or the Esquimaux of Greenland crawl into their winter huts. In the absence of a door some such contrivance is necessary to keep out the wind, and maintain the temperature of the interior.

The long entrance passage, leading to a central chamber, is a marked feature not only of the Etruscan graves, but also of the 'galleried' or 'cham-

[1] Dennis, *Etruria*, vol. i. p. 493.

bered' tumuli which are so numerous in Britain, Scandinavia, and elsewhere, and which have been supposed to belong to the Finnic aborigines. The ancient Turkic graves in Siberia are, moreover, constructed on the same type. The traveller Bell describes them as existing in thousands near Tomsk. There is a passage and a central chamber covered with a mound of earth, within which are found the skeletons of the deceased, buried with all their weapons and ornaments.

The second type of the Etruscan tomb is the cave. At Castel d'Asso, at Cervetri, at Norchia, and at many other places in Etruria, there are hundreds of tombs hollowed out in the low cliffs, the tombs facing each other like the houses in the streets of a town, with lanes of tombs branching out right and left. In one place we have a square or piazza, surrounded by tombs instead of houses.

These cities of the dead are constructed on the precise model of the cities of the living. The tombs themselves are exact imitations of the house. There is usually an outer vestibule, apparently appropriated to the annual funeral feast; from this a passage leads to a large central chamber, which is lighted by windows cut through the rock. This central hall is surrounded by smaller chambers, in which the dead repose. On the roof we see carved in stone the broad beam or roof-tree, with rafters imitated in relief on either side, and even imitations of the tiles. These chambers contain the corpses, and are furnished with all the implements, ornaments, and utensils used in life. The tombs are in fact places for the dead to live in. The position and surroundings of the deceased are made to approximate as closely as possible to the conditions of life. The couches on which the corpses repose have a triclinial arrangement, and are furnished with cushions carved in stone; and imitations of easy chairs and footstools are carefully hewn out of the rock. Everything, in short, is arranged as if the dead were reclining at a banquet in their accustomed dwellings. On the floor stand wine-jars, and the most precious belongings of the deceased—arms, ornaments and mirrors—hang from the roof, or are suspended on the walls. The walls themselves are richly decorated, usually being painted with representations of festive scenes; we see figures in gaily embroidered garments reclining on couches, while attendants replenish the goblets or beat time to the music of the pipers.[1] Nothing is omitted which can conduce to the amusement or comfort of the deceased. Their spirits were evidently believed to inhabit these house-tombs after death, just as in life they inhabited their houses.

In the spirit and intention of these arrangements the Etruscan sepulchres agree precisely with the Egyptian tombs, and with the thousands of graves scattered over the northern hemisphere, and which mark the whole area of Turanian occupancy from Sweden to Algeria—from Siberia to Ireland. The arrangements all indicate one central religious belief, the doctrine of a future life. The religion of the Etruscans, like that of the Chinese and the Ugric nations, consisted essentially in reverence for the spirits of ancestors. Like the Turanian nations the Etruscans needed no temples, since the graves of their forefathers were the spots where their religious observances were performed.

[1] Dennis, *Etruria*, vol. i. pp. 262, 493; ii. pp. 31, 40, 495.

All the Etruscan tombs, whether caves or tumuli, are strictly tombs not for individuals but for families. The inscriptions which they contain show that whole generations were successively buried in the same tomb. It is not uncommon to find eight or ten interments in a single chamber, and one chamber at Toscanella contained no less than twenty-seven sarcophagi.

It has already been observed that there is a notable absence of the remains of Etruscan temples. There is reason to believe that there were temples in some of the Etruscan cities, but they played no conspicuous part in the life of the people, as among Aryan nations. The true temples of the Etruscans were their tombs; they were the sacred places used for the most sacred rites. A singular and characteristic feature which is found in almost every Etruscan tomb is the large antechamber out of which the mortuary chambers open. This was the place where the whole family used to assemble at the annual funeral feast to worship the manes and lares of its ancestors, and make offerings to their spirits. Thus every tomb is in fact a temple.

This system prevails in full force in China and Siberia. It is most characteristic of the Turanian peoples, and is utterly foreign to the thoughts and feelings of Aryan and Semitic races. The Aryans and Semites are temple builders, but they practice no cultus of the dead. On the other hand the Samojeds, the Ostiaks, the Laplanders, the Mongols, and other pagan Ugric nations, have no temples or places of special honour for their idols. The tombs of their forefathers are the places where these tribes assemble for their worship.[1] The pilgrimage of the Chinese emperor to the tombs of his ancestors is the great annual event in Chinese history.

In Egypt and in Asia Minor, as well as in Etruria, we find the same two types of tombs, and the same characteristic features of Turanian architecture. The tent and the cave are the two models on which the house, and its more costly and more enduring imitation, the tomb, have been constructed.

In each of the three countries we have both the tumulus grave and the rock-cut cave; in all three cases we see the possession of great constructive

[1] Klemm, *Cultur Geschichte*, vol. iii. p. 194.

skill, and of artistic taste; effect is produced either by mere size, or by simplicity of outline and massiveness of material. The pyramid of Cheops; the vast mound at Sardis which forms the resting-place of Alyattes, the father of Crœsus; the huge tomb of Porsenna at Clusium; are all constructed on one type. They are all developments of the chambered and galleried tumulus, which is characteristic of the Finno-Turkic race, and which is exemplified alike in the mounds of Orkney or Wiltshire, and of which we find the latest example in the mausoleum of Hyder Ali, the last Tatar king who ruled in India. The resemblances are sometimes most curious and minute. The Cucumella at Vulci, with its towers, is built on the precise model of the turreted tumulus of Alyattes.[1] The tumuli at Tantalais, near Smyrna, or the tumuli of the ancient Lydian cemetery at Sardis, which the Turks call the thousand and one hills, would not be recognised as incongruous structures if they were placed among the six hundred tumuli which constitute the necropolis of Tarquinii.

[1] Dennis, *Etruria*, vol. i. p. 415.

The same similarity also exists between the tombs of the other type, the rock-cut caves, which were employed by all three nations. Round many of the ancient cities of Asia Minor we find ranges of cliffs with hundreds of chamber tombs excavated in their faces, and arranged like houses in a street, closely resembling the cave tombs of Beni Hassan in Egypt, or the chambered cliffs at Cervetri in Etruria.

It may also be observed that the more ancient Etruscan tombs are much more free from traces of the influence of Greek art, and approximate more closely to the Egyptian or Asiatic type, not only in structure, but in the objects deposited, and the religious symbols which are employed. Nevertheless, close though the agreement may be, the Etruscan style is always sufficiently marked—it is always possible to distinguish an Etruscan scarabeus or an Etruscan sphinx from Egyptian work.[1]

[1] Dennis, *Etruria*, vol. ii. p. 51.

§ 2. The Etruscan Priesthood.

We have already had occasion to remark the non-existence of the ruins of any Etruscan temples. Not less significant is the absence of any priesthood, properly so called. The personages who discharged sacred offices among the Etruscans were not the teachers of the people or the servants of the gods; they were rather channels of communication with the spirits of nature and the souls of the departed. They were neither presbyters, priests, nor prophets, but strictly speaking *shamans*. The religion of the Etruscans was distinctly shamanistic. They were distinguished among the nations of ancient Europe as being the chief if not the sole cultivators of the arts of augury, sorcery, and necromancy.

It is to be noted as a strong mark of ethnic affinity that the only ancient rivals of the Etruscans in these arts were the kindred Turanian races of Asia Minor, the Carians, Phrygians, Cilicians, and Pisidians. The proficiency of these nations in the practices of augury is expressly recorded by Pliny, by Cicero, and by Clement of Alexandria. It is true that augury was practised among the Romans, but the whole Roman system was a direct inheritance from the Etruscans, and many of the most eminent of the Roman augurs bore names which clearly indicate their Etruscan descent. In Etruria as in Rome the office of the augurs, haruspices, and fulguriators was to interpret the utterances of the spirits of nature as indicated by the flight of birds, the entrails of animals, and the path of the lightning. Their office was essentially the same as that of their modern representatives, the sorcerers who are called in Lapland and Siberia 'shamans' and 'tadebejos,' or the 'medicine men' of the Mongoloid tribes of North America.

A perusal of the third volume of Klemm's *Allgemeine Cultur-Geschichte der Menschheit* will show the extent to which the Ugric races of Siberia are addicted to the practices of sorcery at the present day. As regards former times, the fact that all the heroes of the Kalevala are gifted with powers of sorcery indicates the estimation in which the practice was held by the ancient Finns.[1]

[1] Castrén, *Finn. Mythol.* p. 275.

§ 3. The Law of Inheritance.

The customs which relate to marriage and the inheritance of property have a remarkable persistency, and therefore furnish valuable evidence to the ethnologist.

Among all Turanian races some 'survival' or 'superstition' may be detected which suffices to indicate the former prevalence of a condition of tribal polyandria, or community of women, all the men belonging to any tribe having at some primæval period possessed common marital rights over all the women.

Survivals indicating the former existence of such a state of society are found universally among the Turanian races; they existed among the Etruscans, the Lycians, the Lydians, the Medes, and the Picts; they are still found among the Lapps, the Samojeds, the Ostiaks, the Mongols, the Kalmuks, the Tunguses, the Kirghiz, the Turkomans, the Nogais, the Koriaks, the Aleutians, and the Esquimaux; they exist among most of the Turanian hill tribes of India, and among all the Mongoloid tribes of North America. Such indications of the ancient practice of polyandria are rare among Aryan and Semitic peoples, and when they are found they may generally be accounted for by some infusion of Turanian blood. It would seem that the Aryans and the Semites had outgrown the polyandrous condition of society at a period not very distant from that at which the separation from the Turanian stem took place.

These survivals of Turanian polyandria are found to assume two chief forms. That which is the most common, and which is usually the last to disappear, is the practice of exogamy. Its origin may be thus explained. If all the men of any tribe possessed common marital rights over all the women, the only way in which the exclusive right to the possession of one woman could be secured would be by the process of forcible capture from some other tribe. The captive would be regarded as belonging exclusively to the captor, and in her case the tribal rights would not exist. As culture advanced this would come to be the universal practice, and long after the ancient communal rights over the tribal women had grown into disuse it would be supposed that no real marriage could be lawfully contracted except with a woman belonging to another tribe, and thus the law prescribing exogamous marriage would gradually arise. Exogamy still prevails among many of the Ugric peoples. Thus the Ostiaks, the Samojeds, the Lapps, and the Tunguses, never marry a woman belonging to their own tribe or family.[1]

The primitive community of women is still more plainly indicated by another, but less frequent survival—the usage of tracing descent through the mother instead of through the father, and of regulating either the inheritance of property, or the descent of the rights of chieftainship in the female instead of in the male line. This survival is a vivid indication of the former prevalence of a state of society in which paternity was too uncertain to be relied upon as the basis of valuable rights, and in which maternity constituted the only relationship that could legally be recognised.

Among the Nairs, Kasias, and other Turanian hill-tribes of India, property descends by the female

[1] Tylor, *Early History*, p. 279.

line. Among the Iroquois, and many other Mongoloid tribes of North America, this also is the rule, the *totem* descending exclusively through the mother. There is reason for believing that the Picts represent the primæval Finnic element in the population of Ireland and Scotland. The Picts were not only strictly exogamous, but the law of descent was in the female line—an arrangement which was a source of unmixed wonder to the Aryan Kelts around them. Herodotus records that the Lycians, also a Turanian race, traced descent through the maternal line, to the entire exclusion of the paternal.[1]

The concurrence of ancient tradition as to an ethnic relation between Etruria and Asia Minor derives immense support from the fact that this Lycian custom, which is absolutely unknown among any Aryan or Semitic race, prevailed also among the Etruscans. We possess many hundreds of Etruscan sepulchral inscriptions. Though they give us little information as to Etruscan customs, on this point their evidence is overwhelming. They testify

[1] Herodotus, i. 173; Fellows, *Lycia*, p. 276; Lubbock, *Origin of Civilisation*, 98, 106; Tylor, *Early History*, p. 281.

in the most plain and conspicuous manner to the invariable Etruscan practice of tracing descent through the mother. In the Etruscan mortuary inscriptions the father's name is not unfrequently added, but that of the mother is hardly ever omitted. The statement of the maternal descent is evidently regarded as of more importance than the statement either of paternity, or age, or sex, or gens.

This practice of stating the maternal descent incidentally supplies a faint indication that the Etruscans were probably exogamous. In the large family tombs the name of the wife does not appear, as a rule, to be one of the names prevailing in the gens of the husband.

Herodotus informs us that among the Lydian damsels public prostitution was considered as a necessary preliminary to marriage. From a chance phrase used by Plautus it would appear that some not dissimilar custom prevailed also among the Etruscans. There can be no more certain evidence of a primitive tribal polyandria than this singular survival, which was abhorrent to the Aryan instinct, but which, among the Lydians and Etruscans, must have been regarded as a sort of necessary and formal satisfaction of ancient tribal rights.

In other respects the position of the wife in Etruria was high. She was her husband's companion, at meals she took her place by his side at the same table, her children bore her name, her tomb was even more splendid than that of her husband. On the Lycian monuments the honour done to the wife is equally conspicuous. Herein the Turanian analogy is followed, rather than the Aryan or the Semitic. The exalted position of the wife in Rome, so different from her position in Athens, may be regarded as an inheritance from the Etruscans. The Turkish practice of female seclusion is apparently of recent adoption, as it differs from the usage which prevails among the Turkomans and other Turkic nations, where the women are neither secluded nor degraded, but are their husbands' helpmates, as in ancient Etruria.

§ 4. THE PHYSICAL TYPE OF BODY.

A few lines may be devoted to the anthropological evidence which bears on the question of the Etruscan affinities. Professor Mommsen has pointed out[1] that the remains of Etruscan art, when free from Hellenic influences, show clearly how wide were the differences in physical characteristics which existed between the Rasenna and the Aryan races. In striking contrast with the symmetrical slenderness of the Greeks and Romans, we find depicted in the Etruscan paintings a short-statured, sturdy race, with large heads and thick arms. The eyes are painted black, the colour of the cheeks is high, the beard is scanty, and the hair is black or very dark, and arranged in small crisp curls. The obesity of the Etruscans was proverbial, and is noted both by Virgil and Catullus.

In all these points the resemblance to the Ugric tribes of Siberia is very striking. The Kazan Tatars, for instance, are described as very short, stout, and swarthy, and with curling black hair. The Mongols are short in stature, and dark in complexion, with black hair, and high-coloured cheeks. Prichard describes the Kirghiz tribes as short, with fat bloated cheeks, the beard scanty, but with

[1] *Römische Geschichte*, vol. i. p. 118.

a natural curl. The Samojeds are short, with a dark brown complexion, small black eyes, and black hair. The Woguls have black hair, scanty beard, and a dark complexion. The Lapps and Finns are a short, dark-eyed race. Haxthausen reports that the Tschermiss have dark skins, dark hair, and dark eyes. Hippocrates describes the ancient Scythians as having bodies gross and fleshy, and with little hair.[1]

But the most distinctive physical characteristics of the Mongolian races are the high cheek-bones, and the oblique angle at which the eyes incline to the nose. In this also the remains of Etruscan art point to the same conclusion as the other evidence. The figures on the later vases and mirrors are to a great extent of the Greek type, and must be set aside in any such comparison. But in the earlier works of art, and more especially when we have what may be regarded as a portrait statue, the Mongoloid type of feature is frequently conspicuous.

[1] Klemm, *Cultur-Geschichte*, vol. iii. p. 138; Prichard, *Natural Hist. of Man*, p. 210; Castrén, *Ethnolog. Vorlesungen*, p. 128; Latham, *Descriptive Ethnology*, vol. i. p. 429.

THE MONGOLIAN TYPE. 63

The development of the cheek-bones is strongly marked in a very ancient bronze portrait bust of an Etruscan lady which has been figured by Dennis, and which might almost be taken for a representation of a Kalmuk woman.[1] The oblique angle at which the eyes slope towards the nose is strikingly shown in the realistic portrait figures on the lid of the great terracotta sarcophagus which has just been added to the British Museum from the Castellani collection. No Aryan ever had such eyes.

§ 5. TYPE OF MIND.

The Etruscans were conspicuously stubborn in temper, highly conservative in their disposition, and orderly in their habits. In this also there is an agreement with other Turanian races. They are orderly and law-abiding, ruled by custom and tradition, with obstinate tempers, and an intensely conservative spirit. The Turanian has none of the fickleness, versatility, and progressiveness, which are

[1] Dennis, *Etruria*, vol. i. p. 429. Compare the statue of *sis*, engraved on p. 427, which presents the same features in a somewhat less marked degree.

among the foremost defects and merits of the Aryan character. We see this conservative spirit manifested in the civilization of China and Egypt. It has been very marked in the history of Hungary, and in the attachment of the Basques to their fueros. Nations of Turanian blood are remarkable for the obstinate sieges which they have endured. The siege of the Etruscan Veii by the Romans is paralleled by the resistance of the Basque Numantia, by the conquest of Liguria by the Romans, and in modern times by the sieges of Silistria and Kars.

Many of the greatest nations have been nations of mixed descent. It is not perhaps an unreasonable conjecture that it was just the Turanian element incorporated by Rome which gave the Latin race its ultimate superiority over other Aryan nations, and supplied the lacking element which was needed in the formation of a great ruling race. The fickle emotional element of the Aryan character has almost always been an element of weakness in nations of pure Aryan blood. It was so in Hellas, it has been so conspicuously among the Kelts. On the other hand we detect among the Romans more or less of the Turanian doggedness and stubbornness, of their conservative law-abiding spirit, of their attachment to ancient customs, of their reverence for parents and ancestors, not to speak of their genius for conquest and for political organisation. It was this stability of character, which characterises the Turanian races, and which we see in its full and unchecked development among the modern Chinese and the ancient Egyptians, that gave Rome some of her leading political virtues, and gave the empire of the world to her, rather than to the keener intellect and brighter intelligence of Athens.

§ 6. Etruscan Art.

Another note of ethnic affinity is the possession of the artistic faculty. This was developed to a surprising degree among the pre-historic Turanian occupants of the Aquitanian caves. It was also characteristic of the Ugric Picts. It exists among the modern Esquimaux. The Turanian nations are more especially characterised by their passion for vivid colour. This is conspicuous in the ornamentation of Etruscan tombs and vases. The colour is always brilliant, and never inharmonious. The primary colours are used in the most daring manner, but the effect is never grotesque or glaring. This Turanian love of colour, and this instinctive skill in its application, is manifested in the paintings on the walls of Egyptian tombs, in Chinese and Japanese drawings, in the personal adornments of the Tunguses and other Siberian tribes, and in the dress and tatooings of North American Indians.

But it is still more conspicuous in the designs in Etruscan tombs, and in those ornamentations of Etruscan vases which have served as models for modern imitation, and which in some cases have never been surpassed. It may be said that the ceramic art of the Etruscans has been the one great permanent legacy which they have bequeathed to the world.

The suggestion may perhaps be allowed that the art of modern Europe owes much to the hereditary transmission of the Etruscan instinct for form and colour. Geographically, ancient Etruria is modern Tuscany. The blood of the mediæval Florentines was probably Etruscan, with but small alien admixture. It was at Florence that the arts instinctively revived at the earliest possible moment after the European cataclysm. The earliest homes of art, the leading schools of colour, were at Bologna, Florence, Perugia, Siena, Lucca, and Parma—cities which belonged, all of them, to the old Etruscan dominion. All the greatest colourists have come from this region. Titian is an apparent exception, but the name of Titian is one of the commonest of the names in the ancient Etruscan sepulchres. Giotto, Fra Angelico, Ghirlandajo, Masaccio, Perugino, Fra Bartolemmeo, Leonardo, Coreggio, Garofalo, Michael Angelo, Raphael, Francia, Guido Reni, Domenichino, and the Caracci, were all Tuscans, and in all reasonable probability may have been ultimately of Etruscan lineage. It may almost be affirmed that, beyond the area once occupied by the Etruscan race, no colourist of the highest rank has ever been born. We may perhaps attribute something of the facile power and genius of these great artists to hereditary instinct, reappearing at last, irrepressibly, after its long eclipse.

§ 7. The Etruscan Isolation

There is another very marked peculiarity of the Etruscans—their singular isolation. Dionysius tells us that 'they were not like any other nation, either in speech or manners.'

Now this isolation is, of itself, an important ethnographic note; it constitutes one of the most characteristic features of the Ugric peoples as distinguished from all other races.

The Aryan and Semitic nations, with hardly an exception, are found stretching over great continuous areas. It is true that they have frequently planted distant maritime colonies for commercial purposes, but their movements by land have been by a system of lateral extensions. They tend to colonise by individuals and families, rather than by tribes and nations. The ultimate results of this tendency are plainly manifested in the ethnological map of the world. The Semitic region in Syria, Arabia, and Egypt, appears as a continuous block; it is unbroken, and it has no detached outliers. So also it is with the Aryan nations. They all occupy continuous areas. We find an unbroken Sclavonic zone stretching across Europe in a great continuous crescent from the Adriatic to the Baltic. There are no outlying fragments of Sclavonic nationalities detached from the great Sclavonic area. It is the same with the Teutonic nations, which stretch continuously from the Danube to the Tay. The nations of Keltic blood are also in occupation of contiguous areas; they inhabit the whole western fringe of Europe—Scotland, Ireland, Wales, Cornwall, Brittany, Galicia. The Latin race is also continuous. So is the Hellenic. So also are the Iranian and the Indic peoples.

This is an absolute note. No Aryan or Semitic people is found separated by any great interval from other nations of kindred race.

An entirely opposite set of phenomena claim our attention when we come to draw the ethnographic map of the Ugric nations. Geographically we find them intermixed and broken up in the most arbitrary manner. The rule among them is dispersion and isolation, instead of congregation. They are scattered here and there in detached patches through sixty degrees of longitude.

The arrangement of the Aryan nations is like that of the sedimentary rocks—regular, orderly, continuous. The Ugric nations, on the other hand, are like the igneous rocks, the traps or the basalts; they protrude themselves here and there, bursting irregularly through the regular aqueous formations —superimposed, confused, discontinuous, eruptive. The deposition of the Ugric peoples has been evidently cataclysmal, rather than secular like that of the Aryans.

The examples are innumerable. On the Don we find an isolated patch of Mongols, separated by an interval of two thousand miles from their nearest Mongolic kinsmen, who occupy the slopes of the Altai. One portion of the Kirghiz Tatars, a Turkic tribe, lives just outside the wall of China, while we have to seek for the remainder of the horde at the other extremity of Asia, three thousand miles away, on the shores of the Caspian. The other Turkic tribes are as widely dispersed. There is an isolated Turkic tribe, the Yakuts, on the Arctic

Ocean, at the mouth of the Lena; there is another Turkic tribe in the Crimea, another on the Wolga, another on the Yenessei, another on the Bosphorus. The Yakuts on the Lena are separated by an interval of four thousand miles from their near congeners, the Seljuks on the Bosphorus.

It is the same with other Ugric tribes. One-half of the Samojeds roam by the shores of the Icy Ocean, the other half are a thousand miles removed, and dwell on the lesser Altai in the centre of Siberia. The intervening space is occupied by Finnic tribes, who themselves are as widely dispersed as the Turks and Mongols. Thus the map shows a Finnic patch in Sweden, a Finnic patch in Hungary, a Finnic patch in Russia, a Finnic patch in Persia, and a Finnic patch in Siberia. The Woguls on the Obi are three thousand miles removed from their near kinsmen the Magyars on the Danube.

If by the aid of comparative philology we thus construct the ethnographic map of the old world, the result is what we have here sketched in outline. The Aryans and Semites are found in occupation of continuous zones, while the Ugric nations are denoted by scattered and discontinuous patches, which are arranged like the squares on a chessboard.

It is easy to see why this should be so. Nomadic tribes, with their tents, their waggons, their herds, their horses, and their camels, ever on the move in search of pasturage, can do, and constantly have done, what the more settled Aryan agricultural races cannot do. They migrate, not by families or colonies, but as a nation. A portion of a Ugric horde, pressed by dearth or by hostile hordes, moves off, and by the title of the sword establishes itself in some desirable spot, removed by thousands of miles from the remainder of the horde, which has been left behind in possession of the ancestral pasturages. There is no need to colonize, it is only necessary to shift the camp.

Throughout the vast region which stretches from Pekin to Vienna, the ethnographic map of the world testifies that this has been the normal habitude of all nations of Ugric blood. They are the meteoric stones of ethnology.

The witness of history agrees with the witness of

ethnology. Ethnology gives us the results; history reveals to us the process by which those results have been attained. We find that the great permanent eruptive conquests and colonizations have as a rule been Ugric—either Mongolic, Turkic, or Finnic.

The Mongols have afforded one of the most recent instances. In the thirteenth century various Turkic and Mongolic hordes, from the neighbourhood of Lake Baikal and the Altai, became united under the standard of Tschengis Khan and his successors. They conquered China, they established themselves at Bagdad and at Moscow, and penetrated into Poland and Silesia. The Tatars in the Crimea and on the lower Wolga are isolated Turkic fragments which were left behind, and which thus mark the passage of Tschengis Khan and the Golden Horde. In the next century Timur or Tamerlane, a Tatar chieftain of Turkic blood, grasped the sceptre of Tschengis Khan, and, nearly repeating the exploits of his predecessor, carried his sword into Persia, Russia, Syria, Anatolia, and India. Baber, a descendant of Timur, completed the conquest of

India, and founded at Delhi that dynasty of the Great Mogul which has lasted to our own days.

About the same time the Mantschus, a Tungusic tribe, conquered China, and established at Pekin the dynasty which still continues to govern the Chinese empire.

Among migrants and conquerors the Turkic race has ever been conspicuous for its migrations and conquests. Though Tschengis Khan was himself a Mongol, his armies were largely composed of Turkic tribes, and his successors were of Turkic rather than of Mongolic blood.

In the sixth century the Avars, a Turkic tribe from the neighbourhood of the Caucasus, established an empire reaching from the Euxine to the Baltic.

The Cumanians, whose Turkic affinities are undoubted, and who seem to have been a branch of the Nogai Tatars, after a long career of conquest in Russia and Poland, finally settled down in Hungary, which they occupied in conjunction with the Finnic Magyars.

One of the latest and more permanent of Ugric conquests is that of the Seljuk, or Osmanli Turks, whose advance from the steppes north of the Caspian, as far as Constantinople, Belgrade, Cairo, and Tunis, is one of the cardinal events in mediæval history.

The Ghusnevids, who established a dynasty in Cabul, were also a Turkic tribe.

The Huns, whose affinities are believed to be Turkic, are first heard of through the ancient Chinese historians, as a fierce and troublesome people who roamed over the steppes to the north of the great wall of China. In the fifth century, under Attila, they fought their way from the Tigris to the Danube, they ravaged Italy, and penetrated as far as Gaul. Had it not been for the sword of Charles Martel, the world would probably have seen a race of Ugric conquerors, speaking a Turkic tongue, establish a Ugric civilization on the Seine, thereby forming a curious parallel to the Magyar colony on the Danube, or to the more ancient settlement which their Rasennic kinsmen established on the Arno and the Tiber.[1]

[1] It may be noted that the name of Attila is of an Etruscan type, and can be explained from Etruscan sources. It is

Second only in importance and magnitude to the wanderings of the Turkic hordes, have been the sporadic migrations of the Finnic tribes who constitute the second great branch of the Ugric race.

It was a Finnic tribe which, in the seventh century, threatened Constantinople, and established the great Bulgaric kingdom on the lower Danube. The Bulgaric name has remained to our own day, although the conquerors have been completely absorbed by their more numerous Sclavonic subjects.

The conquests of the Alans, who were probably also a Finnic tribe, were little inferior in extent and importance to those of the Bulgarians.

In the ninth century another Finnic people, the Magyars, abandoned their ancient pasturages on the lower Wolga, and broke up into two hordes.

still more curious that the Etruscans must have preserved a traditional remembrance of the Huns, who were their neighbours in Eastern Asia. In a design representing the legend of the Trojan horse, the door which shuts in the Greeks is labelled ΗUINS, which shows that the name of the terrible Huns must have been used to mean 'warriors' or 'enemies.' See the woodcut, *infra*.

FINNIC CONQUESTS.

We can trace the wanderings of one branch as far as Persia, but their ultimate fortunes are unchronicled. The second branch established themselves on the middle Danube, and took possession of the wide plains which derive their name of Hungary from the Turkic Huns who had occupied them some four centuries earlier. The Magyars still retain their separate nationality, and though enclosed on every side by Aryan nations, they still speak a Finnic language, which is closely allied to the speech of their nearest known kinsmen, the savage Woguls and Ostiaks, who now occupy the upper basin of the Obi near Tobolsk, separated by a space of two thousand miles from their civilized kinsmen on the Danube.

Within the last few years our knowledge of the migrations of the Ugric race has been most unexpectedly augmented by the great discovery made by Mr. Norris, that the language represented in the second column of the trilingual cuneiform inscriptions is a Finnic form of speech.[1]

[1] *Journal of Royal Asiatic Society*, vol. xv. pt. 1; Cf. Latham, *Descriptive Ethnology*, vol. ii. p. 264.

The great empires of the Euphrates comprised representatives of the three human families. The Persians were Aryans. The Assyrians and Babylonians were Semites. There are many reasons for supposing that the Medes were Turanians, and that the second column of the trilingual inscriptions is written in their language, which was therefore Finnic. This conclusion receives corroboration from several sources. Many of the Median tribe-names are of the Finnic type. Thus the name of the Mardi, one of the Median tribes, contains the characteristic Finn gloss *mart* or *murt*, 'men,' which occurs in the names of a very large number of Finnic tribes, such as the Mord-win and the Komi-murt. The name of the Budii, another Median tribe, is also a Finnic tribe-name which is seen in the tribe-names of the Vod and Wotiaks, and in the town-name of Buda in Hungary. Another Median tribe-name, that of the Matiani, as well as the national name of the Medes, contains the common Ugric tribe-name *mat*, which is the precise equivalent of the Turkic *ordu* (horde) and means 'tent.' The creed of the Medes also connects them with the Ugric races.

THE MEDES.

They not only worshipped the fire and the stars, but believed in a future life. The Magi, who were the Median sacerdotal clan, correspond to the shamans of the other Ugric races. The word *magic*, which we derive from the name of the Magi, testifies to the functions which they exercised. The Magi interpreted dreams, performed incantations, and practised sorcery. The Medes also agree with other Ugric races in having been a free people living in separate villages with a tribal organisation. The very name of DARIUS, the Mede, can be explained from Finnic sources. We know the traditional meaning of the name; it was ὑπὸ Περσῶν ὁ φρόνιμος, ὑπὸ δὲ Φρυγῶν ἵστωρ. The Finnic languages give us both these meanings. In Esthonian *tark* means prudent, and the Lapp equivalent *tjarrok* is rendered 'rigidus, asper.' The name of the Etruscan TARQUIN, which has been borne by many Siberian chieftains, is apparently from the same root, and may be explained as Tark-khan, the 'prudent prince.'

It appears probable therefore that at some remote period, not far removed from that at which the Rasenna established themselves in Italy, another

Ugric people, the Medes, succeeded in effecting a permanent settlement southward of the Caspian.

We see that for more than two thousand years—from the time of the migrations of the Medes and the Rasenna, down to the times of Arpad and Baber—eruptive conquest and settlement have been the habitudes of the Ugric race. Our ethnological conclusions are supported by the evidence of history. Together they establish the fact that throughout an immense period there has been a strong tendency, amounting to an ethnic characteristic, towards national migration and distant conquest, on the part of all the Ugric nations.

The bearing of this conclusion upon our argument is manifest. Encamped among the Aryan races of Italy we find the Rasenna, an isolated race of conquerors, powerful, warlike, with strange customs, strange gods, strange superstitions, and a strange speech. It may be urged that it is most improbable that their original home is to be sought at such a distance as the steppes of Northern Asia. To this it must be replied that instead of there being any inherent improbability that this singular isolated

THE RASENNA.

people should belong to the Ugric race, the whole analogy of history and ethnology ought to teach us that there is the very strongest antecedent likelihood that any such eruptive ethnic fragment would belong to the Ugric stock, among whom such isolations and migrations are the rule, and not to the Aryan or Semitic families, which almost invariably occupy continuous areas, and who are not addicted to intrusive national migrations.[1]

It may also be objected that the Ugric peoples have shown small capacities for such higher culture as we find existed among the Etruscans, and that it is little likely that a nomad Ugric tribe, necessarily in a very rudimentary stage of culture, should have been able to show the way to the Romans in the arts and refinements of civilised life.

In answer to this plausible objection we may urge the case of the Ottoman Empire, which offers a

---

[1] The conquests of the Goths, Vandals, and other Teutonic and Sclavonic races, were the conquests of armies rather than the migrations of nations. In these cases the language and nationality of the conquerors has rapidly disappeared; whereas in the cases of Ugric migrants they have mostly been permanently retained.

striking parallel to that of the Etruscan realm. The Etruscans maintained their national existence for nearly a thousand years. It took them this period to develop the arts and culture of which they were in possession at the time of their absorption by the Latin race. Less than a thousand years ago the Osmanli Turks were a mere wandering horde of Asiatic nomads, living the roving pastoral life which is now lived by their congeners, the wild robber tribes of Turkomans, Usbeks and Uigurs who still roam over the steppes to the eastward of the Caspian. It was only in the eleventh century that the Seljuks, one of these Turkic hordes, first pushed their way into Persia. In the thirteenth century they had advanced into Asia Minor and relinquished their nomad habits. In three centuries more they had extended their sway over Roumelia, Bosnia, Cyprus, and Constantinople.

The results on the Turks themselves of this migration from the steppe to the Bosphorus have been amazing. In the whole history of civilisation there is no such instance of a rapidly acquired culture. The Turks have shown not only great military prowess and the energy of conquerors, but they have developed a remarkable genius for the government and organisation of subject races. They have evinced a great capacity for external polish and refinement, and a taste for Oriental luxury. At first a mere nomad tribe of horsemen, they instinctively took to the sea, and disputed the empire of the Mediterranean with Venetians and Genoese, offering a striking parallel to the development of the piratical marine of the Etruscans. Throughout their history they have remained an exclusive dominant race, never amalgamating or blending with the conquered races, encamped rather than settled in the countries which they have overrun.

If the history of the Rasenna has been repeated in the history of the Osmanli Turks, it has been again repeated in the history of the Hungarians. The Magyars, like the Turks and the Rasenna, are a conquering military aristocracy, encamped among alien races, holding their own in spite of inferior numbers, by virtue of superior capacities for government and organisation.

The Hungarians still retain traces of the ancient

tribal organisation which we see in full force at the present day among the nomad tribes of Siberia, and which has always so greatly facilitated the migrations and conquests of the various Ugric hordes.

This form of political organisation, a tribal despotism, prevailed also among the Etruscans. The Etruscan nation was familiarly known to the Romans as the 'twelve tribes' of Etruria, *duodecim Etruriæ populi*. When the Etruscan dominion was extended beyond the Apennines, it was thought necessary to organise the newly acquired territory on the same twelvefold tribal plan as the parent state. Each of the twelve tribal cities was ruled by its LUCUMO, and the Etruscan league was the confederation of these tribal despots. When we come to examine the etymology of the word lucumo we shall find that it is a Turkic word meaning simply 'the great khan.'

The system of Etruscan government—tribal despotism and tribal federation—is essentially Ugric, and offers a striking contrast to the normal systems of government which prevail among Semitic and Aryan nations. Semitic races tend to a theocracy, while the tendency of the Aryans is to a democratic government in some form, with either an elected or an hereditary chief. The Greek republics, and the village communities of the Hindoos and Teutons, are examples of this tendency, which is manifested in a striking manner by the fact that directly Rome threw off the rule of her Etruscan Lucumo the liberated Aryan people instinctively recurred to a republican form of government.

It is not pretended that any one of these ethnic characteristics which have been discussed in this chapter, if taken singly, is sufficient, by itself, to establish any absolute cogency of proof as to the affinities of the Etruscans. But it may be fairly urged that their cumulative force is great. In every point as to which we are able to institute any comparison, there is a marked and definite resemblance between Etruscan and Ugric institutions, and the claim may therefore be advanced that a *primâ facie* case has been made out. We now come to the discussion of the two tests of affinity which can alone be claimed as absolutely conclusive—Mythology and Language. To the consideration of these two decisive tests the remainder of this book will be devoted.

CHAPTER IV.

THE ETRUSCAN MYTHOLOGY.

Ethnological Value of Mythology—Materials—The Tarunian Creed—Powers of the Underworld—Kulmu—Vanth—Hinthial—Nathum—Death Scenes of Etruscan Art—Charun—Lasa—Mean—Mantus—Amunti—Manes—Lares—Lemures—Genii—Junones—Susnath—Malavisch—The Powers of Heaven—Tina—Thana—Turan—Mearra—Nethuns—Sethlans—Phuphluns—Thesan—Thalna—Cel—The Novensiles—The Æsar—Summanus—Feronia—Ceres—Veda—Thurms—Camillus—List of Ugric words denoting the Sky, the Thunder, the Lightning, and the Sun.

For the purposes of ethnologic research, Comparative Mythology is, in some respects, an instrument quite as safe, and even more handy, than Comparative Philology. As regards the Etruscans this method is especially applicable, since we start with a considerable knowledge of the nature of their creed, but with a complete ignorance of the nature of their speech. Mythology is so intimately interwoven with language that an investigation of the Etruscan mythology will necessarily supply us with the meanings of a considerable number of Etruscan words. We shall thus be able to work from the known to the unknown.

As regards the religious beliefs of the Etruscans, the materials in our hands are, fortunately, ample in quantity, and, to a great extent, unimpeachable as to quality. The monuments of Etruscan art—the vases, the mural paintings, and more especially the engraved mirrors—represent, as a rule, mythologic subjects; and though in the later examples the scenes are mostly taken from the cycle of Greek legend, it is seldom difficult to separate the genuine Etruscan element. The Romans, moreover, incorporated a large portion of the Etruscan theologic system into their own. Those elements of the Roman mythology which are absent from the Greek Pantheon appear to be chiefly of a Ugric character; and even when they are not distinctively Rasennic, they may be attributed with considerable probability to the Finnic substratum upon which the Rasennic element was superimposed.

In the conjoint evidence supplied on the one hand by the Etruscan monuments, and on the other by the non-Hellenic portion of the Roman mythology, it is manifest that we possess ample materials for our investigation. It may indeed be affirmed that our knowledge of the Etruscan mythology is more extensive and more certain than our knowledge of the Ugric beliefs with which it has to be compared. The paganism of the Finnic and Turkic tribes of Siberia is now fast disappearing before the advances of Christianity and Islam; and if it were not for the ancient Ugric creed which is fortunately conserved in the Kalevala, the comparison before us could hardly be attempted with any fair prospect of success.

There is abundant ground for believing that, before the separation of the Finnic and Turkic nations, there was already in existence a common Ugric faith. At some remote period all the Ugric tribes must have worshipped the same Divine Beings by the same names. It appears, moreover, that this primæval faith was shared by some of the most distant congeners of the Ugric race. The ancestors of the Basques, of the Chinese, of the pre-Aryan Dravidian races of India, and even of the ancient

THE TURANIAN RELIGION.

Egyptians, possessed, before they separated, the elements of a common religion, as well as the elements of a common speech.

We shall now endeavour to ascertain what were the distinctive features of this ancient creed, and then to show how far it prevailed also among the Rasennic race.

It is from China that we obtain the earliest, the simplest, and the purest standards of Turanian speech and of Turanian belief.

There are three main elements which are to be distinctly recognised in the Chinese mythology, and which are also to be traced in the beliefs of the Ugric nations.

The Chinese reverence three orders of divine beings:[1]

I. The powers of heaven: namely, the spirits of the sun, of the moon, of the stars, of the sky, of the clouds, and of the thunder.

II. The powers of earth: the deathless terrestrial spirits which represent or inhabit the mountains, the stones, the rivers, the fields, and the trees.

---
[1] See Max Müller, *Science of Religion*, pp. 156, 200, 209, 215.

III. The ancestral powers: the spirits of the departed, who are believed to retain an interest in the concerns of their descendants, and to be able to influence their fortunes.

This threefold system of belief is found to prevail among all the Ugric tribes. Our earliest evidence is derived from the Chinese historians. Many centuries before the time of Attila, the Huns, a Turkic race, dwelt on the frontiers of the Chinese empire. The historic records of the Chinese first mention these HIONG-NU, as they are called, in the time of the dynasty of Shang (B.C. 1766 to B.C. 1134), and they disappear from Chinese history a century or two after the Christian era.[1] These Hiong-nu worshipped, we are told, the sun and the moon, the spirits of the sky and of the earth, and the spirits of the departed. Menander, the Byzantine historian, an envoy of Justinian, gives us much the same account of the religion of the Turkic tribes which he visited in his embassy. As to the beliefs of the Mongols we derive evidence to the same effect from Marco Polo, and other mediæval travellers. Ample information

[1] Klaproth, *Asia Polyglotta*, p. 210.

as to the creed of the ancient Finns may be gathered from the Kalevala, which is a perfect encyclopædia of Ugric mythology. At the present day, according to Castrén, the heathen tribes of Tungusic and Samojedic descent still worship three orders of spirits: the heavenly, the elemental, and the ancestral.

This threefold system of belief, which characterises all the Turanian nations, prevailed also among the Etruscans.

The supreme heaven, the elemental powers, and the ancestral spirits, were the objects of their reverence.

A large portion of this creed was incorporated by the Romans. A certain portion of it is not, however, distinctively Turanian, but is the common property of the Aryan and the Turanian nations.

It will therefore be our safest course to leave to the last the discussion of those mythologic names and beliefs which may or may not have been adopted by the Romans from the Etruscans, and to discuss in the first place the names of those supernatural beings whose names are found exclusively upon the undoubted monuments of Etruscan art, and who were not transferred to the Roman system. It will thus be plain how far we are dealing with that which is of a genuine Rasennic character.

It has been shown in the last chapter that the most obvious indications which connect the Etruscans with the Turanian family, are those derived from the tombs on which they lavished all the resources of their arts and their wealth. We have seen that these costly monuments are the expression of characteristic beliefs connected with the grave and the future life. Hence we may expect to find that those portions of the mythology of the Etruscans which most clearly connect them with other Turanian nations are the beliefs which have reference to death and the world of spirits. The Romans, moreover, found this portion of the Etruscan culture far less easy to assimilate than the usages and beliefs which were connected with nature worship, which, being in harmony with the Aryan genius, were more readily incorporated into the Roman system.

In the death scenes which are such favourite subjects of Etruscan art we find representations of four mythological personages whose characters are unmistakable, and whose names are fortunately preserved. These names are KULMU, VANTH, HINTHIAL, and NATRUM. These four names, like the beliefs which they embody, are all thoroughly un-Roman and un-Aryan in character, and they merit special attention, as they supply us with a crucial test, both philological and mythological, as to the truth of our hypothesis respecting the Ugric origin of the Etruscan race. We shall therefore discuss them with some minuteness.

KULMU

A magnificent marble sarcophagus, evidently the last resting-place of a dame of high degree, was found at Clusium in the year 1826.[1] On the upper part is seen the recumbent effigy of the occupant, while below, on the side of the sarcophagus, ten most touching and instructive figures are admirably

[1] The woodcut is reduced from the engraving given by Micali, *Monumenti*, plate lx. The sarcophagus is figured on a smaller scale by Inghirami, *Storia della Toscana*, plate xxix. The inscriptions are given by Fabretti, No. 564.

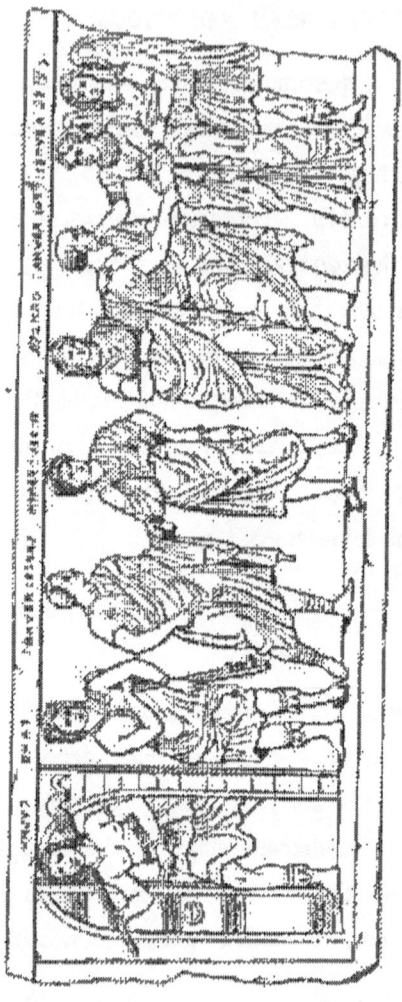

SARCOPHAGUS FROM THE TOMB OF THE APHRODA FAMILY.

NOTE.—The inscriptions are to be read from right to left.

carved in *alto relievo*. At the right-hand side we see the parting between the deceased lady APHUNEI and her husband (LA)RTH APHUNA. A winged messenger from the unseen world, whose name K.. TI is unfortunately partly obliterated, with hand upon the lady's arm, stands behind her, gently but firmly forcing her away. The lady, with a sorrowful but resigned expression on her face, lays her hand lovingly on her husband's shoulder. He, a man in years, bald-headed, and of stately presence, earnestly lays hold of his wife's wrist, vainly striving to detain her. An unmarried daughter, THANCH(VIL), stands behind the father, with her hand on his shoulder, endeavouring to soothe his grief. Then follow a married son, LARKE APHUNA, and his wife, with a married daughter and her husband.[1] Then comes the sepulchre, with its door half opened. By the side of it stands a deity labelled VANTH. Out of the door of the tomb issues another deity labelled KULMU. She bears in one hand the flaming funeral torch, and in the other the emblematic shears. As to the meaning

---

[1] These two figures have been omitted from the woodcut for want of space. The deities are distinguished by buskins.

of the last figure there can be no reasonable doubt. KULMU, issuing from the tomb, and bearing the symbols of dissolution, is obviously intended to be a personification of the SPIRIT OF THE GRAVE.

Here we have a crucial case which will give us valuable aid in deciding as to the affinities of the Etruscan language. We have a very peculiar and unmistakable Etruscan word, as to the signification of which there can be hardly any doubt. It is with a somewhat anxious curiosity that we inquire whether there is any known language, Aryan, Semitic, or Turanian, in which this word KULMU denotes the grave.

The answer is so plain and so decisive that it is a marvel that this well known word alone, should not, forty years ago, have supplied the key to unlock the Etruscan language. That this should not have been the case can only be accounted for by the supposition that no person acquainted with the Kalevala has chanced to be also familiar with the Etruscan inscriptions, or the Etruscan mythology.

In the ancient Finn mythology KALMA is the name of the deity who pre-eminently rules over the grave and its inhabitants.[1] In the Kalevala, which is the storehouse of our knowledge of ancient Ugric belief, the word *kalma* is commonly employed in this sense, though it is occasionally used as a mere equivalent for the unseen world, or 'Hades.' Thus in one passage we read, 'In the earth is the abode of the dead, of those who have disappeared in *Kalma*.'[2] But in the Kalevala the word ordinarily denotes, as has been said, the deity of the netherworld, who presides over the shades of the departed.[3]

The Kalevala represents a very ancient form of Finnish speech. In the spoken language of the modern Finns the pagan mythological element has

---

[1] Die Gottheit, die vorzugsweise über die Gräber und deren Bewohner herrschte, hiess *Kalma*.—Castrén, *Finn. Mythol.* p. 127.

[2] *Kalevala*, Rune 33, vv. 259, 260.

[3] In the Egyptian mythology, ISIS is the goddess of the underworld, and is nearly equivalent in office to the Etruscan KULMU, and the Finnic KALMA. It is very significant to find that in the Kalevala there is a deity called NIISI, and that the names of KALMA and NIISI are interchanged, as if their offices were identical, or as if these were two names borne by the same deity. It is curious to find in the Finnish Kalevala the link between the Etruscan Kulmu and the Egyptian Isis.

nearly disappeared, and we find that the word *kalma* is used ordinarily to denote 'the smell of a corpse.' We have here evidently a linguistic survival of the old belief. It is obvious that the distinctive cadaverous odour floating in the chamber of death must have been identified with the 'Spirit of the grave' supposed to be hovering around the corpse, and when the belief in the latter gradually disappeared, its name came to be applied to the other.

The belief which appears in the Kalevala as to a spirit presiding over the grave has, however, not entirely disappeared from among the Finnic nations. The Siberian Ostiaks, who inhabit the banks of the River Obi, retain more or less of their original heathenism, and still worship a malevolent deity whom they call KULY, who is evidently connected with the grave, since in Ostiak the word *kul* denotes 'death.'

This root *kul*, meaning 'death,' may be traced through the whole region of Ugric speech. We have the Finnish *kuol* 'to die,' and *kalmet* 'deathly white'; in Lapp *kalme* means 'the grave'; while *koloma* in Wogul, and *kuly* in Permian mean 'dead,' and in Wotiak *kolto* means 'the dead.' In Samojed *kolmu* means the 'spirits of the departed,' *khulam* is 'to die,' *kullim* means 'dead' and *kurmo* 'death.' In Hungarian, as usual, the Finnish *k* changes into an *h*, and *halni* is 'to die,' and *halal* means 'dead.'

In Permian the word *kul* has come to mean 'the devil,' and in Ostiak *gühl* has the same meaning. The transition to this sense can perhaps be best explained by a reference to the Turkic GHOUL, the loathsome spirit who haunts the grave-yard, and battens on the corpses. We have also the Turkish *kul* 'ashes,' which may probably be a related word. But in the Turkic languages an initial *k* is frequently dropped, a habitude which enables us to identify with the Finnic forms the Turkic words *ulum* and *ulem* 'death,' and *ul-mek* 'to die.' In the Teleut Tatar, however, the initial consonant has escaped abrasion, and we find the word *jolym* meaning 'death.'[1]

[1] Traces more or less faint of the Etruscan KULMU seem to exist even in the non-Ugric branches of the Turanian family. The Indian KALI, a deity adopted by the Hindoos from the Turanian aborigines, is 'the destroyer.' In Japanese

MYTHOLOGY.

The affinities of these words may be thus exhibited:

Etruscan	K	U	L	M	U	. the spirit of the grave.
Kalevala	K	A	L	M	A	. the ruler of the grave.
Finn	K	A	L	M	A	. the smell of a corpse.
Samojed	K	O	L	M	U	. the spirits of the departed.
Lapp	K	A	L	M	E	. the grave.
Wogul	K	O	LOM		A	. dead.
Hungarian	H	A	L	N	I	. to die.
Ostiak	K	U	L		T	. an evil spirit.
Indian	K	A	L		I	. the destroyer.
Turkish	on ou		L			. the spirit of the graveyard.
Turkish	K	U	L			. ashes.
Ostink	K	U	L			. death.
Finn	K ao		L			. to die.
Turkish		U	L U M			. death.
Coptic				M	OU	. death.
Coptic	KH	O	L			. a cave.

VANTH

On the great Clusium sarcophagus, side by side with KULMU, the spirit of the grave, appears another

koloñ means 'the dead.' The Lesghic *kol* is a 'mouth,' and in Coptic *chol* is a 'tooth,' *khol* a 'cavity' or 'cave,' *mhaou* the 'tomb,' and *mou* 'death.' We may explain and combine these abraded fragments of the ancient Turanian word if we remember that Orcus is represented as the toothed and gaping mouth of Hades, and that the word Orcus may be explained by means of the Basque *oriz*, a 'tooth.'

mythological being, labelled VANTH, who seems to have just opened the door of the tomb, and who bears in her hand what appears to be a huge key, the key of the opened tomb, or possibly a club or other instrument of destruction.

We have another representation of VANTH with which this may be compared. In the year 1857 a splendid tomb was discovered at Vulci, the walls of which are covered with spirited designs of the highest interest and importance. One of these paintings, which is reproduced in the frontispiece,[1] represents the slaughter of Trojan prisoners by Achilleus at the obsequies of Patroklos. Immediately behind ACHLE (Achilleus) stands a mythological personage, who, with upraised finger, is touching him on the shoulder, and evidently prompting him to cut the throat of a Trojan prisoner who kneels before him. This figure is labelled VANTH.

If we compare these two representations we see

---

[1] The woodcut has been taken from the magnificent work of Noël des Vergers, *L'Étrurie et les Étrusques*, plate xxi. See also Fabretti, No. 2162, and plate xl.

that both KULMU and VANTH represent 'death,' but
with a difference. While KULMU represents the
'Spirit of the grave,' VANTH represents rather the act
or cause of death, the taking away of life, or as we
may say, the 'Angel of Death.' The Turkish dictionary supplies us with exactly this sense for the
word VANTH. In Turkish *vani* means 'ready to
perish,' and the substantive *fena* (*vana*) means 'destruction,' 'annihilation,' 'death,' while the same
word used as an adjective means 'dangerous,' 'sad,'
'grievous.' The Etruscan *th* is equivalent to *d* or *t*,
and the suffix *d* or *t* in Turkish commonly denotes
abstract nouns, as in *melekyut* 'sovereignty,' from
melek a 'king, *munidat* 'a proclaiming,' from *munadi*
a 'herald,' *nejdet* 'courage,' *nedamet* 'repentance.'
VANTH, therefore, who prompts Achilleus to destroy
the prisoners, is the 'Spirit of Destruction' personified.
This word can be so completely explained from
Turkish sources that it is hardly needful to trace
the word elaborately through the other Ugric
languages. In the Finnic languages the root appears
with some change of meaning. The Finnish *wana*
and the Hungarian *ven* mean 'old,' a sense closely

allied to the Turkish *cani,* 'ready to perish.' We trace the same general meaning in two of the Yenisseian languages. In the Kot dialect *fenan* means 'ashes,' and in the so-called Yenissei-Ostiak *ben* means 'corrupt,' 'rotten.' The Ude *wai,* 'grief,' and the Lesghi *chuna,* 'death,' seem also to be related words.

HINTHIAL

The tomb at Vulci, containing the painting of the slaughter of the prisoners by Achilleus, enlightens us not only as to the name and nature of VANTH, but gives us another important mythologic word, respecting the meaning of which there can be hardly a shadow of doubt. VANTH, as we have seen, stands behind Achilleus. Behind VANTH the ghost of Patroklos stands gazing, with a smile of saddened satisfaction, on the scene. Over his head is written HINTHIAL PATRUKLES, words which must mean the 'ghost of Patroklos.' We gather therefore that the Etruscan word *hinthial* meant a 'ghost,' or 'spectre.'

104 MYTHOLOGY.

Fortunately this word HINTHIAL occurs again and again on the Etruscan monuments, in such connection that no doubt whatever can remain as to

THE NECROMANCY OF ODYSSEUS.

its meaning. Indeed, so long ago as 1835 Bunsen arrived at the conclusion that HINTHIAL must mean 'ghost.' The great Vulci tomb had not then been opened; but in that year a bronze mirror, now in the Vatican, was discovered at Vulci, containing the scene of the necromancy of Odysseus, from the 11th book of the Odyssey.[1] On the left hand UTHUZE (Odysseus) is seen seated. He has just invoked from the shades the soul of the divine Tiresias. The messenger of the underworld, THURMS AITAS (Hermes of Hades), appears in the centre of the design. He supports in his arms the ghost of Tiresias, who is represented with closed eyes, and drooping corpse-like form. Over the head of this spectre from the grave is written HINTHIAL TERASIAS, words which, as Bunsen suggested, undoubtedly mean the 'ghost of Tiresias.'

On a vase found at Vulci we have a representation of the death of Penthesilea, Queen of the Amazons.[2] On the right, labelled PENTASILA, is the falling corpse, the head drooping, and the limbs relaxed as in death. Just in front is her spirit,

---

[1] Gerhard, *Etruskische Spiegel*, plate ccxl.
[2] Inghirami, *Storia della Toscana*, plate lxxiv.; Fabretti, No. 2147.

labelled MINTHIA, attired in the same manner as the corpse. As in the former scene, TURMUKAS, the messenger of the underworld, advances to conduct the released spirit to the world of shades.

A further illustration of the meaning of the word MINTHIAL is afforded by a most beautiful and instructive mirror which is now in the British Museum.[1] A beautiful being called MALAVISCH is seen seated at her toilet. A spirit called HINTHIAL holds a mirror before her. The word HINTHIAL must here denote the 'image' reflected in the mirror. Our own usage of the words *spectre, spectral, spectrum*, and *speculum*, may suffice to explain how naturally the Etruscan word HINTHIAL would be used to denote either the 'spectre' of the dead, or the 'spectrum' of the living. Savages believe the image in a mirror to be a real being, and if shown their reflected image they imagine they have seen their wraith.

The word HINTHIAL has almost as much ethnological importance as the word KULMU. Its meaning

---

[1] Gerhard, *Etruskische Spiegel*, plate ccxiii.; Fabretti, No. 2475. The meaning of MALAVISCH will be presently discussed. See p. 129.

in the Etruscan language is unmistakeable, and it can be easily traced through the whole of the Ugric languages and the Ugric creeds. The Ugric religions are, as we have seen, Animistic. All visible objects, animate or inanimate, are believed to have a soul or spirit, which either inhabits or protects them. From the Kalevala we learn that the ancient Finns imagined that every stone, every house, every brook, every spring, and every tree, had its guardian spirit or 'soul.' This was called the *haldia* or *haltia* of the object.[1] It can be shown that this Finnish word *haltia* is, letter for letter, the same as the Etruscan word *hinthial*. The Etruscan *th* is universally equivalent to *t* or *d* in other languages, and if we trace the Finnish word *haltia* through the Ugric languages we shall find that several of them have preserved the *i*, the *n*, and the *l* of the Etruscan *hinthial*.

The first syllable of the word *haltia* or *hinthial* may be recognised in the Tungusic *han* or *hane*, and the Mongolic *t'sen*, words which denote the little images of wood or metal which are fabricated by

[1] Castrén, *Finn. Mythol.* pp. 170, 182.

the Tunguses and Mongols to represent the spirits of men and animals, and which are supposed to give to the possessor a certain power over the spirits of the objects which they resemble.[1]

This Tungusic word *han*, an 'image' or 'idol,' will hereafter enable us to explain another Etruscan word, KANA, which is frequently inscribed on works of art, and which has long been recognised as necessarily meaning a 'statue' or 'image.'

Closely related to the Tungusic *han* we have the Turkish words *jan* 'soul,' 'ghost,' *jinn* a 'spirit,' and *jen-aze* a 'corpse.' Among the Turkic tribes of Siberia the initial aspirate has disappeared, and we have the word *ainu*, which is the general name for the spirits of animals and of all natural objects.[2] We find a close approximation to the Etruscan and Finnic forms in the Turkish word *khayal*, a 'spectre' or 'ghost.' This word has lost the *n* of the Etruscan word, but it has retained the final *l* which has been

---

[1] Castrén, *Finn. Mythol.* p. 236; Klomm, *Cultur-Geschichte*, vol. iii. p. 104; Latham, *Descriptive Ethnology*, vol. L pp. 326, 359.

[2] Castrén, *Finn. Mythol.* pp. 186, 220.

abraded in the Finnic form. The Chinese word *shin*, or *jin*, 'spirit,' preserves the Etruscan vowel sound which has elsewhere been changed.

The Tasmanians, Algonquins, Abipones, Zulus, and other tribes of savages, believe that a person's shadow is the same as his ghost. The Greenlanders say a man has two souls, which they identify respectively with the breath and the shadow. The natives of Fiji also believe that a man has two souls, one, which they call his 'dark spirit' is the shadow, the other is his image reflected in water or in a mirror.[1] Bearing in mind this habitude of rude tribes we may expect to find the word HINTHIAL meaning not only a ghost, and the reflection in a mirror, but also a shadow. Even in our English speech the word 'shade' is used to mean both a ghost and a shadow. We may therefore identify with the Etruscan HINTHIAL the Turkish *ghyulghe* a 'shadow,' and the Tatar equivalents *holaga* and *kolatka*.

The equivalence of these words may be thus exhibited:

[1] Lubbock, *Origin of Civilisation*, p. 123.

MYTHOLOGY.

Etruscan	π	I	з	TH	I	A	L	. . . .	a spectre,
	u	E	N	TH	I	A		. . . .	an image.
Finnish	.	B	A	I.	D	I	A	. . . .	a spirit.
Turkish	.	KU	A		T	A	L	. . . .	a ghost
Chinese	.	SU	(	N				. . . .	a spirit.
Turkish	.	J	I	NN				. . . .	a spirit.
Turkish	.	I	A	N				. . . .	a soul.
Mongol	.	T'TS	E	N				. . . .	an idol.
Tungus	.	U	A	N	E			. . . .	an idol.
Etruscan	.	K	A	N		A		. . . .	a statue.
Turkic	.		AI	N		A		. . . .	a spirit.
Karagass	.	H	O	L		A	GA	. .	a shadow.
Koibal	.	S	O	L	AT		SA	. .	a shadow.
Turkish	.	OR		T		D	L	OUE . .	a shadow.

Guided by these analogies, the etymological rudiments of the Etruscan word *Hinthial* are not difficult to detect. In the frontispiece, each of the Trojan captives about to be sacrificed is labelled TRUIALS. The final *s* is here probably a sign of the definite article, as in the Mordwin language. The bilingual inscriptions, as we shall presently see, prove conclusively that the Etruscan suffix *al* is equivalent to the Latin word *natus*. TRUIAL therefore means 'child of Troy,' or 'born at Troy,' and TRUIALS means 'the Trojan.' We shall also see that the syllable *thi* in Hinthial is a root denoting either 'death' or the 'grave.' The first syllable *hin* has

been already shown to mean 'spirit' or 'image.'
Therefore *Hin-thi-al*, a 'ghost,' would be an agglutinated word meaning literally 'the image of the child of the grave.'

NATHUM

On a bronze mirror[1] now in the Berlin Museum we have a representation of URUZTHE (Orestes) about to kill KLUTHUMUSTHA (Clytemnestra). Orestes holds his mother by the hair, and is plunging his sword into her breast. Close beside him, with snake-like hair standing on end, with tush-like fangs in his mouth, and a serpent in either hand, stands a Fury who is labelled NATHUM. The well known legend enables us to identify the Etruscan NATHUM with the Greek Ἄτη, the pursuing Fury who doggedly follows in the track of crime, and even visits on the children's heads the sins of the fathers. We might therefore reasonably expect to find that the Etruscan word NATHUM might mean 'the pursuer.' The

[1] The woodcut is taken from Gerhard, *Etruskische Spiegel*, plate cxxxviii. See also Gerhard, *Gottheiten*, plate vi. fig. 5; Fabretti, No. 305.

Ostiak Samojeds are a race of Siberian hunters, who inhabit the forests on the upper course of the Obi. In their language the word *notam* means to

ORESTES KILLING CLYTEMNESTRA.

'track,' to 'pursue,' to 'follow by the tracks or footsteps.' We have already seen that the Etruscan *th* is equivalent to the Ugric *t*; and the vowel *o*, which is not found in the Etruscan alphabet, is usually replaced by *a* or *u*. The Ugric *notam* is, therefore, the exact phonetic equivalent of the Etruscan NATIUM.

The word is not found in the Finn mythology. It may, however, be noted that Marco Polo relates that the Mongols of his day worshipped a powerful deity whom they called NATAGAI. The name of this god was probably *Natha*, the suffix being evidently *aga*, 'lord.'

It will be observed that beneath the design there is a recumbent figure, which seems to represent Orestes being devoured by a dragon. The inscription is either NUSTHIEEI or NUSTHIEH. The meaning of this word is not absolutely indicated by the design, but the Turkish *niusti*, 'annihilation,' or *ezhdiha*, a 'dragon,' may perhaps furnish an appropriate meaning.

The whole case as to the Ugric affinities of the Etruscan language might safely be rested on these four words that have just been considered—XULMU, VANTH, HINTHIAL, and NATIUM. These words are all of them inscribed on works of art found in recently opened tombs, which have safely preserved their precious secret for more than twenty centuries. The figures over which these four words are written indicate their meaning almost as plainly as if they were accompanied by a Latin translation. These four words are purely Etruscan; no Latin writer transmits them, or gives a hint of their existence. They are utterly foreign to all the Aryan languages. Directly we turn to the Ugric languages we find the precise words, letter for letter, still bearing the precise meanings which the Etruscan words have independently been shown to require. It may be affirmed that the case is more absolutely complete and certain than any that has been brought forward either from the Egyptian or Assyrian monuments. These four words are not arbitrarily selected for comparison. They are the only Etruscan words whose meaning is unmistakably indicated by the monuments. The mathematical chances against these words being accidentally coincident, both in sound and meaning, in the Etruscan and the Ugric languages, can be easily calculated. The chances are many millions to one. Therefore the probability established in the preceding chapter, that the Etruscan language possessed Ugric affinities, may now be said to be reduced almost to a mathematical certainty.

Some other Etruscan beliefs, connected with the unseen world, still remain to be discussed.

In the mural paintings we not unfrequently find, as in the Egyptian tombs, elaborate representations of the events supposed to happen to the soul after death—its journey to the land of spirits, or the judgment pronounced upon it by the rulers of the underworld. The soul, robed in white, is usually on foot, but is sometimes seated in a car, or mounted on a horse, as an emblem of the long journey which has to be undertaken; while a slave attends it, bearing on his shoulders a sack or a vase, containing the provisions for the journey. Some souls are represented as calm and resigned, gliding along with rods in their hands; others are depicted as full of horror and dismay. Attendant spirits, good and evil, are seen contending for the possession of the souls. The good spirits are coloured red, the evil spirits are generally black. The evil spirits usually have their heads wreathed with serpents, a distinctively Turanian emblem, and they bear in their hands a hammer or mallet. Sometimes the hammer is uplifted as in the act of striking, and we see the wretched souls vainly imploring mercy on their knees.[1]

The name CHARU or CHARUN is commonly affixed to one of these demons. He is not altogether the same as the CHARON of the Greeks, whose attributes were probably borrowed partly from Egypt and partly from Etruria. CHARU is armed sometimes with the oar or rudder, as a sign of his office of infernal ferryman; but more frequently he carries uplifted a ponderous hammer, evidently an instrument of torture. He is represented as revolting in appearance, and he is often distinguished by negro features and complexion.[2] In the whole Etruscan mythology there are few representations that occur more universally than this hideous demon with the hammer. This being the case, it is the more worthy of note that we are able to recognise the same per-

---

[1] Dennis, *Etruria*, vol. i. pp. 310, 319, 322; vol. ii. p. 194.
[2] Ibid. vol. ii. p. 206.

sonage in the beliefs which prevail among the Siberian tribes. Pococke, the Oriental traveller, tells that the Turkic tribes which he visited a century and a half ago had a curious superstition. They believed that two black demons dwell in the sepulchre with the dead, and if he be found guilty of any crime, they punish him with hammers. Unfortunately Pococke does not mention the name of these demons; but the black complexion, the hammer, and the office, agree so precisely with the representations of the Etruscan CHARU, that we can hardly refuse to admit the identification.[1] Moreover, the myth of the journey of souls across the river of death, and the office of the infernal ferryman, are both found in the Kalevala.[2] The boat of the dead also occupied a prominent position in the belief of the old Egyptians.

The name CHARUN may be explained from Ugric sources. The suffix -un occurs repeatedly in the names of Etruscan deities, and is probably an

[1] See Dennis, *Etruria*, vol. i. p. 310; Preller, *Römische Mythologie*, p. 460, 461.
[2] Castrén, *Finn. Mythol.* p. 132.

abraded form of *aina*, a 'spirit,' or of *jum*, 'god.' The first syllable of the name may be either the Turkic *kara* 'black,' or it may be from a root which denotes an 'oar' and a 'river.' A 'river' is *schur* in Wotiak, *schor* in Zirianian, *ky* in Samojed, *chor* in Lesghi, and *agar-su* (*su*=water) in Turkic. An 'oar' is *kyur-ek* in Turkish, and *kürn-ak* in Koibal Tatar. CHARUN would thus mean either the 'black spirit' or the 'ferryman.'[1]

In addition to the malevolent demons, we find two attendants on the departed soul who are of gentler aspect and milder nature. They seem to be decreeing or recording Fates, and bear the names of LASA and MEAN. They are represented with stylus and paper, recording, as in the Egyptian monuments, the judgments pronounced against the deceased.[2]

LASA perhaps means the 'gentle' one. In Wogul *las* and *lasy* mean 'gentle,' 'slow,' and in Hungarian *lassa* and *lassan* have the same meaning. Among the Samojeds, and also among the Ostiaks,

[1] It need occasion no surprise that we do not find KERBEROS on the Etruscan monuments. He is an Aryan conception, and may be identified with the Vedic *Çarvara*.

[2] Dennis, *Etruria*, vol. ii. p. 63.

LOSI, LOS, LUOSO, LUOS, LOII, or LONCII, are either worshipped as guardian deities, or are regarded as serviceable spirits ready to do the bidding of the shaman.[1] But as Christianity and Mahometanism have advanced, the usual result has followed. The Gods of the earlier creed become the devils of its successor. Thus in Yenissei *liitze* means the 'devil,' and in Samojed the word *loose* has the same signification.

The Turkish phonetic equivalent of the Finnic *l* is *j*. The word *lasa* would therefore become *jasa*, and the Turkish dictionary gives the word *jesa*, with the signification of 'judgment' or 'retribution.' This sense brings us near the Chinese *le*, 'fate,' which is probably the original source of the Etruscan LASA.

The Etruscan deity MEAN seems to have been a guardian spirit taking charge of the souls of the dead. At the present time MEAN and KULT are two of the minor deities, malevolent rather than kind, who are worshipped by the Siberian Ostiaks. We may without much hesitation identify them with the

[1] Castrén, *Finn. Mythol.* pp. 188, 221.

MEAN and KULMU of the Etruscans. The Ostiak MEAN is the same as the old Finnish deity MANA, who is represented in the Kalevala as the ruler of TUONELA, the land of the dead.¹

This remarkable name, MEAN, which so unmistakably connects the Etruscan pantheon with the mythology of the Kalevala, contains the same root as the names MANES, MANIA, and MANTUS.

These names may be conveniently discussed together. The MANES were the deified spirits of the dead. The worship of ancestral spirits, under the names of MANES, LARES, and LEMURES is well known, as it was adopted by the Romans from the Etruscans, and became an integral and important part of Roman belief, and an essential mark of difference between the religions of Greece and Rome.

From Festus, Servius, Macrobius, and Varro, we learn that MANTUS and MANIA were the King and Queen of the underworld. Representations of both are believed to exist on the Etruscan monuments, though unfortunately no names have as yet been found attached to the representations. The deity

¹ Castrén, *Finn. Mythol.* p. 127.

who is supposed to be MANTUS is figured as an old man, with crown, wings, and torch. MANIA, the mother of the Lares, was a still more fearful deity, propitiated by human sacrifices. In connection with these words must be taken the MUNDUS, the pit at Rome which was considered to be the mouth of Orcus, and the MANDUCUS, a symbolic effigy with gaping jaws which was borne aloft in Roman games and processions to represent the underworld.

We have just seen that in the mythology of the Kalevala the ruler of the land of the dead was called MANA. This word means 'under the earth,' or 'belonging to the earth,' being the locative or possessive case of *ma*, a word which means 'the earth' in all the Finnic languages. From *mana* we get *mana-la*, the 'underworld,' literally 'the place of Mana,' and *manalaiset* the 'people of the underworld,' which is the chief name given in the Kalevala to the spirits of the departed.[1]

The MANALAISET of the Kalevala are to be identified with the MANES of the Romans and Etruscans.

---

[1] Castrén, Finn. *Mythol.* pp. 123-128; cf. Weske, *Vergleich. Gram.* p. 95.

MANTUS, the Etruscan diespiter, seems to be the father of the Manes, the *t* being derivable from the Turkic *ata*, 'father.'

The Ugric root which underlies all these words is of vast antiquity, anterior to the first separation of the Turanian family. This appears from the fact that the ancient Egyptian name for the kingdom of the dead was *amenti*, a word radically identical with the *manala* of the Finnic Kalevala, the realm of the Etrusco-Roman *Mantus*, and of the Cretan *Minos*.[1]

Uniting these long separated fragments of the Turanian creed and speech, we see that the underworld, *amenti* or *manala*, was inhabited by the manes, or *manalaiset*, the souls of the departed, who were the children of *Mania*, and were ruled over by *Mantus*, the king of souls.

The LARES were the spirits of virtuous ancestors, while the LARVÆ were the spirits of evil men. The root of the two words is probably the same. It means the 'Lords' or the 'Great Ones.' In the

---

[1] Compare the Lydian Manes, the Phrygian Mania, the Egyptian Menes, the Tibetan Mani, the Siamese Manu, and the Indian Menu.

forms Lar,[1] Larth, Larthi, and Larthia, the word is extremely common in the Etruscan sepulchral inscriptions, being used either as a personal name, or as a title denoting rank, and equivalent to 'lord' or 'lady.'

It is easy to understand how the spirits of deceased ancestors, who were believed to rule the fortunes of their descendants, came to be ordinarily designated as 'the lords.'

The analogies of this characteristic word are not far to seek. The Albanian language has preserved many elements of the neighbouring Etruscan speech, and there can be little doubt that the Albanian word λjάρτε, which means 'high,' 'magnificent,' is identical with the Etruscan *Larthi*.[2] If the word be transliterated into a Ugric form, we should expect to find the *l* becoming a *j*, or a *dj*.[3] This phonetic

---

[1] Lars, the Roman form, is still used as a personal name among the Lapps. Lessing, in his Norwegian journey, was accompanied by a Lapp named *Lars*. Klemm, *Cultur-Geschichte*, vol. iii. p. 64.

[2] The *la'da* of the Lycian inscriptions, which means 'wife' or 'lady,' may possibly be an abraded form of the Etruscan *larthia*.

[3] See Schott, *Altaische Sprachengeschlecht*, p. 119.

law enables us to recognise the Etruscan word *lar* in the Samojedic *jeru*, which means 'lord,' 'master,' or 'prince.' In the Taigi, which is a dialect of the southern branch of the Samojeds, we find the form *djar* with the same meaning. This brings us to the title of the Russian emperor, the *Tzar*, an appellation which is doubtless of Tataric origin. In the Finnic languages we find the same root, *ejer* meaning 'high,' and *suur* 'great,' while in the Hungarian we have the abraded form *ur*, a 'lord.' The supreme god of the Lapps is DJERMES, the 'lofty one,' a name identical with the Esthonian TARA, 'god,' and the Wogul TAROM, 'heaven.' SAR-AKKA, the 'ancient lady,' is the name of a tutelary deity whose images are used by the Lapps to protect their flocks from evil.[1]

There is every reason to believe that the Romans derived from the Etruscans their practice of keeping in their houses little images to represent the LARES of their ancestors. It is more than curious to find that this ancient custom still prevails among the northern Ugric tribes. When a man dies the Ostiaks make an image of the deceased, and preserve it in

[1] Castrén, *Finn. Mythol.* pp. 142, 178.

the house or tent for three years, treating it with exactly the same respect as if it were the deceased person. The Samojeds and Mongols do the same. It is still more worthy of note that the Tschuwash call these tutelary images of their ancestors by the name JER-ICH,[1] a name which we have seen is etymologically identical with the Etrusco-Roman LARES.[2]

The general name for the spirits of the dead, including both Manes, Lares, and Larvæ, was LEMURES. We only possess this word in its Latin form, and it is manifest that the last syllable is only the Latin plural termination. In the word LEMUR we recognise the Etruscan plural termination, *ar* or *ur*, and it would therefore appear that the root is *lem*. The LEMUR were the spirits of ancestors, and remembering that the Etruscans traced descent through the mother and not through the father, we might expect to find that the word means 'maternal ancestors.' This is actually the case. The Turkish word *li-umm* means 'on the mother's side,' 'maternal.' The

---

[1] The suffix *ich* denotes the plural.
[2] Castrén, *Finn. Mythol.* p. 179; Castrén, *Ethnol. Vorles.* p. 116; Lubbock, *Origin of Civilisation*, p. 229; Klemm, *Cultur-Geschichte*, vol. iii. pp. 119, 194.

liummar, lemur, or *lemures* would therefore be 'those of the mother's side,' the spirits of the maternal ancestors.

In the Turanian spirit-world a prominent place is taken by the guardian spirits who were believed to be the constant protectors of the persons to whom they were attached. This doctrine also takes its place in the Etruscan mythology, and from thence it penetrated into the Roman system. Every human being was believed to have his protecting spirit, whose sex corresponded to the sex of the protected person. Every man had his GENIUS, and every woman had her JUNO. These words have not yet been recognized on the monuments; we only possess them in their Latin guise, and they are evidently accommodated in form to an assumed Latin etymology. But if these words were, as is doubtless the case, borrowed from the Etruscans, there is no difficulty in detecting a Turanian source. We have seen that in Chinese the word *shin* or *jin* means 'spirits.' These *shin* are of three classes—celestial, terrestrial, and ancestral. The ancestral spirits, the spirits of kings, sages, and families, are called *jin kwei*. This word *jin* pervades all the Ugric languages. The JINNS of the 'Arabian Nights' are probably to be regarded as ultimately not Semitic, but Turanian. The word *jinn* in modern Turkish denotes the 'genii,' the spirits of Nature, a race of intelligent beings with unsubstantial bodies of the nature of smoke. The Turkish *jan* 'soul,' and other related words, have already been enumerated (p. 108 *supra*), and will suffice to explain the Etrusco-Latin word GENIUS, which denotes a man's soul, or his protecting and inspiring spirit.

The word JUNONES, which was the name of the protecting spirits of women, if it is not merely a differentiated form of the word *genius*, may be referred to the root *jen*, *jum*, or *gun*, which, as we shall presently see, is the most universal of all Ugric names for divine beings.[1]

It is doubtful whether the PENATES belonged to the Etruscan system. They may, perhaps, be identified with the BUNI, who were formerly wor-

[1] See p. 159, *infra*.

shipped by the Tunguses as protecting spirits, though, since the introduction of Christianity, they have come to be regarded as evil demons.[1]

We find on Etruscan mirrors representations of two protecting or guardian spirits, who are called SNENATH and MUNTHUCH. They seem to be guardians of the health. SNENATH may with some confidence be identified with SUONETAR, who is represented in the Kalevala as the deity in charge of the veins and sinews of the human body.[2] In the Kalevala she is represented with a distaff spinning fresh veins and sinews for the wounded. In the Etruscan mirror where she is depicted she has in her hand an object which looks like a spindle whorl. The Turkish *sihhat*, 'health,' may serve to show that the word is common to both the great branches of the Ugric stock.

In the mirror representing the toilet of MALAVISCH, already referred to (p. 106 *supra*), MUNTHUCH holds MALAVISCH by the chin and brow, apparently directing her face in the direction of the 'mirror,'

[1] Castrén, *Finn. Mythol.* p. 185.
[2] Ibid. p. 187; Gerhard, *Etr. Sp.* pl. cxi.

ZIPNA or VIPNA,[1] which HINTHIAL holds before her. If MENTHUCH is 'eyesight,' we may identify her with MENNU, the Finnic deity who had charge of the eyes.[2]

MALAVISCH, or MALAKISCH, as the name is sometimes written, has been identified somewhat arbitrarily with Helen or Venus. She cannot be Venus, as in the mirror in the British Museum TURAN (Venus) is looking on while the toilet of MALAVISCH is being performed.[3] Nor can she be Helen, who bears her Greek name, ELINAI, in the scenes in which she appears. It is possible that the solution may be found in the *Maahiset*, who, in the Finn mythology, are the 'fairies,' or spirits of natural objects. The Esthonian form of the word is *Maallused*, which indicates an abraded *l*, and an original form *maal-ahiset*, which corresponds pretty closely with the Etruscan MALAKISCH or MALAVISCH. The Turkish

---

[1] The same word ZIPNA or VIPNA is written over another mirror in a design in the British Museum, representing the meeting of Ceres and Proserpina. Gerhard, *Etrusk. Spiegel*, plate cccxxiv.

[2] Castrén, *Finn. Myth.* p. 117; Fabretti, Nos. 2475, 2487, 3054 *ter*, 2494 *bis*.

[3] Gerhard, *Etrusk. Spiegel*, plate ccxiii; Fabretti, No. 2475; see also Nos. 2507, 2508, 2497.

mal, 'fortune,' may be a related word, and possibly throw some light on the meaning of the Etruscan name.

We have now traced to their Ugric sources the more peculiar and characteristic features of the Etruscan belief as to the world of spirits. It will in the next place be necessary to attempt the more difficult task of identifying the higher Etruscan deities, the heavenly and terrestrial spirits, and, as far as may be, of sifting out from the Roman mythology its chief non-Aryan elements.

The supreme deities of the Etruscans, with their nearest Aryan equivalents, were as follows:—

Etruscan	Aryan
1. Tins	Jupiter, Zeus, Zeus.
2. Thana	Diana, Janua.
3. Turan	Venus Urania.
4. Menrva	Minerva, Athena.
5. Nethuns	Neptune.
6. Sethlans	Vulcan.
7. Phuphluns	Bacchus.
8. Thesan	Aurora.
9. Thalna	Juno.
10. Usil	Apollo, Helios.
11. Summanus	Summanus.
12. Novensiles	The Thunderers.
13. Æsar	The Gods.

These Etruscan names can be traced in the Ugric mythologies, and their meaning can be explained from the Ugric languages.

Though the names given to the supreme deity by the Turanian nations differ widely in form, they are ultimately reducible to the same elements, and all testify to the same primitive objects of worship. The Turanian and the Aryan mythologies agree in this—all the supreme deities resolve themselves ultimately into the chief celestial phenomena, the 'dawn,' the 'sky,' the 'sun,' and the 'thunder.' The Semitic nations, on the other hand, have, from the earliest times, shown themselves capable of a far higher conception of Deity than the mere nature worship of other races. With them God was the Ruler. They worshipped EL the 'Mighty,' ADONIS the 'Lord,' MOLOCH the 'King,' RIMMON the 'Exalted.' Their supreme Deity was POWER.

The names of the chief Turanian deities are derived from two simple roots, *ten*, 'high,' and *sil* to 'pierce.' The first root explains the names of the 'sky' gods and the 'thunder' gods; the second explains the names of the 'sun' gods and the

132   *MYTHOLOGY.*

'lightning' gods. Words derived from these two roots can be traced in scores of languages, with endless phonetic variations, and are used to denote the sky, the day, the night, the dawn, the thunder, the lightning, the sun, the stars, the moon, the wind —in short, every celestial phenomenon and every celestial being.

For convenience of reference, and to avoid constant repetitions, the leading variations in sound and meaning which these roots assume in the Turanian languages have been tabulated at the end of the chapter.

TINA

The supreme Etruscan deity was TINA; he corresponds to the Aryan Zeus, and is a personification of the heaven.

Among the Chinese we find the simplest and most primitive forms of Turanian language and belief. The central object in the Chinese creed is TIEN,[1] a word which originally meant the 'sky,'

[1] See Max Müller, *Science of Religion*, p. 204.

and afterwards the 'sky god.' To this root we trace *teng-ili* (heaven-place?), and *teng-ri* (heaven-man?), the Hunnic, Turkic, and Mongolic names for 'heaven' and 'God.' The Hungarian word for 'God' is IS-TEN, the 'lofty spirit,' or the 'spirit of heaven.' The Turkoman *tin*, 'night,' and the Tschetschenz *dini*, 'day,' are almost identical in form with the Etruscan TINA.

THANA

This word is only a phonetic modification of TINA. The Kirghiz *tang*, and the Tschjulim *tan* mean the 'morning,' and in Tobolsk and Teleut Tatar *tan* means the 'light.' The Etruscan *th* being equivalent to the Latin *d*, the Etruscan THANA is phonetically identical with the Roman DIANA. In the Finnic languages a Turkic *t* often becomes *j*. Thus in Zirianian 'God' is *jen*, and *jomu* in Tscheremis. Hence it would appear that JANUS and JUNO, both 'heaven-gods,' belong to the Finnic substratum, while TINA, THANA, and DIANA, are probably Rasennic.

TURAN

Although a Turanian etymology seems to be preferable, it cannot be denied that perfectly adequate explanations of the names of TINA, THANA, DIANA, and JUNO, can be supplied from sources purely Aryan. This, however, is not possible in the case of TURAN, a word which is unmistakably non-Aryan. The name occurs constantly on Etruscan mirrors, and owing to its not having been adopted by the Romans, there are no phonetic complications. TURAN is a personification of the 'sky,' agreeing closely in character and office with Venus Urania. In Ostiak and Wogul the word *torum* means both 'heaven' and 'God.' TARA is the supreme 'heaven-god' of the Esths. The Etruscan TURAN may be compared with the *turjan tythi*, 'the daughter of heaven' or 'heaven maiden,' who appears in the Kalevala.[1] It seems probable that the Egyptian ATHOR may be identified, both philologically and mythologically, with the Etruscan TURAN. If this identification be correct, it would serve to show the

---

[1] Castrén, *Finn. Mythol.* pp. 50, 53, 211, 216, 312, 345.

immense antiquity of the TURAN worship, and would be one of the many indications of a distinctively Finnic element in the population of ancient Egypt.[1]

MENRVA

If we may judge from the frequency with which the names occur on works of art, TURAN and MENRVA or MENERVA, were held in higher estimation than any other Etruscan deities. The prevalence of the Menrva worship is shown also by the fact that in Rome the name of the Turanian MINERVA completely displaced that of the Aryan ATHENA. The close correspondence in function of the two deities made this more easy.

One of the surest conclusions of comparative mythology is the identification of the Homeric ATHENA with the Vedic DAHANA, the 'dawn.' But with respect to Minerva no passable etymology has ever been suggested. The usual *pis aller* derivation

[1] On an Etruscan mirror TURAN is styled TIFANATI. The word *Tifa* is probably only the Latin *Diva*. The latter part of the name is probably that of ANAITIS, the eastern name of Venus.

from the Latin *mens*, although adopted both by Cox and Preller, must be summarily rejected by the instinct of every comparative mythologist. The substitution in Rome of MINERVA for ATHENA was so absolute, that we may expect to find that the two names, though philologically so diverse, are really identical in their primitive significance. It is, therefore, most satisfactory to discover that MINERVA, a pure Ugric word, has precisely the same meaning as the Aryan word ATHENA. MENEVA, like DAHANA, is the 'dawn.' The first syllable, *men*, obviously denotes the 'heaven,' the 'sky.' The Hungarian *meny*, the Mordwin *manen*, the Permian *immyn*, and the Ostiak *noman*,[1] all mean 'heaven.' The signification of the next syllable *er* is not much more difficult to discover. We find it throughout

[1] This form throws considerable light on the etymology. In Samojed *nom* means 'God,' and *men* means 'house.' The Ostiak word *noman* 'heaven,' of which the Permian and Hungarian words are abraded forms, would therefore be the 'abode of God.' The Latin word *numen* seems to be the same as the Ostiak *noman*, and to be derived from the Finnic substratum of Italy. It may be noted that in Yakut *māna* means 'broad,' 'extended,' and *māna tanara* means 'the immeasurable heaven.' MANITOU is the North American 'heaven-god.'

the whole range of Ugric speech, signifying either
'red,' 'sunrise,' 'east,' 'dawn,' or 'early.' 'Red' is
ur in Wogul, and *veres* in Hungarian. The Mongolic *ör*, and the Hungarian *vira*, mean the 'dawn.'
The Lapp *ar-et* and the Turkish *er-te* mean 'early
in the morning' (literally 'red heaven'). In Mandshu *d-er-gi* is the 'east.'¹ In the Ostiak mythology,
ŎRTIK, the special favourite of TURUM (heaven) is
probably a personification of the dawn, and the
same word, ŎRDOG, has come to mean 'the devil'
among the Hungarians.² The desinence *va*, which
is very common in the Ugric languages, remains to
be accounted for. It may be the old Ugric definite
article *vas*, it may be a participial desinence, or
possibly it may be a sign of the inessive case. But
whatever may be its precise significance, there can
be no doubt that MENERVA or MENRVA denotes the
'red heaven' or the 'dawn.'

This interpretation of the name and nature of
the Etruscan MENRVA may throw light on some of
the obscure Minerva myths. Thus the two Me-

¹ See Schott, *Altaische Spr.* p. 62.
² Castrén, *Finn. Mythol.* p. 62.

nervas who occasionally appear together on the same mirror, and whose relations have so much perplexed Etruscan mythologists, are seen at once to denote respectively the morning and the evening twilight. The Menerva myths will probably show themselves capable of illustration, if not of explanation, from the Kalevala.¹

NETHUNS

A deity called Nethuns, who appears on an Etruscan mirror, is probably the same as NEPTUNUS, who was completely identified by the Romans with

---

¹ The root *men*, in MENRVA, appears also in the name of WAINA-MOINEN, the chief hero of the Kalevala, who goes with his comrades in a life-long quest of SAMPO. The Finn word *wana*, 'old,' shows that Wainamoinen is the 'ancient heaven,' (Ju-piter), while Sampo seems to be the twilight. Thus, when Sampo plunges into the sea, the land becomes dark, and there is no more sun, but when Sampo is washed up again the sun immediately re-appears. The esoteric meaning of the Finnic mythos would thus seem to be the same as that of the great cycle of Aryan legend—the daily pursuit by the solar heroes of the golden-haired Dawn. The wool and swan's feathers of Sampo are probably the white cumulus clouds, and correspond to the shirt of swan's feathers in the Aryan legend of the swan maidens.

the Aryan POSEIDON. I believe that Neptune, like Poseidon, will prove to be ultimately a solar, and not a marine deity. One indication is afforded by a mirror found at Vulci, on which are depicted together THESAN, USIL, and NETHUNS, who apparently represent the 'dawn,' the 'rising sun,' and the 'risen sun.' The etymology of the word points to the same conclusion. The suffix, which appears several times in the names of Etruscan deities, means 'God.'[1] The first syllable is explained by the Hungarian word *nap*, which means the 'sun,' and also the 'heaven.' The Samojedic words *nup*, *nub*, *nop*, and *num*, which mean 'heaven,' 'sun,' 'god,'[2] and the Ostiak *nai*, the 'sun,' are evidently related forms. The name of JAPAN is only a European corruption of NIPON, which means 'sun-source' or the 'east.' The connection between the Finnic and Egyptian mythologies has already been remarked. It is not impossible that the Samojedic *nub* may explain the name not only of the Etruscan

---

[1] See p. 141, *infra*.
[2] See Castrén, *Finn. Mythol.* p. 17; Klaproth, *Sprach-Atlas*, viii.

140 MYTHOLOGY.

Neptune, but of the Egyptian NOUB, NUF, or ANUBIS, who is distinctly a solar deity.

SETHLANS

SETHLANS was the Etruscan fire-god, and corresponds to the Roman Vulcan. The first syllable of the name means 'fire' in most of the Turanian languages. In the Hungarian, which often offers a close approximation to Etruscan forms, we have *suto*, 'a baker,' *sütes*, 'roasted,' and *sutet*, 'quickly baked.' The letters *s* and *t* being interchangeable, we may identify this root with the Ostiak *tut*, 'fire.' We have the abraded forms *siu* and *tu* in Samojed, *sa*, *so*, and *sie*, in Lesghi, and *su* in Basque, all meaning 'fire.' In the Turkic dialects of Siberia the former instead of the latter part of the root has as usual been abraded, and we find the words for 'fire' are *oot, ut, ud, od, ot*, and *oth*. The last word preserves the aspirate, as in the Etruscan name. The suffix *-lans* is found also in the names of NETHUNS, PHUPHLUNS, THESAN, and JUNO. It is probably the Ugric word for 'God,' as appears by comparison with the Permian LUN, 'god,' a form of the Finnic *jum* or *jen*. The Ostiaks have a similar form, *lung*, *long*, or *lonch*, being the general name which they give to their idols.

PHUPHLUNS

The Etruscan city of PUPLUNA (Populonia) was under the protection of PHUPHLUNS, an Etruscan deity who corresponds to the Roman Bacchus. The suffix -*luns* is evidently the same designation of divine beings which is found in SETHLANS and NETHUNS. I am inclined to explain the first syllable of the name by means of the PÄIVÄ and POHJOLA of the Kalevala. Phuphluns would thus be a solar deity, in fact, the 'sun' himself; and the analogy with the Aryan Dionysos would be perfectly maintained.

THESAN

It has been usually assumed that the Etruscan deity THESAN corresponds to the Latin AURORA, and is a personification of the 'sunrise.' The suffix -*an* is probably *aina*, a 'spirit' or 'deity,' while the prefix may be referred to the wide-spread Ugric root *tus*, which signifies 'fire,' 'star,' 'sparks,' 'dust.' Hence the Burjät word *tujan*, 'sunbeams,' which may suffice to explain the Etruscan name.

THALNA

THALNA is doubtless equivalent to JUNO, and means the 'day.' She appears on numerous mirrors, and is frequently represented as assisting at the birth of solar deities, such as Apollo, Minerva, or Dionysos. The root is seen in the Ostiak *tschel*, *chatl*, the Samojed *jale*, *tala*, and the Andi *tljal*, *tshsal*, words which all mean the 'day.' The suffix -*na* would be a common Finnic desinence, which signifies 'belonging to.'

USIL

Among the treasures of the Vatican Museum is a bronze mirror from Vulci, on which are depicted three deities, NETHUNS, THESAN, and USIL.[1] USIL

---

[1] Fabretti, No. 2097. See p. 139, *supra*.

THE SUNRISE.

bears a bow, and is evidently intended for APOLLO. From a passage in Festus it would appear that *ausel* was a Sabine word meaning the 'sun.' Hesychius says that among the Etruscans *ausel* meant the 'dawn.' We may conclude, therefore, that the USIL of the monuments personified the 'rising sun.' The ramifications of the wide-spread Turanian root *sil* are traced on p. 154. It may here suffice to say that in Samojed *tschel* is the 'sun,' and in Permian *asal* is the 'morning.'

NOVENSILES

The DII NOVENSILES are stated to be the nine great Etruscan gods who possessed the privilege of hurling thunderbolts. The name does not occur in the Etruscan inscriptions, and may probably be Sabine, and therefore Finnic, rather than Rasennic. The latter portion of the name, *-siles*, apparently contains the Finnic root *sil*, 'piercing,' 'bright,' which we see in the Wogul *sely*, the Wotiak *sil-aka*, and the Samojedic *tschillirn*, words which all mean the 'lightning.' It is no less evident that in *noven*, the former portion of the name, we have the Finnic and Samojedic word *nom, num, numma,* or *noman,* which means 'heaven' and 'God.' The word NOVENSILES would, therefore, signify the 'lightning gods,' or the 'heavenly lighteners.' It has not been found possible to make a list of so many as nine thundering deities; and it is obvious that the real meaning of the name being unknown to Roman writers, the interpretation and the orthography have been accommodated to suit a plausible Latin etymology.

ÆSAR

According to Suetonius ÆSAR was an Etruscan word which meant 'God.' Since *aesar* also means 'God' in Erse,[1] the statement of Suetonius has been brought forward as a proof of the Keltic affinities of the Etruscans. It is quite possible that the word may not be really Rasennic, but, like several other so-called Etruscan words, may have belonged to the Keltic conquerors, who dislodged the Rasenna from

---

[1] Compare the Teutonic *Æsir,* 'gods,' and the Vedic *Asura.* See Cox, *Mythology of the Aryan Nations,* vol. I. p. 335.

the valley of the Po. It is, perhaps, equally probable that the word may have been among those, and they are many, which the Irish Kelts adopted from Ugric tribes who preceded them in Ireland.

But, however this may be, it is as easy to explain the word ÆSAR from Ugric, as from Aryan sources.

Castrén asserts that all the Altaic nations reverence as the highest deity, ES, who is evidently the visible heaven, the sky.[1] Among the Turkic races of Siberia the word *asa*, or *yzyt*, is 'God.' Among the Yenisseians the word *ais*, *eis*, or *es*, means both 'heaven' and 'God,' and *'asa* denotes the devil. The Mongols call their tutelary idols *esan*, and *ser* is heaven in Lesghi. This root *es* may be taken as the source of the Etruscan word ÆSAR. The suffix *-ar* is the Etruscan plural termination, which we find in such words as *klen-ar*, 'children,' and *tul-ar*, 'tombs.' It may be identified with the suffixes *-lar* and *-nar*, which are respectively the signs of the plural in the Turkic and Mongolic languages.

[1] Castrén, *Finn. Mythol.* p. 229.

SUMMANUS

SUMMANUS was the god who emitted such lightnings as flew by night. He belongs apparently to the non-Aryan element in the Roman mythology, though there is no direct evidence that he was an Etruscan deity. The name may be explained by reference to the Samojedic *chaimmn* or *chaimuno*, which means 'thunder,' and its Finnic analogies.[1]

According to Stralenberg the Yakuts, a Turkic tribe on the Lena, call their chief deity by the name SAMAN, and the priests of the Siberian Mongols are universally called SHAMANS, which is probably a related word.

FERONIA

Varro informs us that the Sabine name of Juno was FERONIA. If the Sabines could be proved to have been Aryans, we should have to identify Feronia with the Vedic VARUNA, the overarching firmament. But if, as seems more probable, the

[1] See p. 154.

Sabines belonged originally to the Finnic substratum, we might refer the name to the Albanian PEREXDI, 'God,' a word which seems to be related to the Phrygian Βερεκύνδαι, which meant δαίμονες, and which we may identify with PERKUNAS or PERUN, the thunder-god of the Lithuanians, and DURCHAN, the chief god of the Mongols.

CERES

The name of CERES is also probably Ugric, as is indicated by the Ostiak *kyra*, and the Lapp *aker*, which mean a 'field,' and the Wotiak *giri*, a 'plough.' Moreover, according to Bishop Agricola, KEKRI was the Finn harvest god. CERIE was a goddess worshipped by the Marsi, an Italian hill-tribe whose name proclaims them to have been of Ugric blood.[1] The word meant 'creator,' as we learn from the Salian hymn, where the words *cerus manus* are translated *creator bonus*.[2] The word

---

[1] MARSI means the men, and the root is of constant occurrence in Ugric tribe names. See p. 78, *supra*.
[2] See Preller, *Röm. Mythol.* p. 70.

is also found in the Etruscan inscriptions bearing the same sense. Thus at the entrance to one of the tombs at Vulci there is the carved figure of a man, with the inscription,

    EKA : SUTHIK : VELUS : EZPUS : KLENSI : KERINU.'

Here the word *ker-in-u* must mean 'made' or 'carved,' and, as we shall see hereafter, the inscription must be translated,

    'Here a tomb Velus Ezpus piously made.'

VESTA

There can be little doubt that the most primitive element in the religion of Rome was the worship of Vesta and Janus.[2] It has been already shown that JANUS may not impossibly have been originally a Finnic, and not an Aryan deity. The identity of the word VESTA with the Greek ΠΕΣΤΙΑ raises a strong antecedent probability that the Vesta worship was an Aryan cultus. On the other hand, the nature

---

[1] Fabretti, No. 2183.
[2] Preller, *Röm. Mythol.* p. 57.

of the cultus is Turanian rather than Aryan, ranging with the Siberian worship of household spirits. The antiquity of the Vesta worship also, makes it probable that it may have been derived from the Finnic substratum, which the Aryans must have found in Greece as well as in Italy. If this be the case, the names Vesta and Hestia are at once to be explained by the Ugric *eiesta*, a word which means the 'hearth' among the Karelian Finns.

TURMS

TURMS or TURM was the name of an Etruscan deity who presided over boundaries, and acted as the messenger of the underworld. Till we are better acquainted with the phonetic laws which regulated the transliteration of Greek words into the Etruscan speech, it cannot be absolutely affirmed that the word TURMS is not the linguistic equivalent of HERMES, who has been identified with the Vedic SARAMEYAS, the 'rising wind.' But if, as seems more probable, TURMS is a genuine Rasennic name, there are two possible explanations of the word.

TURMS may have been a sky god, like the rest, and the name, like that of TURAN, may be referred to the Wogul *torum*, 'heaven.' There are, however, reasons for supposing that the office of heavenly messenger belonged rather to CAMILLUS, and that TURMS was primarily the god of boundaries. In that case we may refer the name to the root *tur* (cf. Turkish *dur-mak*, to 'stand'), which in many Ugric languages means something high or pointed, something placed or fixed, hence a post or pillar.[1]

CAMILLUS

We gather from a fragment of Callimachus that the Etruscan name of Mercury was CAMILLUS.[2] According to Servius the name given by the Etruscans to youthful priestesses was CAMILLÆ. The attendant minister of the Flamen Dialis at the sacrifices was called CAMILLUS, a name which, like

---

[1] So the Aryan root *mark*, a 'boundary,' seems to underlie the name of MERCURY, who was represented by an upright stone.

[2] See Müller, *Die Etrusker*, vol. ii. p. 71.

other Roman sacrificial terms, is presumably of Etruscan origin. It appears, therefore, that the Etruscans gave this name both to the messenger of the gods and to the messengers of the priests. We may take it that the word meant a 'bearer' or 'messenger' in Etruscan. The word is widely spread throughout the Turanian languages, and signifies a 'bearer,' a sense which applies equally to the messenger of the gods, to the servitor at the sacrifices, and to the CAMEL, whose office is to bear the burdens of the Mongolian nomads across the steppes of Central Asia, and whose name may, perhaps, be ultimately of Turanian rather than of Semitic origin.

In the Albanian language, which preserves so many Etruscan words, we have the precise word χαμαλ, a 'carrier,' a 'porter.' This leads us to the Turkish *hammal*, a 'porter,' a 'carrier,' and to the Tungusic *ugam*, to 'load on the back,' to 'carry,' and the Finnish *kanda*, to 'bear.' We have also in Albanian χαμ,[1] a 'riding-horse,' a word which may

---

[1] Compare the Basque *sam-aria*, a 'beast of burden,' and the Armenian *sam-bik*, a 'mare.'

perhaps throw light upon the legend of the fleet Camilla, who, according to Virgil, was suckled by a mare.

These investigations show that the Etruscans held clearly the two great doctrines which have ennobled the superstitions of the Turanian nations, and which form a portion of the religious heritage of the world into the possession of which the Semites and the Aryans have at length now likewise happily entered. The central object of the Turanian belief was a Supreme God, the great beneficent protecting power of Heaven. They believed also, as firmly as we do ourselves, in a future life and in a future judgment—they held that according to the deeds done in the body, so the future state will be.

We may take comfort in the thought that the Heavenly Father whom they ignorantly reverenced did not leave them without some faint witness of Himself, but dimly guided them to a glimmering knowledge of the Eternal Goodness, and gave them also in their darkness the solace of that blessed hope of immortality which is the stay and refuge of the Christian life.

THE HEAVENLY POWERS.

LIST OF URIC WORDS DENOTING THE POWERS OF HEAVEN.

TINA	Mongol	DEN	high.
	Turkish	TEN-LU	big.
	Chinese	TIEN	heaven, God.
	Hungarian	IS-TEN	God.
THANA	Turkic	TAN	light, dawn.
	Finnic	TANO-LI	heaven, God.
	Yakut	TANGARA	heaven, God.
	Turkic	TANG-RI, TENGRI, TARI	heaven, God.
TURAN	Esth	TARA	God.
TURM	Tscherkess	TORA	God.
TURMS	Tschuwash	TORA	God.
	Wogul	TAROM	heaven, God.
	Ostiak	TOROM, TOURUM	God.
DIANA	Turkic	TAN	light.
	Turkic	TUIN, TJUN	night.
	Turkic	EJUN, KUN, OGN	day, sun.
	Basque	EGUNA	day.
	Lesghian	XINA	day.
	Abasian	DJUAN	heaven.
	Samojed	CHU	dawn.
	Lesghi	CHU	night.
	Mordwin	JON-DOL (heaven-fire)	lightning.
JUNO	Lapp	AIJAN-TOL	lightning.
JANUS	Permian	SCHUNDY	sun, day.
	Permian	JEN, JEN-LON	God.
	Basque	JINCOA	God.
	Tungus	NJANGJA	heaven.
	Tscheremis	JOMA, JOMU	heaven, God.
	Finn	JOMA-LA	God.
	Lapp	JABMEL	God.
	Permian	GYMA-LA	thunder.
	Finn	JUMU	thunder.

MYTHOLOGY.

SETH-LUNS PHUPH-LUNS	Samojed . NUM, LOM . . God, thunder Permian . LUN . . . day. Ostiak . LUNG . . . gods, idols. Thibetian . NAM . . . God.
NOVEN-SILES NUMEN	Ostiak . NOMAN . . . heaven. Wogul . NUMAN . . . high.
MEN-RVA MIN-ERVA	Permian . INMEN . . . heaven. Mordwin . MÄNEX . . . heaven. Hungarian . MENY . . . heaven.
SUMMANUS	Yakut . SAMAN . . . God. Samojed . CHAI-MUN, KAL-NOM . thunder.
NETHUNS NEPTUNE	Samojed . NUM, NOM, NED, NOR . heaven, God. Hungarian . NAP . . . . sun, day. Ostiak . NAI . . . . sun.

From the root *sil*, to pierce, we have

NOVEN-SILES	Tungus . SILIN . . . lightning. Turkic . JASIL, JILDRIM . lightning. Permian . SILAKA . . . lightning. Wogul . SALT . . . lightning. Samojed . TSCHILLIEN . lightning.
USIL	Samojed . TJELL . . . sun. Turkic . CHWEL . . . sun. Samojed . JELE, TEL . . day. Ostiak . TSCHEL . . . day.
THALNA	Andi . TLJAL, TSHZAL . day. Lesghi . SAAL, ZALLA . God. Lesghi . DELU, DELI . thunder. Wogul . TSCHOCEL . . thunder. Samojed . KAL-NOM . . thunder.
THESAN	Permian . TYSEL . . . star. Hungarian . TÜZ . . . fire.
SETH-LUNS	Wogul . TAUT . . . fire. Samojed . SIU, TU . . . fire. Turkic . UT . . . . fire. Tschetschens SUTA . . . star. Hungarian . SUTES . . . roasted.

CHAPTER V.

THE DICE OF TOSCANELLA; OR, THE ETRUSCAN NUMERALS.

Bilingual Inscriptions—The Rosetta Stone—Discovery of the Inscribed Dice—Supreme Philological Importance of this Record—Formation of Numerals—Fingers, Hands, and Toes—Determination of the first six Etruscan Digits—The remaining Numerals—Mortuary Inscriptions—The Radix—The Ordinal Suffix—The Etruscan System Vigesimal— -ty, -teen, and ten—Siemsathrms—Numeral Adjuncts.

ALTHOUGH correspondences of creeds and customs may raise a strong presumption as to ethnic affinities, language, after all, is the ultimate test of race. It is the only test which is thoroughly complete and satisfactory. To the investigation of the Etruscan language the remaining portion of this book will be devoted.

The failure of the numerous attempts that have been made to explain the Etruscan inscriptions must be attributed to the want of a key to determine the nature of the language. The success attained by Young and Champollion in deciphering the Egyptian inscriptions must be attributed to the fortunate discovery of the Rosetta Stone, which contained a bilingual inscription of sufficient length to disclose the nature of the Hieroglyphic writing and the structure of the Egyptian language.

No Etruscan 'Rosetta Stone' has yet been found. We possess, it is true, seventeen so-called bilingual inscriptions, but when they come to be examined they prove to be most disappointing. None of them contain more than four words, many of these words are so defaced as to be illegible, and the remainder appear to be only proper names. The seventeen bilingual inscriptions, taken together, do not give us the absolute Latin equivalent of a single independent Etruscan word. At the most all that it has been possible to affirm respecting them is that they assign a positive meaning to one suffix.

It is possible that the excavations which are going on among the Etruscan tombs may yet furnish what has so long been anxiously sought in vain—an Etruscan Rosetta stone—a bilingual inscription long

DISCOVERY OF THE DICE. 157

enough to establish the nature of the Etruscan grammar, and to supply the meanings of half-a-dozen genuine Etruscan words.

But though no such inscription has as yet been found, a discovery has been made, which, for the purposes of the present inquiry, has proved itself to be as invaluable as the Rosetta inscription was to Champollion and Young. If it had not been for the two DICE OF TOSCANELLA I should not have been able to convert into something like certainties those vague suspicions as to the affinities of the Etruscan race which have been set forth in the third chapter of this book.

During a long series of years the brothers Campanari have been patiently pursuing their excavations among the tombs in the neighbourhood of Toscanella, the presumed site of the ancient Etruscan city of Tuscania.

So long ago as the year 1848, by a piece of great good fortune, they discovered in a tomb a pair of Etruscan dice, which, instead of being marked in the usual manner by pips, had an unknown word inscribed in Etruscan letters on each of the six faces.¹ It was perceived at once that these six words must presumably represent the first six Etruscan numerals. The six words are: MACH, THU, HUTH, KI, ZAL, and SA, but there is no clue to inform us how these six words are to be allotted to the first six numerals.

The importance of this discovery can hardly be overrated. Here, manifestly, is the key to the great Etruscan secret. If the affinities of a language are once known, the language can be ultimately spelt out; it is only a matter of time and labour. Now in all languages the NUMERALS are among the most unerring indications of linguistic affinity. They are only surpassed in philological importance, if indeed they are surpassed, by the personal pronouns, and the case endings of the nouns.

Strange to say this great and fortunate discovery has hitherto received no adequate attention. A quarter of a century has elapsed since the dice were found, without their having been forced to yield up their secret. Lorenz and Pott have fruitlessly

---

¹ *Bullettino dell' Instituto di Corrispondenza Archeologica*, (Roma) 1848, pp. 60, 74.

discussed them, but Mr. Robert Ellis seems to have been the only person who has really appreciated the importance of these dice. He has made an ingenious attempt to explain them in accordance with his hypothesis that the Etruscan is a language belonging to the Aryan family, but he is ultimately compelled to acknowledge the existence of the singular fact, the real cogency of which he does not seem altogether to appreciate, that in a language which he asserts to be an Aryan form of speech, there exist numerals which are hopelessly non-Aryan in character.

Dr. Donaldson and Lord Crawford do not seem to have been aware of the existence of the dice; at all events they make no mention of a discovery which would alone suffice to prove that their hypothesis as to the Gothic affinities of the Etruscan language cannot be maintained for an instant.

The secret of the dice is an open secret. He who runs may read. Not only are these six numerals clearly and decisively Ugric, but in several cases they actually supply the ancient forms from which the modern Ugric numerals must have been derived, and thus enable us to connect apparently unrelated numerals in various Ugric languages.

The analogy of all known languages makes it almost certain that the Etruscan numerals are abraded fragments of ancient words denoting members of the body, such as finger, hand, arm, toe, foot, or eye. Therefore the Ugric languages ought not only to supply numerals similar to the Etruscan numerals, but also to furnish appropriate etymologies for the words by which they are denoted.

The six words on the Dice of Toscanella are, as has been already stated, MACH, THU, HUTH, KI, ZAL, and SA. We will discuss these words one by one, and endeavour to ascertain, first their meaning, and then their value.

MACH

This word appears to have meant a finger in the ancient Ugric speech. In seventeen of the Tatar dialects belonging to the Turkic family the word *bar-mach* denotes a 'finger,' and in Turkish *mikh-lab* means the 'clawed foot' of a bird or animal. In

Lesghi a 'finger-nail' is *maach*, and in Burjät it is *ko-moh-on*. In Tungusic dialects we find that *umuk-kotschar* and *amuk-utshon* mean a 'finger.' It is obvious that the most natural way of denoting the numeral ONE would be by holding up the forefinger, and pronouncing its name. This seems to have been the method adopted by most of the Ugric peoples. In the Tungusic dialects, according to Klaproth, the numeral one takes the forms *amukon, umukon, omukon, ummukon*, and *ommukon*, which are obviously derived from the Tungusic word for a 'finger.' But it is instructive to find that in one dialect the middle syllable of *umukon* is abraded, in another the first, and in another the last, and thus we get the shortened forms *umon, amu*, and *mukon*, 'one.' The same takes place in Samojed. In the Motor dialect 'one' is *om*, and in Tymisch it is *ockúr*. In the Finnic languages the *m* is altogether lost, and 'one' is *aku* in Wogul, *akt* in Lapp, *egy* in Hungarian, and *ogy* in Ostiak. The Turkic word for 'one' is *bir* or *ber*, which is evidently derived from the first syllable of *bar-mach*, a 'finger,' in the same way that the second syllable has given rise to the Finnic, Samojedic, Tungusic, and Etruscan forms of the numeral. In the Armenian, an Aryan language, which has incorporated numerous Turanian vocables, we find 'one' is *miak*. The Greek μία, radically distinct from the Aryan εἷς, may possibly have been derived from the Turanian aborigines of Hellas.

There can be little doubt that the Etruscan numeral MACH represents 'one.' It seems to be most closely related to the Turkish *bar-mach*, a 'finger,' and it gives an ancient and unabraded form from which both the Samojedic *om* and the Finnic *aks* may have been derived.

THU

It has been usually assumed that the Etruscan THU is an Aryan numeral, equivalent to 'two.' The phonetic resemblance can, however, be accounted for without making this assumption. The word *thu* is an abraded fragment of a primæval word, the common property both of Aryans and Turanians. In Ugric, Malayic, and Caucasic, as well as in Aryan languages, this ancient word denoted the 'hand' or 'arm,' and from it have been derived the Aryan numerals 'two' and 'ten,' as well as the Turanian numeral which signifies 'five.'

In Yenissei the 'hand' is *ton*, and in Kamtschadkan it is *tono*. In Samojedic dialects the 'hand' is *uden, utem, uda, huthe*, or *oda*, and the 'arm' *utte* or *udu*. In Thuschi the 'hand' is *tota*. Coming to the Finnic family of languages, the 'fingers' are denoted by *tjute* in Lapp and Zirianian, by *tula* and *tulet* in Wogul, and by *tschun* in Permian.

Throughout the Turanian region we find that this word for 'hand' has been the source of the numeral used to denote 'five,' though the dialectic changes are often so great as to leave unchanged no single letter of the root.

The ancient Egyptian is a Turanian language which rivals the Etruscan in antiquity. In Egyptian 'five' is *tu* or *tit*, a form which is phonetically identical with the Etruscan *thu*, the Etruscan *th* being equivalent to *t* or *d*.

Among the Caucasic languages 'five' is *tchu* in Tscherkess, *chu-ba* in Abase, *schu-go* and *chuyal* in

Lesghi, *ba*, *yo*, and *gal* being only desinences denoting 'number.' In Tungus 'five' is *tun-ga* or *ton-ga*, forms which closely resemble the Yenisseian *ton*, a 'hand.' In the Finnic languages the same root may be discerned in the Ostiak word *uet*, the Hungarian *öt*, the Wogul *at*, and the Permian and Lapp *wit*, all meaning 'five.' In Esth, Suomi, and Karelian the *t* changes to *s*, and 'five' is *wis*, *wisi*, and *wiisi*. These forms are valuable, as they enable us to identify the Turkic words *wes*, *bes*, and *bisch*, 'five,' which have permuted every letter of the root.

It will have been noticed that this numeral has not yet been traced in the Samojedic dialects. Here we have a totally distinct word for 'five,' namely *samlik* or *samblag*, which seems originally to have meant 'birds.' But though the original Turanian word for five has now been lost in Samojed, there is a very curious indication that a word *tun* or *tu*, 'five,' must at some former period have existed in the language. The present words for 'six' in various Samojedic dialects are *much-tun*, *muk-tut*, *mo-tu*, and *mut*. Now *much-tun*, the least abraded and the most archaic of these forms, is obviously a compound of *much* 'one,' and *tun* 'five,' as in the case of the Etrusco-Roman numeral VI (= V+I). This curious piece of evidence is of the greater value inasmuch as *tun*, 'five,' has been wholly lost in Samojed, while *much*, 'one,' has in some dialects been replaced by another word, and in the others has undergone phonetic changes which totally destroy the resemblance to the primitive form. But the compound numeral has survived to this day in a form so little changed that we may believe that Lars Porsenna or Tarquin might have recognised the Samojedic *much-tun* as an intelligible expression for 'six' in his own Rasennic speech.

HUTH

The word *much-tun*, 'six,' the formation of which is so manifest in Samojed, is especially valuable as it enables us to explain certain obscure and abraded words for 'six' which we find in other Ugric languages. At first sight there seems to be no resemblance between the Samojedic *much-tun* and the Etruscan *huth*, but there exists a complete sequence of Ugric words for 'six' which makes it easy to connect the forms, and to show that they are radically identical.

We have seen that in the Finnic languages the Etruscan *mach*, 'one,' appears in the abraded form of *aku*, while the Etruscan *thu*, 'five,' is represented by the forms *at, uet, öt,* and *wit*. Therefore the Finnic word for 'six,' if in its method of formation it followed the Samojedic analogy, might be expected to take the forms *aku-at, aku-ot,* or *aku-it,* i.e. I + V = VL. This is exactly what we find to be the case. In Wotiak 'six' is *ku-at*, in Zirianian it is *kwait*, in Mordwin and Mokscha it is *kota*, in Lapp and Wogul it is *kot*. In Hungarian, as usual, the *k* is changed into an *h*, and the word for 'six' is *hat*, a form which closely approximates to the Etruscan *huth*. The vowel it is true is different, but in the Ostiak, which is the nearest congener of Hungarian, we find the forms *chut* and *kut*, which preserve the Etruscan vowel sound unchanged. The Suomi and Esthonian *kusi* and *kuus* follow the analogy of the Finnish words for 'five,' and change the *t* into *s*.

It will have been observed that this word for 'six' has not yet been traced into either the Turkic or the Caucasic languages. It will presently be shown that in these languages an entirely different method of formation has been followed, and 'six' is two threes, instead of being one and five.

KI

There are two Ugric words which denote the 'hand' or 'arm.' One of them, *tun* or *thu*, has, as we have seen, been usually taken to denote 'five.' The other, *ki*, which we will now proceed to trace, has been employed to signify 'two.' It is obvious that holding up one hand with the fingers extended would be a natural primitive sign for 'five,' while holding up both hands or arms would be an equally natural way of denoting 'two.' In any language where there are two primitive words denoting 'hand' or 'arm,' one of them will be almost certainly used to mean 'five' and the other to mean 'two.'

Now in Zirianian and Wotiak we find that *ki* signifies 'hand.' In other Finnic languages we have the less abraded forms *ket*, *kat*, *kez*, *kezi*, and *kässi*. In the Turkic languages a 'hand' is *kal* or *khal*; in Lesghic it is *kiaa*, *koda*, *kak*, and *kuik*, and in Mingrelian it is *khe*. The same root has survived in widely separated branches of the Turanian family, and we may discern it in the Burmese *ka*, the Siamese *kha*, and the Basque *escu*, words which all signify a 'hand.'

The next step in the argument is to prove that this widely spread word for 'hand' is used throughout the Ugric languages to mean 'two.' We have already seen that one of the Etruscan numerals, which cannot mean 'five,' is *ki*. In the Turkic dialects we have a very close approximation to this form, the words *iki*, *ike*, or *ikke*, running through the whole series with the signification of 'two.' In Yenissei 'two' is *kina*, and in Ostiak it is *ki*, which is precisely the same as the Etruscan form. Turning to the other Finnic languages we have *kik* in

Wotiak, *kük* in Permian, and *kaks* in Esthonian, words for 'two' which seem to be reduplicated forms, signifying 'hand-hand.' In Tcheremis 'two' is *kok-tot*, in Lapp *kuek-ta*, and in Hungarian *ket-to*. In these cases both of the Ugric words for 'hand' seem to have been combined in order to obtain a distinctive word for 'two.' The same principle appears in Samojed, where 'two' is *ky-dy* in the Motor, and *kid-de* in the Tawgi dialect. In the Turanian languages of the Caucasus the root may be traced in the Avar and Anzuch, where 'two' is *ki-go* (*go* is only a desinence) and in Thuschi and Tschetschenz, where it is *schi*.

It may be noted that the Aryan numeral for 'five' corresponds to the Turanian numeral for 'two,' while the Aryan words for 'two' and 'ten' are ultimately the same as the Turanian word for 'five.' This would seem to indicate that the separation of the Aryan and Turanian families took place at a period when the two words for 'hand' and 'arm' were already in existence, but before the art of numeration had been attained.

ZAL

In all languages the most widely spread names of numerals are those denoting 'one,' 'two,' and 'five,' the names of which almost universally denote, as we have seen, 'finger,' 'arms,' and 'hand.' To denote 'one' a finger was held up, to signify 'two' the arms, while 'five' was indicated by the expanded hand. So far there is a general agreement among almost all races. But the methods of denoting the numerals 'three,' 'four,' and 'six,' show considerable diversity. We either find compound numerals such as *much-tun* and *huth*, or else the feet, toes, or eyes are called into requisition. This is the case with ZAL. The root of this word is manifestly to be sought in the Finnic *jalka, jwolke, jalyn, jaly, jal,* or *lal,* the Hungarian *gyalog,* the Mongolic *kül,* the Turkic *ajak,* the Tungusic *khalgan, halgan, algan,* and the Samojedic *uju.* All these words mean a 'foot,' and are closely related to the Koibal *sala,* 'finger,' the Turkic *chal,* and the Tungusic *tjalan,* a 'hand.'[1] This word enters largely into the Turanian

[1] See Schott, *Altaische Spr.* p. 63.

systems of numeration. The unabraded form of the Etruscan *zal* may be recognised in *jalon*, which represents the number 'three' among the Yukagir, a tribe of eastern Siberia, whose language preserves an unusually large number of Etruscan forms. In Tungusic dialects 'three' is *gilan, ilan,* or *elan*. In the Tschudic languages the *j* becomes a *k*, and 'three' is *kolm* in Esth and Lapp, *kolmi* in Suomi, *cholym* in Ostiak, and *korum* in Wogul. In Hungarian we have as usual the further change of *k* to *h*, and 'three' is *harom*. In Kubitschi and Akuscha, two Lesghic languages, 'three' is *quial*.

Although the Turkic languages possess the Ugric word *chat*, 'hand,' we find that a quite disconnected term for 'three' has been adopted, namely, *us* or *utsch*, which seems to be an abraded form of *kus*, 'eyes.' Finger, hand, eye, is perhaps a way of counting one, two, three, as natural and convenient as finger, hand, foot. But it is worthy of note that the Turkic tribes must at some remote period have possessed the same word for three, and therefore the same mode of counting, as the rest of the Ugric nations. This appears from the dialect of the Nogai Tatars, in which *ol-tuz* is 'thirty.' Since in Nogai *tuz* means 'ten,' *ol* must have meant 'three.' The Osmanli, in which 'thirty' is *o-tuz*, shows the radical in a still more abraded form. The same root, preserving the vowel sound of the Etruscan *zal*, is found in the Turkic word for 'six,' which is *al-ty, al-te, al-ta,* and *ol-ta*. This is supposed to be a compound word meaning 'hands thrice,' or 'three twos.'

The ancient Etruscan numeral for 'three' may similarly be detected in the higher compound numbers of some of the Caucasic languages. Thus in Tschetschenz and Inguschi 'three' is *koe*, a word apparently bearing no relation to *jal* or *zal*. We find, however, that the Ugric numeral has been conserved in the word *jal-ch*, 'six,' which is plainly a compound of *jal* or *zal*, 'three,' and *schi* or *ki*, 'two'; the mode of composition being the same as in the Turkic word *al-ty*, 'six.'

SA

Of the six numerals which are inscribed upon the dice of Toscanella, the only one that now remains to be identified is sa. If the preceding analysis be correct, this word must denote the only remaining number, and will signify 'four' and not 'six,' as the Aryan analogies might lead us to suppose.

In the formation of the numeral for 'four,' there is a great diversity among the various branches of the Ugric family, hardly any two of them agreeing. Probably the separation of the Ugric stems took place at a period anterior to the full development of the power of counting consecutively beyond three, a number which forms a common limit to the powers of numeration possessed by uncultured tribes. We might therefore antecedently expect that the Ugric analogies in the case of the Etruscan term for 'four' would be more faint than in other cases.

The root of the Etruscan numeral *sa* is to be sought in the Samojedic *sai* and the Permian *sin*, which signify an 'eye.' From this source apparently are derived the words which denote 'four' in the Yenisseian dialects, which owing to their remoteness and isolation have preserved many points of analogy with the Etruscan. Here we have the forms *sa-gem*, *si-em*, *se-ga*, *tscha-ja*, and *si-a*, 'four.' The last syllable in these words is a suffix denoting 'number,' and therefore *sa* or *si* is the radical denoting 'four.' The Chinese and the Siamese have also preserved this numeral. In both of them 'four' is *si*.

There are also some indirect and obscure traces of this numeral in Finnic and Turkic languages. Thus in Wogul 'seven' is *sa-tje*, apparently a compound equivalent to IV + III (*sa* + *zal*). Again, the second syllable in the Turkic *se-kis*, 'eight,' seems to be the Ugric numeral for 'two.' Therefore *se-kis* would be twice *se*, and *se* must have denoted 'four.'

We have now discussed all of the six numerals whose names are written on the dice of Toscanella. As to the remaining numerals there is no such safe ground to tread upon, and the possible limits of error are less narrow. The materials available for the investigation are, moreover, extremely scanty. The Etruscan mortuary inscriptions, of which we possess many hundreds, contain, as a rule, nothing

THE HIGHER NUMBERS.

beyond names, parentages, and ages. Fortunately there are nine inscriptions in which the age of the deceased has been written in words, instead of in figures, according to the usual practice. A careful analysis of these nine precious records will, I believe, enable us to detect the principles of the Etruscan system of numeration, and to recover several important numerals.

I transcribe those portions of these nine inscriptions which relate to the ages of the deceased persons, omitting, for the sake of simplicity, the names and parentages. The numbers attached are those in Fabretti's list. I have given what appear to be the most probable readings,[1] indicating by brackets the letters which are doubtful or conjectural.

---

[1] VARIOUS READINGS.

No. 2,108.   KEALCH:S, Fabretti; KEALCHS, Lepsius; KEAL:CHS, Campanari.

No. 2,335 d.   AVILSKIS·MUVALCHL..., Fabretti.

No. 2,070.   SEMPHALCHLS, Fabretti. The Etruscan M and S resemble each other very closely, and are often interchanged in transcription.

No. 2,340.   AVILS...ACHS·MEALCHLSK, Fabretti, Lanzi; AVLS...IACHS·MEAI·CHLSK, Forlicesi.

No. 2,033 bis D. c.   In the text Fabretti reads SESPHS, and in the glossary SEMPHS.

No. 2,108. Inscription on a sarcophagus from Toscanella, now in the British Museum. It bears the effigy of a man in the prime of life:

AVILS : KIS : KEALCHILIS

No. 2,335 d. Inscription on the side of a sarcophagus from Tarquinii:

AVILS KIS · MUVALCHL(S)

No. 3,335 a. Another epitaph from the cover of the same sarcophagus:

AVILS : THUNESI : MUVALCHLS

No. 2,070. Inscription on a sarcophagus from Vitorbo, bearing the effigy of an aged man:

AVILS : MACHS SEIS:PHALCHLS

No. 2,340. Inscription written on the wall of a tomb at Tarquinii. The inscription records that the deceased was a PUIAM, or 'maiden:'

AVILS · [M]ACHS · MEALCHLSK

No. 2,093 bis D. c. Inscription over the figure of a youth, on the wall of a tomb at Orvieto:

AVILS · SESPHS

No. 2,104. Inscription on a cinerary urn from Toscanella. The inscription records that the deceased was a SECH, or 'daughter:'

AVILS · SAS

No. 2,119. Inscription on the cover of an ossuary from Toscanella:

AVILS : TIVRS : SAS

No. 2,071. Inscription on a sarcophagus from Norchia, bearing the effigy of an aged man:

AVILS : KIEMZATHRMS

It will be proved in the next chapter that the word AVILS, which in every case precedes and indicates the numeral, is a word meaning the 'age,' and nearly equivalent to *ætatis*.

The most superficial inspection of these inscriptions will suggest three important general observations :—

1. It will be noticed that in the first five inscriptions the age of the deceased is expressed by two words. These words, therefore, presumably denote the higher numbers; numbers certainly above ten, and probably above twenty. The second words are :—

   KE-ALCHLS

   MUV-ALCHLS (twice)

   SESPH-ALCHLS

   ME-ALCHLSK

In all these cases the suffix, ALCHLS, is the same, or nearly the same, and it will occur to everyone that it probably denotes what is technically called the *radix* of the system of numeration. The value of this *radix* is a more difficult question, and must be reserved for further discussion.

2. In the next place it will be observed that in eight out of the nine inscriptions there is another word, which does not itself contain the suffix *alchls*, but usually precedes a word which does. We have:—

   KIS (twice)
   MACHS (twice)
   SAS (twice)
   THUNESI

It may be conjectured that these four words represent some of the digits, or numbers less than ten. Three of them, KIS, MACHS, and SAS, will be recognised at once as presumably connected with the numerals KI, MACH, and SA, which were obtained from the dice, since the only difference is the addition of a final *s*.

3. Fourteen out of the fifteen numeral words in these nine inscriptions terminate with this letter *s*. The dice prove that this final *s* is not an integral or necessary part of an Etruscan numeral. It may be conjectured that this suffix is the sign which distinguishes the ordinal from the cardinal numbers. If so the Etruscan ordinals would follow the analogy

of several Ugric languages, in which the ordinals are denoted by a sibillant suffix appended to the cardinals.[1] But a more positive indication is forthcoming. In one case, MEALCHLSK, the suffix is not -s, but -sk. This is a valuable instance, as it doubtless presents a more archaic form of the suffix. The final k might easily be extruded, but it could not have been intruded. Now in Karagass Tatar, a Turkic language, we find this precise form, the ordinal suffix being either -ske or -eske.[2]

Since MACH, KI, and SA have been shown to be 'one,' 'two,' and 'four,' it would appear that MACHS, KIS, and SAS mean 'first,' 'second,' and 'fourth.' In determining the meaning of the remaining words we may therefore discard the final s in every case.

If we compare the two Etruscan numbers, KIS MUVALCHLS, and THUNESI MUVALCHLS, it appears that THUNESI must represent one of the digits. As all of the first six digits have been already determined,

[1] E. G. The ordinal suffix is -scha in Tscheremis, -tschi in Mandschu and Turkic, -mas in Yenissei, and -san or -ken in Burjät. See Schott, Tatar. Spr., p. 77.
[2] Castrén, Koibal. und Karagassischen Sprachlehre, p. 18.

THUNESI will represent either 'seven,' 'eight,' or 'nine.' The first syllable is apparently *thu-* or *thun-*, which we have seen means 'five.' It is just possible that *-esi*, the latter part of the word, may be an abnormal form of the ordinal suffix, but there seems to be a much greater likelihood in identifying it with *se, zia,* or *sa,* 'four.' The digit THUNESI would therefore be 'nine,' or 5+4. This analysis is confirmed by a comparison with the Turkic words for 'nine,' *togus* and *tohus,* which are, apparently, abraded forms of *tong-usa,* or 5+4.

We now approach the important question of the *radix* of the Etruscan system of numeration. There can be little doubt that the *radix* is denoted by *-alchl,* the suffix which appears in the numerals KE-ALCHL, MUV-ALCHL, ME-ALCHL, and SESPH-ALCHL. This suffix *-alchl* seems to be a reduplicated form, equivalent to *lch-lch*. The simple root would therefore be *lch* or *lk*. This root *lk* denotes 'ten' in various Ugric languages. In Lapp 'ten' is *lokke* or *logie,* a word allied to the Lapp suffix *-lokk,* 'all,' and to the Thushi ordinal suffix *-loghe.* In Tscheremis and Wogul we have the abraded forms *lu, lou,* and *lawa*, 'ten.'[1] This root *lk* is frequently used as a Ugric equivalent of the English numerical suffix *-ty*. We have examples in the case of the Lapp *kuahte-logis*, 'twenty,' the Koibal *i-lix* and the Turkish *el-li*, 'fifty,' or the Tscheremis *kut-lu*, 'sixty.'[2] If *lch* denoted 'ten,' the reduplicated form *lch-lch* would mean 10+10, and *-alchl*, the Etruscan *radix*, would be 'twenty.'

The study of the Turanian systems of numeration makes it not improbable that the Etruscan system might prove to be a combination of the decimal and vigesimal methods, a system resembling that which we employ when we speak of 'three score and ten,' or 'four score and twelve,' or that which the French use when they denote 'ninety-five' by *quatre-vingt quinze*.

Such a vigesimal-decimal system of notation is now found among the Ainos, a Tungusic tribe

---

[1] Also in Yukahir, a Yenisseian language, *lekhlon* must at some former time have denoted ten. This may be proved thus: In Yukahir *malhiyalon*=6=2×3. Since *yalon*=3, *malki* must have been 2. Again *malhielekhlon*=8=10−2. Therefore *lekhlon* must have meant 10.

[2] Cf. Scholl, *Tatarisch. Spr.*, p. 76.

of Eastern Siberia. We also find it employed by the Avars, the Didos, the Anzuchs, the Abkasians, the Udes, and other Caucasic tribes,[1] as well as by the Basques.

If *-alchi*, the Etruscan radix, be 'twenty,' then since KI means 'two,' KE-ALCHL would be two score, or 'forty,' and ME-ALCHL would be one score, or 'twenty,' *me* being apparently an abraded form of MACH, 'one.'

The discovery of Sanskrit has elucidated numberless obscure points of Aryan philology, and in the same way we may expect that Etruscan will throw unexpected light on existing Ugric languages. We have here an instance to our hand. The Turkic systems of numeration are decimal, but there is one Turkic numeral which is entirely anomalous, and which Turkic scholars have confessed their inability to explain.[2] In Turkish 'forty' is *kerk*. In Tschuwash we have the form *hirih*, and in

---

[1] See Schiefner, *Sprache der Uden*, p. 8; Rosen, *Sprache der Lazen*, p. 9; Pott, *Die quinare und vigesimale Zählmethode*, pp. 81–87; Pott, *Sprachverschiedenheit in Europa an den Zahlwörtern nachgewiesen*, p. 73.

[2] See Schott, *Tatarisch. Spr.*, p. 76.

Koibal Tatar the still more archaic form *kerik*, which is phonetically equivalent to *ke-lik*. The first syllable obviously denotes 'two,' and therefore *lik* must mean 'twenty.' We instantly recognise the Etruscan vigesimal suffix *alchl*, and perceive that in this anomalous Turkic numeral we have a unique survival of the ancient vigesimal notation which, in all the remaining numbers, has been replaced by the more convenient decimal system. The Etruscan *kealchl*, 'forty,' must be the archaic form of the Turkish *kerk*, but without the light thrown by the Etruscan, the Turkic form would ever have remained, as it has so long remained, unexplained and inexplicable.

The Etruscan system being vigesimal, a distinct root denoting -*teen* would be required. Now if we compare KE-ALCHL and ME-ALCHL on the one hand with MU-V-ALCHL, SES-PH-ALCHL, and SES-PH on the other, it appears that *ph* or *v* denotes -*teen*. This conclusion is supported by the Ugric analogies. In Samojed and Wogul the words *tei, bi, bü,* and *lu* mean 'ten.' In Hungarian -*ven* is equivalent to the English -*ty*, as in *het-ven*, 'seventy,' and the Hungarian *ven* is again equivalent to the Turkish *on*, 'ten.'[1]

This *v* or *ph*, 'teen,' occurring as it does in the middle of long compound numerals such as MU-V-ALCHL and SES-PH-ALCHL, must be an abraded relic of some longer word which meant 'ten.' What this word was is indicated by the inscription No. 2,119, which reads AVILS TIVRS SAS.[2] Since SAS means 'fourth,' TIVRS can hardly be anything else than 'tenth,' and TIVR SA would be 'fourteen.' The Ugric analogies fully bear out this supposition. The Permian *dass*, the Wotiak *das*, and the Hungarian *tiz*, all mean 'ten.' In Tscheremis the word for 'ten' must formerly have been *deshi*, as is shown by the existing numerals *kan-dashe*, 'eight' (i.e. 10−2), and *in-deshe*, 'nine' (i.e. 10−1). The Tschudic languages now use other words to denote 'ten,' but at some former time 'ten' must have been *tesa*, as appears from the numbers 'eight' and 'nine,' which in Esthonian are *kat-tesa* (10−2) and *ut-tesa* (10−1). The Samojedic 'nine,' *ne-esa*

---

[1] Schott, *Tatarisch. Spr.*, p. 76.
[2] See p. 176, *supra*.

(10 1), also points to *esa* as a primitive word for 'ten.'

We may probably regard the Etruscan *v* or *ph*, 'teen,' as a highly abraded representative of TI·V·R, 'ten,' retaining only a single letter of the original word.

SES-PHS therefore would be 'fourteenth,' or if the true reading be SEM·PHS, it might be 'seventeenth,' since the Finnic *sisem*, the Tschuwash *sitsche*, and the Turkish *site*, all denote 'seven.' It is also just possible that KIS, instead of being 'second,' may be identical with the Turkic *segis*, 'eight.'

Only one numeral now remains to be considered. In the last of the inscriptions, No. 2,071, the age of the deceased is denoted by AVILS KIEMZATHRMS. This word must denote a very high number, since the sarcophagus bears the effigy of an aged man, *uomo vecchio*. There is no detached digit, and it is therefore probable that KIEMZATHRM stands for either 'seventy,' 'eighty,' or 'ninety.' Since SESPHALCH has been shown to be ninety, our range is limited to seventy and eighty.

The numeral KIEMZATHRM offers no points of

comparison with the other Etruscan numerals, and seems to be altogether anomalous in its mode of formation. The word entirely baffled me for a long period, and it was only while these sheets were passing through the press that I stumbled, almost by accident, on the solution now presented. It is a solution which I trust the reader will consider to be as thoroughly convincing as it is undoubtedly curious.

The word is not only anomalous in the Etruscan system, but scores of Ugric languages may be searched without their yielding any analogous word. The key is to be found in one remote dialect only —the speech of the Ariner, a Yenisseian tribe which was visited by G. F. Müller in 1735.[1] The tribe has probably been long extinct, since Müller found only ten men surviving at the time of his visit. He succeeded, however, in collecting a small vocabulary of their language, which seems to be an extremely primitive form of Ugric speech, containing as it does both Finnic, Samojedic, Turkic, and Tungusic

[1] See Klaproth, *Asia Polyglotta*, p. 168.

forms, and offering several marked points of analogy with the Etruscan.

In this singular language 'eighty' is denoted by the word *kinamantschauthjung*. If this jaw-breaking word be divided into syllables, the resources of the Yenisseian languages explain its mode of composition quite plainly, and show that *kina-man-tschau-thjung* must mean 'twice forty.' To begin with the end of the word, from the Yenisseian *chaijung*, 'ten,' we get the suffix *thjung*, which evidently means -ty. We find also that *tschaju* is the word for 'four,' and *schaithjung* that for 'forty.' The first part of the word, *kina-man*, must mean two ones, or twice, since *kina* is 'two,' and *man* may be compared with the Etruscan *mach*, 'one.'

Comparing the Ariner and Etruscan forms, it is evident that they correspond very closely, and enable us, from Etruscan sources alone, to explain the formation of the Etruscan numeral. We have,

Ariner: KINA-MAN-TSCHAU-THJUNG.

Etruscan: KI E M   Z A THR M.

Guided by the Yenisseian analogies, the elements

of the Etruscan word are manifest. ZI is 'two,' and ZM is the abraded form of *mach*, 'one,' which we find in ME·ALCHL. Therefore KIEM is 'twice'; ZA is equivalent to *sa*, 'four'; THR is an abraded form of TIVR, 'ten'; and M, as before, means 'one.' THRM is therefore ten-ones or '-ty,' and ZATHRM is four-ten-ones or 'forty.' Therefore KIEMZATHRM is twice forty, or 'eighty,' and KIEMZATHRMS is the ordinal, 'eightieth.' When the clue is once obtained, every letter of the Etruscan word can be explained from Etruscan sources. Nor should we omit to notice that not only is this singular numeral by itself of great philological value, but the rudiments of which it is composed demonstrate that we have been correct in our interpretation of four other Etruscan numerals, namely, ZI, MACH, SA, and TIVR.

The symmetry of the Etruscan system is remarkable. It proceeds by a geometrical progression. Twenty is twice ten; forty is twice twenty; and eighty is twice forty.

Summing up the results which have been attained, we have the following list of Etruscan numerals:—

MACH is one.
KJ is two.
ZAL is three.
SA is four.
THU is five.
HUTH is six.
SEM is possibly seven.
KIS is possibly eight.
THUNESI is nine, or possibly second.
TIVR is ten.
TIVR SA is ten and four, or 14.
SEMPH or SESPH is either seventeen or fourteen.
ME·ALCHL is one score, or 20.
MACH ME·ALCHL is one score and one, or 21.
MU·V·ALCHL is one score and ten, or 30.
KI MUVALCHL is one score and ten and two, or 32.
THUNESI MUVALCHL is one score and ten and nine, or 39.
KE·ALCHL is two score, or 40.
KI KEALCHL is two score and two, or 42.
KIEMZATHRM is twice two score, or 80.
SES·PH·ALCHL is four score and ten, or 90.
MACH SESPHALCHL is fourscore and ten and one, or 91.

In several cases we can test these results.

The sarcophagus No. 2,108 bears the figure of a man in the prime of life, and the inscription, AVILS KIS KEALCHLS, tells us that he died in the forty-second year of his age.

The sarcophagus No. 2,070 bears the effigy of an aged man. He died in the ninety-first year of his age, AVILS MACHS SESPHALCHLS.

No. 2,033 shews the effigy of a youth, and the record is that he died either in his seventeenth or his fourteenth year, AVILS SEMPHS or AVILS SESPHS.

The 'maiden' in No. 2,340 died in her twenty-first year, AVILS MACHS MEALCHLSK.

No. 2,104 records the death of a 'daughter' who died in her fourth year, AVILS SAS.

In No. 2,071 the age is expressed by AVILS KIEM-ZATHRMS, or eighty, and the effigy is that of an aged man.

In these six cases only, out of the nine, are there any means of determining whether our results are probably correct, and in every case the test bears out the analysis.

From another source we may, however, obtain

a curious verification of our identification of the Etruscan KI with the Turkish *iki*, 'two.'

In Etruscan inscriptions the word KLENAR, 'children,' is found conjoined with numbers. In the tomb of the Alethnas family at Viterbo there are two inscriptions,[1] which record in words the number of children born to the deceased. One of these inscriptions mentions KLENAR KI, or 'two children,' and the other KLENAR ZAL ARKE, or 'three male children.' I transcribe the whole of the first inscription, with an interlinear translation:

ALETHNAS. V. V. THELU · ZILATH.   PARCHIS
Alethnas V. V. Thelu is buried (here). (His) ancestor

ZILATH :   ETERAV ı KLENAR ı   KI ı
is buried (here); (the) younger children two (of)

AKNANASA   VLSSI ı ZILACHNU :   KELUSA
Aknanasa his wife he buried (here); (viz.) Kelusa

        RIL XXVIII   PAPALSER . AKNANASA   VI
(aged) years 28 (and) Papalser Aknanasa (aged) 6.

MANIM   ARKE   RIL LXVII
I myself the husband (lived) years 67.

We are as yet hardly in a position to attempt

[1] Fabretti, Nos. 2,055, 2,056.

the verbal analysis of the inscription. The reader must for the present take the interpretation on trust. References to the several words will be found in the Glossary at the end of the book. This inscription is here given because it affords an independent corroboration of our previous conclusions as to the meaning of *ki*. We are told that Alethnas and Aknanasa his wife had 'two children'— KLENAR KI—whose names and ages are separately recorded.

In the Etruscan inscriptions we repeatedly meet with words which the preceding investigation has shown to be numerals. The words next adjacent to these numerals are usually either NAPER, TENE, RAS, or RASNE. Thus in the great inscription from Volterra we have HUTH NAPER. In the great Perugian inscription, which is apparently a conveyance of land for sepulchral purposes, we have the following phrases:—

    NAPER XII
    NAPER KI
    HUT NAPER
    NAPER S

SA RAS
THU RAS
SA TENE

It has long since been recognised that these words, NAPER, RAS, and TENE, must denote something connected with weights, measures, or numeration. Their precise significance is difficult to determine. The Turkish numeral adjuncts, *nefer*, *ras*, and *dane*, meaning respectively 'souls,' 'head,' and 'corn,' which are used in the numeration of men, of animals, and of things, would supply the required explanation if it could be shown that they are genuine Ugric terms, and not, as seems more probable, borrowed by the Turks from the Arabic or Persian.[1]

[1] See Kasem-Beg, *Gram. Türk. Tatar. Spr.* p. 58.

CHAPTER VI.

EPITAPHS.

Epitaphs Recording the Age of the Deceased — The Five Etruscan Formula — The Four Etruscan Words — Their Significance determined — The Ugric Analogies: leine — lupu — avil — ril — Epitaphs not Recording the Age: cilach — thni — tular — The Formula aka suthi nesl—suthina—The San Manno Inscription.

More than three thousand mortuary inscriptions have been found in the Etruscan tombs. When they come to be examined a most disappointing sameness is found to pervade them. By far the larger number contain nothing beyond an enumeration of the names of the deceased person. In many cases, however, the parentage, and sometimes also the age, is added.

The inscriptions which record the AGE are of considerable philological value, inasmuch as they make constant use of four important Etruscan words, namely, AVIL or AVILS, RIL, LEINE, and LUPU.

One or more of these four words usually occupies a position immediately adjacent to the numerals which express the age. These four words are of such importance that it will be well for us to examine them with some minuteness.

Guesses as to the meaning of these constantly recurring words have, of course, been freely hazarded, and it has been usually believed that the meaning of two of them has been certainly ascertained. Niebuhr has summed up the prevalent belief when he observes that 'among all the Etruscan words of which explanations have been pretended, only two, AVIL RIL, *vixit annos*, seem to have been really explained.'[1] We shall presently discover that Niebuhr might easily have satisfied himself that even this interpretation, which has been repeated by almost every subsequent writer, could not possibly be correct.

The inscriptions which record the age of the deceased resolve themselves into five recurring formulæ.

[1] Niebuhr, *History of Rome*, vol. I. p. 90.

I. The most frequent formula, of which there are forty-nine instances, consists of the name, the word RIL, and a numeral. For instance:

KUMLNAS · LARTH · VELUS · RIL · LXXXIIIIII

(Fabretti, No. 2,106.)

II. The second formula contains the name, the word AVIL or AVILS, sometimes spelt AIVILS, and a numeral. For instance:

LARIS : SETHRES : KRAKIAL : AVILS : XXVIII

(Fabretti, No. 2,109.)

Occasionally we have AVIL instead of AVILS, as:

THALEIVIAIMAXRAKE
AVIL XXXIIII   (Fabretti, No. 88.)

III. The third formula contains the name, a numeral, and both of the words AVIL and RIL. Thus we have:

S · SVETIV : L
AVIL : RIL · LXV   (Fabretti, No. 340.)

IV. The fourth formula consists of the name, a numeral, and the two words LUPU and AVILS. For instance:

ARNT · THANA · LUPU · AVILS XVII   (Fabretti, No. 2,136.)

THE FIVE MORTUARY FORMULÆ. 197

V. The fifth formula contains the name, a numeral, and the words RIL and LEINE. For instance :

A · PEKNI

RIL · LIII · LEINE   (Fabretti, No. 333.)

These five formulæ have now to be interpreted.

Following the inductive method which has been employed in the two preceding chapters, I shall first endeavour, from internal evidence alone, to determine the probable meanings of the four words, RIL, AVIL or AVILS, LUPU, and LEINE. I shall then examine whether the results that have been obtained are in accord with the evidence derived from the Ugric vocabularies.

If we compare the five Etruscan formulæ with mortuary inscriptions in Latin, or indeed in almost any other language, there arises a very strong presumption that the four Etruscan words which are used in connection with the age of the deceased must signify 'lived,' 'died,' 'years,' and 'age.' No other meanings for these words have ever been suggested, and it is difficult to see what other possible meanings they could bear. It is, however, by no means so easy to appropriate one of these four meanings to each of the four Etruscan words.

By taking the four words, 'years,' 'age,' 'lived,' and 'died,' in combination with a name and a numeral, it is manifestly possible to construct five mortuary formulæ, and no more. Let M. stand for the name, and LX. for the numeral.

The formulæ will be these:—

    I. M. LX. YEARS.
   II. M. AGE LX., or, M. AGED LX.
  III. M. AGE LX. YEARS.
  IV. M. LIVED LX. YEARS.
   V. M. DIED, AGED LX.

It will be observed:

1. Either of the nouns 'age' or 'years' can stand by itself in a formula, in combination with a proper name and a numeral.

2. This is not the case with the verbs 'lived' and 'died.'

3. It is possible to have the two nouns together in one formula.

4. This is not the case with the two verbs.

5. The verb 'lived' can only be used in association with the noun 'years,' and the verb 'died' with the noun 'age.'

Let us now compare the Etruscan with the English formulæ, and apply to them our five rules.

The Etruscan formulæ are:

    I. M. RIL LX.

    II. M. AVILS LX., *or*, M. AVIL LX.

    III. M. AVIL RIL LX.

    IV. M. RIL LX. LEINE.

    V. M. LUPU AVILS LX.

It will be observed:

1. Either of the words AVILS and RIL can stand by itself in a formula in combination with a proper name and a numeral.

2. This is not the case with the words LUPU and LEINE.

3. It is possible to use the two words AVIL and RIL together in one formula.

4. This is not the case with the words LUPU and LEINE.

5. The word LEINE is invariably associated with the word RIL, and the word LUPU with AVILS.

Comparing the five Etruscan rules with the five English rules, we see that there is no escape from the conclusion that RIL and AVIL must be the two nouns, and LEINE and LUPU the two verbs.

The third Etruscan formula

M. AVIL RIL LX.

must therefore be equivalent to the third English formula,

M. AGE LX. YEARS.

Therefore the words AVIL RIL cannot possibly mean, as Niebuhr supposed, *vixit annos*.

We have next to ascertain which of the two Etruscan nouns means 'age,' and which means 'years.'

To determine this point it may be noted that we have the two forms AVIL and AVILS, which would correspond to 'age' and 'aged,' whereas RIL is always unchanged in form, and would correspond to 'years' in the English formulæ.

If the meaning of any one of the four words is

absolutely ascertained, the meanings of the other three are necessarily determined by our rules.[1]

If RIL means 'years,' it follows that AVIL means 'age,' while LEINE, the verb which is always joined with RIL, must mean 'he lived,' and LUPU, the verb which is always joined with AVIL, must mean 'he died.' (See Rule 5.)

From the internal evidence which indicates the meaning of these words we now turn to the surer ground of the Ugric analogies.

LEINE.—We have seen that LEINE must be an Etruscan verb in the third person singular of the præterite tense, and that it probably means 'he lived.' The suffix *e* may be safely taken as the sign of the third person singular, since in numberless Ugric languages, Turkic, Mongolic, and Finnic, the third person singular of the præterite ends either in *e*, *u*, *i*, or *a*. The root, therefore, is LEIN. Now, in Hungarian, from the verb substantive *lenni*, 'to be,'

---

[1] A bilingual inscription of very dubious authenticity would, if it were genuine, settle the meanings of these words. The Etruscan words, *air. xzii* are accompanied by the Latin translation, *ætatis xvii*. See Fabretti, No. 90; Müller, *Die Etrusker*, vol. i. p. 64.

are derived the words *leny,* 'existence,' and *ile,* 'living.' In Lapp and Samojed the forms *lei* and *ilei* mean 'he was.' In Turkic languages the present participle of *ol-mak,* the verb substantive, is *olan* or *ulan,* 'being.' In Samojedic dialects *ilen, ila,* and *ilin-de* mean 'living' or 'alive,' and in Finn, Lapp, and Wogul, *elen-da, elem,* and *olmt* mean 'life.' It is therefore almost absolutely certain that the Etruscan word LEINE meant 'he was alive,' or 'he lived.'

The correspondencies may be thus exhibited :—

Etruscan	.	.	.	L	EI	N	E	. . .	he lived.
Hungarian	.	.	.	L	E	NI	I	. . .	to be.
Hungarian	.	.	.	L	E	N	Y	. . .	existence.
Turkic	.	.	O	L	A	N		. . .	being.
Samojed	.	.	I	L	E	N		. . .	living.
Finn	.	.	E	L	E	N	DA	. . .	life.
Wogul	.	.	O	L	A	N	T	. . .	life.
Lapp	.	.		L	EI			. . .	he was.
Samojed	.	.	I	L	EI			. . .	he was.

LUPU.—The other verb, LUPU, 'he died,' is also derived from the Ugric verb substantive. In the Turkic and Tataric languages *olup* or *ulup* is the gerund of the regular auxiliary verb, and means 'in being,' 'in existence.' Hence the Wotiak *ulep,* 'life,' and the Yakut equivalent, *olloruput*. Now, if a verb were formed from the gerund *olup*, the third person of the præterite would probably take the form *olupu*. Such a word would in Etruscan almost certainly be devocalised, and become LUPU, 'he was in existence,' which would be a euphemism equivalent to 'he died.' Among all nations there is an instinctive natural tendency to denote death by some indirect form of expression. The English phrases 'he is gone,' 'he is no more,' 'the departed,' 'dissolution,' or the German expression *der Seliger*, may sufficiently illustrate this natural usage of denoting 'death' in some periphrastic mode.

The usual form of this word in the Etruscan inscriptions is LUPU. In one instance, however, we have LUPUM, and in two cases LUPUKE. According to Turkic grammatical analogies, LUPUM might mean either 'death' or 'I died,' and LUPUKE 'the person who died,' the 'deceased.'[1] But the existing materials are hardly sufficient to enable us to deter-

---

[1] Kasem-Beg, *Gram. der Türk. Tatarisch. Spr.*, §§ 110, 114, pp. 37, 38.

mine with certainty the precise significance of these two Etruscan forms.

AVIL, AIVIL, AVILS, 'age.'—In the frontispiece (Figs. 7 and 9), the name of AJAX is spelt AIVAS. This shows that the Etruscan letters *aiv* were equivalent to *aj*. The word AIVIL would, therefore, be equivalent to *ajil*. Now, in Turkish, *ajil* means 'future,' 'to come,' and the differentiated form *ejel* means 'the appointed time of death.' The word has been supposed to be of Arabic origin, but I should be inclined to connect it with the Turkic and Mongolic words *jil*, *djil*, and *zil*, which mean 'year.' We have also the Turkish *el-ni*, 'life,' and *wilem*, 'death,' the Coptic *hello*, 'an old man,' the Basque *il*, 'to die,' and other Turanian analogies.

The form AVILS, which is of much more frequent occurrence than AVIL, remains to be explained. We have seen (p. 110) that the suffix *s* is the sign of the Etruscan definite article. The source of this definite article is probably the pronoun of the third person. In most of the Ugric languages the noun has a personal declension, and the suffix *s*, *se*, or *si*, is used to denote this declension in the third person singular.

Thus, in Tscheremis we have *atja*, 'father,' and *atja-se*, 'his father;' *kid*, 'hand,' and *kid-se*, 'his hand.' In Lapp we have *atzja*, 'father,' and *atzja-s*, 'his father.' In Turkic, *ata*, 'father,' *ata-si*, 'his father;' *ana*, 'mother,' *ana-si*, 'his mother.'[1]

Since AVIL means 'age' in Etruscan, AVILS would mean 'his age,' or 'her age,' or possibly only 'the age.'

RIL.—It may be safely affirmed that RIL, 'years,' is not an Aryan word. Even Dr. Donaldson admits that it bears no resemblance to any synonym in the Indo-European languages.[2] We must not, however, expect to find the word in an unchanged form in the Ugric languages, which as a rule studiously avoid an initial *r*.[3] But the Etruscan speech shows a marked partiality for this letter, often introducing it in a seemingly needless manner, as in the well-

---

[1] Schott, *Tatar. Spr.*, p. 63; Kasem-Beg, *Tatar. Gram.*, p. 74.

[2] Donaldson, *Varronianus*, p. 193.

[3] The Turkish words beginning with *r* are all importations from the Arabic or Persian. See Schott, *Tatarisch. Spr.* p. 29.

known case of the transliteration of the Greek name APOLLO into EPURE.

We cannot, therefore, expect to find the word RIL in an unchanged form in any Ugric dialects. If it exists anywhere it will be in the Lesghic languages, which occasionally allow of an initial r. Now in Avar, Tschari, and Kabutsch, three Lesghic languages, we find the word *ridal* meaning 'summer.' The word for 'summer' would naturally be taken to mean 'year,' as we see from our own usage in speaking of a person having seen so many summers when we mean he has lived so many years.

The question now arises, under what forms are we to seek for the word RIL in those languages which do not tolerate an initial r? Now we find that when the letter r occurs at the end or in the middle of Hungarian and Mongolian words it is frequently dropped in the corresponding Turkic words, or it becomes either *z* or *dj*.[1] Also this Turkic *dj* is equivalent to a Finnic *t*. Hence we should expect to find that the Etruscan RIL would take the form *il*, *zil*, or *djil* in Turkic languages, and *til* in Finnic.

[1] See Schott, *Tatarisch. Spr.*, pp. 28, 29.

This is exactly what we do find. In the various Turkic dialects the words which denote a 'year' are: *djel* (Koibal), *tschil* (Yakut), *djil* (Kirghiz), *jil* (Osmanli, Uigur, and Teleut), *il* (Kasan, Nogai, Bamba, and Qasach). In Mongolic languages a 'year' is *djil, djill,* and *dil,* and *zil* in Burjät.

The Ostiak often exhibits forms which are transitional between the Turkic and Finnic languages. In the Ostiak dialects a 'year' is *djel, jal, all,* and *al,* while in Wogul the transition to the Finnic form is complete, and we have *tal* and *taal,* a 'year,' with which the Avar *thahel,* a 'year,' may be compared. The Ugric nations who live by the shores of the Arctic Ocean, instead of counting their years by 'summers,' as in the Caucasus, naturally counted them by 'winters.' Hence we find that 'winter' is *teli* in Wogul, *telli* in Ostiak, *tel* in Hungarian, and *tahee* in Lapp, Esth, and Finn.

All these related words for 'year,' 'summer,' and 'winter' are probably to be traced ultimately to the Turanian word which means 'sun,' which is *usil* in Etruscan, *tjell* in Samojed, and *ra* in Egyptian.[1]

[1] See p. 154, *supra*.

The Etruscan words AVIL, 'age,' USIL, 'sun,' and RIL, 'year,' would thus appear to be only differentiated forms of the same root.

We have now determined the Etruscan equivalents of the words *vixit, obiit, annos,* and *ætatis*, which, in Latin mortuary inscriptions, are of constant occurrence in juxtaposition with the numerals which denote the age of the deceased. But the analogy of Latin inscriptions would lead us to expect to meet with other recurring phrases, not associated with numerals, and equivalent in meaning to *conditur, sepultus est, hic jacet,* and the like.

ZILACH.—Now in the Etruscan inscriptions there are two recurring words, ZILACH and THUI, which seem to meet these requirements. The word ZILACH and its derivatives appear frequently in inscriptions on stone coffins, and, I believe, in no other positions. Hence it has been commonly assumed by Etruscan antiquaries that ZILACH must necessarily mean a 'sarcophagus.' The first syllable of the word ZIL-ACH seems to be the wide-spread Turanian root *sil*, which means to 'pierce,' and the second the equally wide-spread root *ach*, which means a 'stone.'

would therefore be a pierced or hollowed stone, a 'sarcophagus.'[1]

We find the derived and contracted forms, ZILACH, ZILACHNU, ZILACHNKE, ZILACHNUKE, ZILACHNTHAS, ZILATH, and ZILC. I take the first form to mean simply a 'sarcophagus;' the second, 'he was coffined;' and the third and fourth, 'the person coffined.' The suffix -*thas* occurs in other Etruscan words, and, as we shall hereafter see, has probably a participial significance. The two last forms may be equivalent to the first.

THUI.—The other word, THUI, is of more philological importance. We have seen that in the Kalevala MANALA means 'the underworld.'[2] The word TUONELA is frequently used as a synonym for MANALA. The words are strictly parallel in formation, and contain the same two suffixes, -*na* and -*la*. TUONELA means 'the place belonging to the dead.' One of the eight ancient Hiongnu or Hunnic words preserved by the Chinese historians is *teulo*, which meant a tumulus erected over graves. The composition of

---

[1] A stone is *achtas* in Wogul, *acha* in Basque, and *tasch* in Turkic. In Abasc *aicha* is iron.
[2] See p. 121, *supra*; Castrén, *Fin. Mythol.* p. 128.

the word is obvious; it is simply 'the place of the dead.' With *teulo* we may compare the Yenisseian *du-no*, 'dead,' the Tschetschenz *dalar*, to 'die,' the Samojedic *tulau*, to 'bury,' and the Finnic and Mongolic *tül*, to 'burn.' The analogy between death and sleep did not escape these ancient word-makers. In Yenissei *tul-uk* is a 'bed,' in Yakut *tül* is a 'dream,' and 'sleep' is *tül-uk* in Tschuwash, and *dusch* in Turkish.

We have already met with this wide-spread Ugric root in the word *hin-thi-al*, and it would be a matter of surprise if it were not found in the mortuary inscriptions. It is doubtless to be recognised in THUI, which would be a verb in the third person singular. Perhaps it may be best rendered by *jacet*, thereby preserving the ambiguity between death and sleep which is indicated by the Ugric analogies. A few instances of its occurrence may be given. Thus: THUI·LART:PEITANI·LARTHALISA[1] would mean (*Here*) *lies Lart Petrni Larthalisa*; and LARTIKAIS THUI[2] would be *Larti Kais lies* (*here*). In one instance we have

[1] Fabretti, No. 192.
[2] Ibid., No. 1029 *bis*.

a touching memorial apparently recording the death of the son and the survival of the father:

LARTHVETE ARNTHALISA · THUI - LARTH VETELINE[1]

Larth Vete Arnthalisa is dead: Larth Vete lives.

TULAR.—Connected with THUI is the word TULAR, which is occasionally inscribed with other words on large blocks of stone which have probably served either to close sepulchres or to mark their position.

Thus we have

TULAR : HILAR ..[2]

and
TULAR : RASNAL[3]

If we compare this word TULAR with the *tuonela* of the Kalevala and the Hunnic *teulo*, 'a tumulus grave,' and remember that *-ar* is the Etruscan plural suffix, and that *la* is the Fiunic word for 'place,' we may conclude that TULAR means the 'places of the dead,' and TULAR RASNAL would denote the tombs, or sepulchral niches, belonging to Rasnal.

In the great Perugian inscription we have TULARU, which is probably a verb equivalent to *sepelit*.

[1] Fabretti, No. 427. [2] Ibid., No. 937.
[3] Ibid., No. 1044.

With the exception of TULAR, the sepulchral words which have as yet been discussed are found to occur invariably in mortuary inscriptions, being usually inscribed upon ossuaries, tegulæ, sarcophagi, or the inner walls of tombs. There is another common formula which is never found in such positions, but invariably over the entrances to tombs. The formula is either EKA SUTH, or EKA SUTHI, or EKA-SUTHI NESL, and is frequently followed by a proper name.

Thus the inscription EKASUTH, and nothing else, has in three separate instances been found written over the outer doors leading to sepulchres.[1] More frequently, however, a proper name is added, as

EKASUTH'LATHI ALKILNIA [2]

or

EKASUTHILARTHAL R·USPU KILISAL [3]

Sometimes the word NESL is appended as

EKASUTHINESL TETNIE... [4]

[1] Fabretti, Nos. 2084, 2085, 2086.
[2] Ibid., No. 2031.   [3] Ibid., No. 2031 bis.
[4] Ibid., No. 2089.

or the words of the formula are divided, instead of being run together, as

EKA : SUTHI : NESL : PAN ...[1]

The general meaning of the formula, from the position in which it is invariably found, cannot admit of much doubt. It is always inscribed at the entrances to tombs, either on the lintel of the outer door, or on the stone which closes vaults. Hence it must mean 'Here is the tomb,' 'This is the tomb of . . . ,' or something of the kind.

EKA.—It has long been conjectured that EKA, the first word in the formula, must mean 'here,' 'in this place.' We shall meet with the word again, as it occurs in no less than twenty-three inscriptions, and in every case the sense of 'here' is found to be appropriate. Ugric analogies are not wanting. The singular Yenisseian languages, which offer so many marked points of agreement with the Etruscan, have conserved the precise word, still bearing the precise sense required. In the Imbazkisch dialect *egii* means 'here;' in the Yenissei-Ostiak dialect *eyei* has the same meaning, and in the Kott dialect

[1] Fabretti, No. 2132.

eca means 'at,' while *ut-iga* means 'here,' literally 'just here,' *ut* meaning 'just,' 'quite.'[1] The word may be traced in the Finnic and Turkic languages. Thus in Ostiak *tege* (=ut-iga) means 'here,' and in Karagass Tatar *tega* means 'thither.'[2]

SUTHI.—It is probable that the Carian and Etruscan languages were nearly related. Nine Carian words have come down to us. One of these is σοῦα, which, we are told, was equivalent to the Greek τάφος, a 'tomb.' Assuming that this is the meaning of SUTHI, it is probable that the Turanian root which underlies it will mean either to 'burn' or to 'bury.'

We have already seen that SETHLANS was the Etruscan Fire-God, and it has been shown (p. 140) that *seth*, the first syllable of the name, must have denoted 'fire' in Etruscan. It may here suffice to note that in Hungarian *sut* means a 'fireplace.'

We may conclude that the Etruscan SUTHI meant

---

[1] Castrén, *Jenias. Sprachlehre*, pp. 146, 148, 150.
[2] These adverbs and postpositions are apparently derived from a wide-spread root meaning a 'place' or 'enclosure.' Compare the Turkic words *iyi*, a 'boundary,' *aga* and *ekin*, a 'field.' In Basque *kia* means a 'place.'

originally 'place of cremation,' and hence, when interment began to supersede cremation, it would naturally come to mean a 'tomb.' The formula EKASUTHI ... would therefore mean 'Here is the tomb of . . . ' In the inscription given on p. 148, we have EKA SUTHIK. This would probably be the diminutive, 'a little tomb,' while EKA SUTHIS (Fabretti, No. 1937) would mean 'Here is his tomb.'

We have seen that the formula occurs only at the entrances to tombs. In one instance, however, we have engraved, not on a door, but on a sarcophagus, the words

EKA : SUTNA : ARNTHAL : PIPINANAS : SETHRESLA.[1]

The form SUTNA might be derived from the instructive case, denoting, therefore, the result of burning, and the inscription would mean, *Here (are) the ashes of Arnthal Pipinanas Sethresla.*

The word SUTHINA is frequently found engraved on statues, dishes, and other votive offerings found in tombs,[2] and can hardly mean anything except an 'offering.' Offerings to the deceased were at first

[1] Fabretti, No. 2130.
[2] Ibid., No. 2604.

made by burning the article offered with the corpse. The word SUTHINA must have meant originally a burnt offering, a sacrifice, and so would easily come to denote any object placed in the tomb and dedicated to the uses of the deceased.

Occasionally the formula EKA SUTHI contains the additional word NESL, the meaning of which is less obvious, as EKA:SUTHI:NESL:PAN.... The Turkish word *nessl* means 'progeny,' 'race,' 'posterity.' It is usually assumed that the word has been borrowed from the Arabic; but the Samojedic *natschel*, 'young,' indicates possible Ugric affinities. If the word be of a genuine Ugric origin, EKA:SUTHI:NESL... would mean 'Here is the family tomb of . . . .' Otherwise the Hungarian *nesz*, a 'fore-wall,' may perhaps indicate the meaning, and the formula might be rendered, 'Here is the front wall of the tomb of . . . .'

Near Perugia there is a spacious and magnificent tomb, popularly called the 'Tempio di San Manno.' Over an archway in this tomb is inscribed a celebrated inscription,[1] which illustrates the meaning of

[1] Fabretti, No. 1915.

some of the words discussed in this chapter. The inscription begins thus:

KEHEN : SUTHI : HINTHIU : THUES : SIANS : ETVE : THAURE : . . .

Here, instead of the usual external formula EKA SUTHI, we have KEHEN SUTHI. When we come to the celebrated inscription on the statue of the orator, we shall see that KEN must have meant 'this' in Etruscan. Probably KEHEN is only an archaic form of KEN, and KEHEN SUTHI would therefore mean 'This is the tomb.' The Yenisseian words *tscheañ*, 'people,' 'folk,' and *tschañ*, 'guest,' may indicate the meaning of SIANS, and the other words have already been discussed. The following conjectural rendering may therefore be offered, *This is the ghost chamber of the sleeping folk of Etve Thaure.*

CHAPTER VII.

WORDS DENOTING KINSHIP.

The Philological importance of words denoting Kinship — The Matronymic suffix -al — The Patronymic -al — Uyric affinities — The suffix -nal — Puia, 'maiden' — Ipe, 'sister' — Klan, 'son' — Etera and Agalletora, 'younger child' — Sech, 'daughter' — The suffix -isa, 'wife' — Kinship illustrated by the records in the tombs of the Lekne, the Herini, and the Petruni families — Words denoting husband, wife, and widow — The Agglutinative Structure of the Etruscan language.

THE monotonous catalogues of proper names which constitute the records of the Etruscan tombs are, as a rule, diversified only by statements as to AGE and statements as to KINSHIP. The phrases which denote age have been discussed in the last chapter—the not less important vocables which express kinship remain to be considered.

Words which distinguish the primary degrees of kinship—such words as wife, mother, son, daughter, child, brother—are of almost unequalled philological importance as evidences of the affiliations of languages and nations. Among the endless mutations and diversities of human speech these simple words stand forth as eternal witnesses to the primæval unities of race. Whatever other elements a language may absorb, create, or throw off, these primary words descend almost unchanged as a fundamental portion of the inalienable linguistic heritage of long-separated branches of the same stem; and therefore, in their ethnological value, they rank with the pronouns, the numerals, and a score or so of familiar household words, such as those which designate the principal members of the body, the domesticated animals, and certain matters of everyday use and necessity, such as tools, weapons, and articles of food.

Such being the philological and ethnological importance of the words which denote kinship, it is the more fortunate that one of them, which is of constant, nay almost of perpetual recurrence in the Etruscan inscriptions, should also happen to be the sole Etruscan word of which we possess a positive and indubitable Latin equivalent.

The Etruscan suffix *-al* or *-nal*, which appears in

hundreds of the mortuary records, occurs also in five of the bilingual inscriptions. In the next chapter these bilingual inscriptions will be given at full length. It may now suffice to state that the Etruscan suffix -*al* or -*nal* is uniformly represented in the bilinguals by the Latin word *natus*. We have the following equivalents:—

Etruscan.	Latin.
KAIN·AL.	CAINNIA NATUS.
KAHATI·AL.	CAFATIA NATUS.
ARNT·NAL.	ARRIA NATUS.
VAR·NAL·(ISIA.	VARIA NATUS.
VAR·NAL·ISLA.	VARIA NAT.

In the first three cases there are no complications, but in the last two we find a second suffix, -*isa* or -*isla*, which is not represented by any word in the Latin version. It is an honourable title pertaining to the mothers of the persons to whom the inscriptions refer, and will be explained hereafter.

It will be noted that in each of the five instances the Etruscan suffix -*al* or -*nal* is translated by the Latin word *natus*, and never by *filius*. Moreover, the word to which it is appended as a suffix is in every case the name of a woman, who is obviously the mother of the person to whom the inscription relates. An instance will make the usage clear. Thus, in the tomb of the Kupsna family, we have the epitaph:

ATH : KUPSNA · AU · KNEVIAL [1]

According to the usage of the records, this denotes ATH KUPSNA, whose father was AULE KUPSNA, and whose mother was KNEVI KUPSNASA. In the same tomb we find the epitaph of the mother, who is styled

LARTHI · KNEVI · KUPSNASA.

LARTHI was the mother's personal name, KNEVI her maiden name, and the word KUPSNASA denotes that she married a man whose family name was Kupsna. The word KNEVI-AL in her son's epitaph records his maternal descent from the KNEVE family. It appears, therefore, that -al was the Etruscan MATRONYMIC SUFFIX. Since it is used indifferently in the epitaphs of men and women, it cannot mean distinctively either 'son' or 'daughter,' but 'child,' and may be translated 'mother's child of . .' or 'born of . . .'

The fact that the descent on the mother's side is

---

[1] Fabretti, No. 494 bis, d.

so constantly recorded, while that on the father's side is frequently omitted, is, as we have seen (p. 57), a peculiarity of the highest ethnological importance. But a result of this usage is that although the matronymic suffix occurs so perpetually in the inscriptions, there is not a single mortuary record which gives us the corresponding patronymic suffix. This defect is fortunately supplied by a small statue found at Picenum, which is plainly intended to represent Apollo. It bears the inscription JUPETRUL EPURE, words which evidently mean 'Jupiter's child, Apollo.' We conclude, therefore, that the Etruscan patronymic suffix was -ul, evidently a differentiated form of the matronymic suffix -al.

The word HEL, used as an independent word, and not as a suffix, seems also to have been occasionally used to denote 'father's child.' Thus one epitaph runs:

AR·SEMTHNI·AULES HEL·VERIAL ːKLAN.[1]

This may be taken as the designation of ARNTH SEMTHNI, who was the HEL or 'father's son' of Aule, and ·AL or 'mother's son,' of Veri.

[1] Fabretti, No. 1756. See p. 232, infra.

The ethnological importance of this suffix, and the fact that it is the only indisputable Etruscan vocable whose Latin equivalent is known with absolute certainty, may justify us in examining in some detail the question of its linguistic affinities. Fully to produce the whole evidence from more than one hundred languages would be tedious and superfluous. Wherever languages of the Ugric type are spoken, from Nova Zembla to the Nile, from the wall of China to the Pyrenees, there we find manifest traces of this ancient word, still bearing its ancient signification, and denoting either son, daughter, child, boy, or girl.

Beginning with the far north-eastern steppes of Asia, we find that *uli* means a 'child' in Ochozk, one of the Tungusic dialects. In three of the Turkic languages of Siberia, namely, in the Yenissei, Tobolsk, and Bashkir Tatar, 'son' is *ul*, a word which, letter for letter, corresponds to the Etruscan patronymic -*ul*, 'father's son.' In Bunbu, Kirghiz, and Kasan Tatar, a 'son' is *aul*, a form which may exactly represent the sound of the Etruscan matronymic -*al*. In Osmanli *oghul*, usually pronounced *oul*, means 'son,' and in Karagass Tatar *ol* is a 'boy.'

In other Turkic languages we find the various forms *uu, uul, oul, iuul, jouul, ogul, ughul, oghul, oylu, oulou, ochly, olyun, ulan, lan, oglan*, and *oghlan*, all meaning either 'son,' 'boy,' or 'child.' [1]

The Etruscan matronymic suffix is occasionally -*nal* instead of -*al*. The distinction in the usage is merely phonetic, the *n* having been elided except when the suffix follows a vowel or a liquid. But this original *n*, which has been wholly lost in all the Turkic languages, and which was in process of disappearance from the Etruscan, has been faithfully conserved in Finnic speech. Thus in Wotiak and Ziriauian we have *nyl*, a 'daughter,' while in Samojed *neo* is 'son,' and *nelled* is 'daughter.' In the Tungusic languages this *n* often becomes *m*, and we have *omolgi* and *ongolgi*, 'son,' 'boy,' and in Mandschu, *omolo* and *ongolo*, 'son.' In the Yenisseian languages the *n* changes to a *d*, and we find *dal* and *dyl*, a 'child,' *fig-dyl*, a 'boy,' and

---

[1] See Schott, *Tatar. Spr.* p. 32; Schott, *Altaische Spr.* p. 79; Klaproth, *Sprachatlas*, xxxvi.

kim-dyl a 'girl.' In Tschulim Tatar *bala* means 'son,' and in Koibal it means 'boy.' The sequence of Turkic forms is so complete that it will be convenient to take them for reference while enumerating related words which occur in other Turanian languages.

Thus we may compare the Turkish *oulou*, 'boy,' with the Coptic *alou*, 'boy;' the Kangaz Tatar *olgan*, 'son,' with the Lapp *alge*, 'son,' and the Basque *al-aba*, 'daughter;' the Tschuwash *jouul*, 'son,' with the Samojed *jile*, 'son,' and the Lapp *juglo*, 'child.' The Bashkir Tatar *ulan* and *lan* bring us to the Hungarian *leany*, 'girl,' and *leanka*, 'daughter,' while the Turkoman *ogul*, 'son,' explains the Ostiak *oggui*, *eury*, and *eua*, and the Wogul *agi*, and *aa*, 'daughter,' and the Samojedic *iga* and *i*, 'son.' The Yakut *uu* a 'son,' approximates to the Caucasic forms, examples of which are the Tschetschenz *ua*, 'son,' and the Lesghian *uas*, 'son,' and *jas*, 'daughter.'

The Turkoman *ogul* also explains the Ostiak *pagul* a 'son,' an intermediate Finno-Turkic form which enables us to trace the connection of the Ostiak *pachy*, *pach*, *poch*, the Samojed *pagam*, the Tschud *peiga*, *poika*, and *poiu*, the Lapp *peiвas*, the Wogul *puum*, *puu*, *pu*, and *py*, the Wotiak *pi*, and the Hungarian *fiu*, all of which mean 'son.'[1]

These Finnic forms, of which the Esthonian *poia* may be taken as the type, enable us to explain the word PUIA, which occurs in some four-and-twenty Etruscan epitaphs. In all these cases the names seem to be exclusively female names, and in none of them can it be affirmed with any certainty that the deceased was a married woman. In one case only is the age recorded, and in this instance it is twenty-one. The word PUIA is, therefore, probably equivalent to unmarried daughter or 'maiden.'

We find also, but more seldom, the forms PUIUS, FUIUS, PUIAM, PUIAK, PUIL, and PU. The first two of these may mean 'his daughter,' the third 'my daughter,' and the fourth may be either 'little daughter' or 'our daughter,' according as we are guided by the Turkic or the Hungarian analogy.

[1] Compare the Mongol *bagha*, Mandschu *bujo*, Finn *poika*, and Turkish *uak*, which all mean 'little.'

The word PUIA is usually placed at the end of the inscription, thus:

THANA . ALPHI . TITUIS . PUIA.[1]

Sometimes it is the first word, as

PUIA : KUMNIS : THUKERNA.[2]

Sometimes it comes in the middle, as

KAPH PUIA . L . ACHUPN . . .[3]

meaning, probably, *Kaphati, daughter of L. Achupna*. In one case we have

THANA . MANI . IPE . PUIA.[4]

which may perhaps be rendered, *Thana, sister of Mani, a maiden.*

The word IPE, which occurs in the last of these inscriptions, is also written IPI and APE. Its meaning is indicated by the Kirghiz *apa*, the Bashkir *apai*, and the Teleut *ege*, which all mean an 'elder sister.'

We have also an inscription on a statue of Apollo which contains the words EPUL (A)PE ARITIMI. We shall presently discuss the whole of this inscrip-

[1] Fabretti, No. 1,527. [2] Ibid., No. 637.
[3] Ibid., No. 1,080. [4] Ibid., No. 1,681.

tion, when it will appear that these words mean either 'Apollo's sister Artemis,' or, not improbably, ' Apollo, brother of Artemis.'

In a few of the mortuary inscriptions we have two matronymics, the second of which exhibits the additional suffix *k*. For instance:

LARTH ALETHNAS ATHNTHAL·RUVPHIALK KLAN....[1]

KAMNAS:LATH LARTHALS ATNALK KLAN.[2]

Possibly the maternal descent is here recorded through two generations. Since ·AL denotes ' child,' ALK might denote ' grandchild,' and the *k*, as in some other instances, would be a diminutive, a usage for which Ugric analogies are not wanting.

There are three other Etruscan words which designate children. These words are, KLAN, ETERA, and SECH.

In tracing the affinities of the matronymic suffix we have met with the word *oglan*, which means ' son ' in the dialects of the Turkoman and the Qasach Tatars. This form is of special interest, not only because it is apparently a very primitive and un-

---

[1] Fabretti, No. 2,058.   [2] Ibid., No. 2,335.

abraded form, from which several of the other Turkic words for 'son' may have originated, but also because it enables us to explain the very common Etruscan word KLAN, which means 'son,' or perhaps 'eldest son.' The marked tendency to devocalisation which characterises the Etruscan language accounts for the loss of the initial vowel of the Turkic word, so that there can be no hesitation in identifying the Turkoman *oglan* and the Etruscan KLAN.

Though the meanings of the Etruscan words ·UL, ·AL, and KLAN have long ago been correctly surmised, yet it has never been even conjectured that they possessed the close linguistic affinities which undoubtedly subsist between them, and which are so plainly revealed by the connecting series of Turkic words for 'son' which has been given above. No one can doubt that the Bashkir *ul* is to be identified with the Turkoman *oglan*, and hence the relation between the Etruscan ·UL and the Etruscan KLAN is no less certain.

The word KLAN occurs in about seventy epitaphs, and is invariably used as a title or designation, following immediately after the names of the deceased, and preceding the record of the age. Thus we have

AULE PATLINS·RUPENIAL KLAN.[1]

As to the exact significance of the word we are fortunately not dependent on mere conjecture or analogy. It occurs in one of the bilingual inscriptions, which runs thus:

Etruscan: V ·KAZr   K KLAN
Latin: C, CASSIUS C F.[2]

The second inscription appears to be word for word a translation of the first. The Etruscan word KLAN would therefore correspond to the Latin F., which of course stands for *filius*. We must therefore assume that KLAN primarily meant 'son.'[3]

That it may have been specially used to denote 'eldest son' is not improbable. The chief evidence is derived from two sarcophagi which were found in

---

[1] Fabretti, No. 1,697.   [2] Ibid., No. 460.
[3] The Erse *clund*, and the Gaelic *cluin*, 'children,' and the modern Scotch *clan*, a 'tribe,' may be regarded as non-Aryan words, borrowed by the Kelts from the Pictish or Ugric substratum. The Latin *cliens* is the Etruscan KLAN.

the tomb of the Venete family at Perugia. The first bears the inscription

SE VENETE LA·LETHIAL KLAN.[1]

On the other we read

LA·VENETE LA·LETHIAL·ETERA.[2]

These records evidently refer to two brothers whose personal names were Sethre and Larth, of which SE. and LA. are common contractions. The family name VENETE occurs in all the nine inscriptions which were found in the same tomb. The third word in each inscription is LA., which, according to Etruscan usage, must represent the father's name, Larth. The next word LETHIAL shows that SETHRE and LARTH were both children of the same mother, Lethei. But while one brother is called a KLAN, the other is an ETERA. Many years ago it was suggested by K. O. Müller[3] that KLAN meant 'eldest son,' and ETERA 'younger son.' Although we must absolutely reject Müller's derivation from the Greek ἑτέρα, yet he was probably right in his guess as to the meaning of the Etruscan ETERA. In Koibal Tatar *oti* means

---

[1] Fabretti, No. 1,397.   [2] Ibid., No. 1,396.
[3] Müller, *Die Etrusker*, vol. i., p. 446.

'younger child,' and the unabraded form of this Ugric word is shown in the Yakut words *edder* and *öder*, and the Tungusic *edör*, which mean 'young.' The same signification attaches to the Yenisseian words *eti* and *ete*, and the Kamasin *üttei*, which have all lost the final *r*. It is therefore nearly certain that the Etruscan word ETERA meant either 'young son' or 'younger son,' and the purport of our record (No. 1,396) is either that LARTH VENETE died young, or that he was the younger brother of SETHRE VENETE.

It does not, however, follow, as has been usually assumed, that KLAN necessarily meant 'eldest son.' The tomb of the Semthni family, also at Perugia, affords some additional evidence as to the meaning of these words. Here we have another pair of epitaphs, also referring to two brothers, Arnth and Aule, sons of the same father and mother, who are both of them designated as KLAN. We have

AR·SEMTHNI·AULES HEL·VERIAL·KLAN.[1]

AU:SEMTHNI:AU HEL VEREAL:KLAN.[2]

[1] Fabretti, No. 1,756. [2] Ibid., No. 1,757.

Another Perugian inscription, not improbably from the same tomb, commemorates a third brother. It runs

> AU : SEMTHNI : ETERA
> [. . .] HEL · VEREAL.[1]

I have not met with any other instance in which two brothers bear the same prænomen. Possibly No. 1,906 was the first born, and died young—ETERA. Nos. 1,756 and 1,757 may have been twins, sharing the rights of primogeniture and the designation of KLAN, one of them (No. 1,757) succeeding to the vacant paternal prænomen.[1] It is possible, however, that No. 1,757 may have been the first born and have died young, so that No. 1,756, the second son, would succeed to the designation of Klan, while No. 1,906, born after the death of No. 1,757, took the father's prænomen.

There is another very curious illustration of the meaning of ETERA, which I am surprised to find has never been noticed by any writer. Hesychius informs us that AGALLETORA was an Etruscan word equivalent to the Greek παῖς, a 'boy.' The elements of *Agall-etora* are evidently to be found in the

[1] Fabretti, No. 1,906.

Turkoman *ogul*, 'son,' and the Yakut *edder*, 'young.' Therefore *Agalletora* would mean 'young son.' This looks as if the ETERA of the inscriptions meant 'young' rather than 'younger,' and that KLAN simply meant 'son,' and not 'eldest son,' as has been usually assumed. Moreover KLENAR, the plural of KLAN, which occurs in the phrases KLENAR KI and KLENAR ZAL (which have been discussed in Chapter V. p. 191), must mean either 'sons' or 'children,' and cannot possibly signify 'eldest sons.' The word KLEN-AR-ASI, which occurs in the San Manno inscription, would be 'his sons,' or 'his children.' Once or twice the word seems to denote a female child, as

PHASTI·KUINTI·SALES·KLENS PUIA.[1]

And in another inscription we have the phrase KLAN PUIAK.[2]

The word SECH, sometimes written SAK and SEK, is found in numerous inscriptions which relate exclusively to women. It seems to be the feminine correlative of the masculine word KLAN, as it occurs in the same way at the close of the epitaph. We may render

[1] Febretti, No. 1,653.   [2] Ibid., No. 987.

it 'daughter,' or 'girl,' or possibly 'eldest daughter.' The Ugric correspondences are numerous. In Turkish *say-ird* denotes a 'female slave in the Sultan's harem,' and the word is also used to mean a 'servant' or 'apprentice.' In Hungarian, *fele-sey* means a 'woman,' and in Zirianian *sotsch* is a 'sister.' In Burjät *ba-sag-an* is a 'young maiden,' in Tungus *a-satk-an* is a 'daughter,' and in Lapp *sakko* denotes 'offspring.' In Tscherkes *shiz* is a 'woman,' *psah-sey* a 'girl,' *soopshaz* a 'daughter,' and *sagh-oo* a 'boy.'

The appelations SECH and PUIA are not synonymous, being sometimes applied to the same person, as in the inscription,

PUIA · AKLNIS · NUPHRZNAS PARMNIAL SECH.[1]

There are two or three inscriptions which seem to indicate that the word SECH was applicable to a married woman. Thus we have

PHA : TUTNIE : KUTLISNEI : TETINASA : TLESNAIL) : SEK.[2]

and again,

VEIZI : KUMERESA : VARNAL: SEK.[3]

[1] Fabretti, No. 1,541.   [2] Ibid., No. 749.
[3] Ibid., No. 940.

Not the least interesting of the words denoting kinship is this suffix -ISA, -ESA, or -ASA, which appears in the two last inscriptions, and which is sometimes cut down to -s. We have already met with it in the bilingual equivalents given on p. 220, where we saw that KAIN-AL is translated CAINNIA NATUS, and that VAR-NAL-ISA is also translated VARIA NATUS. These instances show that the word *natus* is solely the equivalent of -NAL or -AL, while there is nothing in the Latin which corresponds to the Etruscan suffix -ISA. The suffix constantly occurs in the epitaphs of men, but solely as a suffix in the matronymic word. It must therefore be regarded as an appellative, relating not to the deceased, but to his mother. It is of still more common occurrence in the epitaphs of women, but here it is usually appended directly to the surname borne by the husband's family. Thus PHRAVN-ISA denotes the wife of Phravna, or as we should say, 'Dame Phravna,' whereas the matronymic PHRAVN-AL-ISA designates the 'son of Dame Phravna.'

In order to make clear the normal usage of this suffix it may be well to give a few inscriptions in which it occurs. In the tomb of the Kvenle family at Siena there is an epitaph which runs thus:

THANA METHLNE KVENLESA.[1]

This denotes a woman named Thana, who by birth belonged to the Methlne family, and who was married to a Kvenle. In the same tomb we have the epitaph of her son, which runs:

AU · KVENLE METHLNAL.[2]

He bears the family name Kvenle, and takes his matronymic, Methlnal, from the Methlne family to which his mother belonged by birth.

In the tomb of the Lekne family at Clusium we have, among others, the four following epitaphs[3]:—

1. **THANCHUVIL SESKTNEI LEKNESA**
2. **LARTHI VUISINEI LEKNESA**
3. **V · LEKNE · V · SESKTNAL**
4. **A · LEKNE VUISINAL**

No. 1 is a woman of the Sesktne family who married a Lekne, and No. 3 is her son. No. 2 is a woman of the Vuisine family, who also married into the Lekne family, and her son is No 4.

[1] Fabretti, No. 373. [2] Ibid., No. 378.
[3] Ibid., Nos. 405, 408, 411, 409.

The mode in which these kinships are ordinarily denoted is well exhibited by the epitaphs found in the tomb of the Herini family at Clusium. This tomb contained eight urns, bearing the following inscriptions[1]:—

1. LTH · HERINI : UMRANAL
2. LTH : HERINI : LTH · RATHUMSNAL : KLAN
3. AR · TUTNA : KLANIU : RATHMSNAL
4. THA : TLESNEI : HERINISA · PULUPHNAL
5. ATH : HERINI : LTH : TLESNALISA
6. LTH : HERINI : TLESNAL
7. THANIA : TUTNEI : KLANTUNIA : RATHUMSNAL
8. ... HERINI : ATH : VIPINAL

The explanation of these records seems to be as follows:—No. 4 was the mother of No. 5. By birth she belonged to the Tlesna family, whose tomb also exists at Clusium. Her own surname was Tlesnei, the feminine form of Tlesna. She married No. 2, and therefore took, in addition to her own, her husband's surname Herini, with the suffix -*isa*, equivalent to 'Dame.' This suffix also appears in

[1] Fabretti, Nos. 495–502.

the matronymic of her son, No. 5, who is called Tlesnalisa, or 'son of Dame Tlesnei.' He also bears as his third name a patronymic, which is the same as the first name of his father, No. 2. The father of No. 2 is No. 1. He married a widow, who was by birth one of the Rathumna family. Her first husband was a Tutna, a family whose tomb also exists at Clusium. This widow seems to have brought into the Herini family two children by her first husband. These were a boy, No. 3, and a girl, No. 7. These children are called respectively Klanin and Klantunia. These words do not appear to have been Etruscan proper names, and may mean 'stepson' and 'stepdaughter,' or possibly may denote illegitimacy. The Genealogical Table which follows will make clear the kinships of the remaining members of the family. The names printed in italics are those of persons whose epitaphs are not among those in the tomb, but whose existence and respective kinships are sufficiently indicated by the Etruscan system of nomenclature.

KINSHIP.

GENEALOGICAL TABLE OF THE HERINI FAMILY.

```
...Tutus...=........Rathamnei...      ...Herini...=....Usarei...
             |                                |
   ┌─────────┼─────────┐          (1) Larth Herini Umranai.
   |                   |                      |
(3) Arath Tutus  (7) Thana Tutnei        ...Tlesma...=...Pulaphnei...
Klania Rathumnal. Klaniania Rathumnal.              |
                                   ┌────────────────┼──────────────┐
                                   |                |              |
                          (2) Larth Herini Larth=(4) Thana Tlesnei  
                              Rathumnal.          Herinia Puluphnai.
                                   |                              |
                        ┌──────────┴───────┐           (6) Larth Herini
                        |                  |               Tlesnal.
                 (5) Ath Herini=...Vipei...
                     La-rh Tlesnalisa.
                                |
                     (8) Herini Ath Vipinal.
```

THE PETRUNI FAMILY.

The tomb of the Petruni family at Perugia contains another very instructive set of thirteen epitaphs, and is especially interesting as the series closes with a Latin inscription.

We have first a sarcophagus bearing the effigies of a man and a woman, and the two inscriptions

1. LA ∴ TITE · PETRUNI · VE · KLANTIAL
2. PHASTI · KAPZNEI · VE · TARCHISA CHVESTNAL TUBURTHIR

Then comes another sarcophagus, also with the effigies of a man and a woman; on the lid is the word TUBURTHI, and below the two inscriptions,

3. VETI : PETRUNI : VE : ANEINAL : SPURINAL : KLAN :
4. VEILIA : KLANTI : ARZNAL

No. 5 bears the effigy of a man and the inscription
LS · TITE PETRUNI LS VESTI

No. 6 has the effigy of a man and the inscription
LS ı TITE : FETRUNI : VELUS : KLANTIAL

No. 7 has the effigy of a man and the inscription
VL · TI · PETRU · HAMPHNAL

No. 8 has the effigy of a man and the inscription
LS · TITE · PETRUNI · LS · KASPRIAL

No. 9 has the effigy of a woman and the inscription
VE · PETRUNI · LA · KAPIZINAL
10. AULE : TITES PETRUNIS :
11. AULE : TITES ([PE]TRUNIS VELUS : T · ETERA
12. PHASTI TITIA PETIS
13. L. PETRONIUS · L · F · NOFORSINIA.[1]

It is hardly needful, after the explanations which have been already given, to go through these names in detail. No. 2 seems to have married a Tarchna as her second husband. The Genealogical Table which follows will explain the rest. The places of Nos. 5, 10, and 11, are uncertain. The word TUSURTHI will be explained presently.

There are few Etruscan words which possess plainer Ugric affinities than the suffix -ISA. In all the branches of the Ugric stock[2] this word *isa*, with various phonetic modifications, is used as a title implying originally the respect due to age, and subsequently coming to bear the meaning of master or mistress, lord or lady, thus corresponding very closely with the Italian signor and signora.

Thus in Turkish *issi* means 'master,' 'lord,'

---

[1] Fabretti, No. 1,242-1,252.
[2] See Schott, *Altaische Spr.* p. 95.

GENEALOGICAL TABLE OF THE PETRUNI FAMILY.

```
... Petruni ... = ... Hamphnei ...
                  |
   (7) Vl : Ti : Petru : Hamphnal = ... Spuriei ...        ... Klauti ... = ... Arznei ...
                           |                                           |
   (10)? Aule   (11)? Anle Titea    (3) Veli Petruni Ve : Anciual = (4) Veilia Klauti Arznal.
   Titea        Petrunis Velus T : clan.        Spuriual Klan.
   Petrunis.
                              |                                           |
                ... Kapnus ... = ... Checaluci ...        (6) La : Tito Petruni
                              |                                Velus Klantial.
                (1) La : Tito Petruni. = (2) Phasti Kapranei Ve.       (5)? La : Tito Petruni
                     Ve : Klantial.       Turclnas Cluvasimal.              Le Vesti ...
                              |
       (8) La : Tito Petruni = ... Nuphrznei ...    (9) Ve Petruni    ... Pete ... = (12) Phasti Titu
            Le : Kaprial                                 La : Kapznal.                  Peltsa[s] ...
                                                         (unmarried daughter.)          (married daughter.)
       (13) L. Petronius L. F. Noforninia.
```

'owner;' *essa-let* means 'nobility of birth'; and *asch* or *esch* means a 'comrade,' or 'peer.' The Yakuts, a Turkic tribe in Siberia, call their formidable foe the white bear, *ese*, the most respectful title in their language, equivalent to monseigneur or grandfather. In Finn and Esth, *isä* or *issa* is a 'father,' and *isä-nta* is 'master of the house.' In Hungarian 'God' is *is-ten*, in Mongolic *etsen* is 'Lord' or 'master,' and related words are applied in various Siberian languages to honoured female relatives—as *ese*, 'sister;' *edschi*, 'mother;' *adscha*, 'aunt;' *ascha*, 'wife of an elder brother.' In Burjät, a Mongolic language, *izi* means both 'wife' and 'mother,' *nagasa* is 'aunt,' *eg-ese* or *ig-isi* is 'sister,' and *es-ega* is 'father.' In several of the Turkic dialects *bisa* or *bysa* means 'wife,' and in all of them *kis* or *kys* means 'daughter.' The root extends from the Arctic Ocean to the Caucasus. Thus in Samojed *pug-itscha* is a 'woman,' while *fis* is a 'wife' in Tscherkes, and *yase* is a 'maiden' in Lesghi.

In a few of the Etruscan inscriptions the suffix takes the form *-isla* instead of *isa*, but there is no indication which will guide us in assigning a distinctive meaning to the words. It is possible that the *l* may be a vestige of the Turkic *ulu*, 'great' or 'chief'; and when a man had more wives than one the suffix -*isla* may have denoted the head or chief wife.

It is very significant, from an ethnological point of view, that no word for 'father' has as yet been detected in the inscriptions. The words denoting husband and wife are also somewhat doubtful. The analogy of the Turkish *erkek*, a 'male,' may indicate that the word ARKE, which occurs in one or two inscriptions,[1] may mean 'husband;' and the Turkish *evli*, 'married,' and *evle-nish*, 'marriage,' give a certain probability to the supposition that the difficult word VLSSHI may mean 'his wife.'

These, however, at the best are extremely doubtful and uncertain words. But there is another word concerning which we may speak with much greater confidence. This is TUSURTHI, which appears twice in the inscriptions in the tomb of the Petruni family, and which occurs repeatedly in the curtailed forms SURTI and SURTES.[2]

The analogies of the Etruscan SURTI may be

[1] See p. 191, *supra*.
[2] Fabretti, Nos. 2,055, 2,335. See p. 241, *supra*.

found in the Samojed *seri* a 'widow,' and *sereatem* 'to celebrate a wedding.' The Karagass Tatar *erduk*, 'widow,' seems to be the same word deprived of its initial consonant. The other Etruscan form, TU-SURTHI, exhibits a prefix *tu* which in numerous Ugric languages denotes marriage or the loss of virginity. Thus, in Samojedic dialects, *thoi*, *tune*, and *tuia*, mean 'marriage;' a wedding is *toi* in Koibal Tatar; and in other Turkic languages a 'widow' is *dul-kari* (*kari*, 'woman'), *tul-kizi* (*kizi*, 'person,' 'maid'), or simply *dul*.

The words TUSURTHI and TUSURTHIR occur in the Petruni tomb on the two double sarcophagi which each contained the bodies of a married couple. Probably the feminine TUSURTHI means 'wife,' while TUSURTHIR, obviously a plural word, denotes 'wedded pair.' The usage on the monuments seems to indicate that SURTI meant 'widow,' and SURTES, 'widowed dame' or 'a widow.' Thus

PHASTI : SURTES [1]

may mean *Phasti, a widow*. We have also the parallel inscriptions :—

[1] Fabretti, No. 1,780.

LTH · ANIS · SURTES [1]

LATHI · KAI · SURTES [2]

THANA · ACHUNI · LA · TITES · SURTES [3]

This is the designation of Thana, by birth of the Achuna family, daughter of Larth, wife of Tite, a widow.

VEILIA : SURTI : VELKZNAL : SEK [4]

would designate *Veilia, a widow, daughter of Velkzni.*

KAPZNAS · SURTUI : PLAUTI : AR : PUM [5]

would be *Dame Kapzna, widow of Plauti. Ar. Pum.*

Striking as are the strict and universal correspondences of meaning between the Etruscan and Ugric words which denote kinship, the grammatical significance of the usage of those which are employed as suffixes is of still greater ethnological import. All the Ugric languages belong to the agglutinative class, the distinguishing feature of which is the system of gluing on to the root suffix after suffix. Qualifying or explanatory words, which in Aryan languages would appear either as pre-positions or as

[1] Fabretti, No. 1,501.   [2] Ibid., No. 1,907.
[3] Ibid., No. 1,580.
[4] Ibid., No. 1781.   [5] Ibid., No. 1272.

independent words, are in the Ugric languages successively glued on as post-positions, the order in which we should arrange them being usually reversed. Now the mode in which the Etruscans employed the suffixes -*al* and -*isa* is beyond all question distinctly agglutinative. It may be confidently asserted that the mere existence of such a word as TLESN-AL-ISA or VAR-NAL-ISA is of itself sufficient to establish the agglutinative character of Etruscan grammar, and thus to set at rest for ever the question of the linguistic affinities of the Etruscan tongue. It is an inexplicable marvel that this obvious and unmistakable feature of the Etruscan language should have so long escaped recognition.

CHAPTER VIII.

THE BILINGUAL INSCRIPTIONS.

The unsatisfactory character of the Bilinguals—The nine Inscriptions—Comparison of the Etruscan and Roman systems of Nomenclature—The Roman Agnomen corresponds to the Etruscan Matronymic—The Latin equivalents of the five Etruscan female names: Kakati, Tari, Kiarthi, Thapiri, and Veni—The cognomen and the patronymic—Meaning of Aelche—The prænomen—Latin equivalents of Ath, Arth, and Vele.

THERE are seventeen so-called BILINGUAL INSCRIPTIONS—that is, there are seventeen Etruscan mortuary records which are either followed or preceded by a Latin inscription which is presumably a version of the Etruscan. But as regards any practical utility for the study of the Etruscan language this number must be reduced to nine. The other eight records are either mere transcriptions in Latin letters of Etruscan proper names; or they are so mutilated, and the readings consequently so uncertain, as to be useless for any practical purposes; or they are only seemingly equivalent, proving on examination to relate to different members of the same family.

Even the nine inscriptions which remain are most disappointing. They consist almost exclusively of proper names, and only supply us with the direct Latin equivalents of one, or at most, of two, Etruscan vocables. These have been discussed in the last chapter. We have seen that the Etruscan suffix ᴀʟ, translated by ɴᴀᴛᴜs, means 'mother's child,' that ᴋʟᴀɴ, translated by ꜰ., means 'son,' and that the untranslated suffix ɪꜱᴀ is equivalent to 'dame.'

In addition to these direct results there are others of an indirect character. An analysis of the bilinguals shows that in several cases the Latin names are not identical with the corresponding Etruscan names, being apparently translations, instead of transliterations only, of the corresponding Etruscan names

The greatest obstacle in the investigation of the affinities of the Etruscan language has been the difficulty of discovering test-words, as to the real meaning of which there exists any independent and certain indication. In every case in which such a word can in any way be found, and shown to bear the same meaning in the Ugric languages as in the Etruscan, another link is thereby added to our chain of proof. Hence a careful examination of these apparently barren bilinguals may prove ultimately to be fruitful of positive and valuable results.

I will begin by transcribing from Fabretti the nine bilinguals.

THE NINE BILINGUAL INSCRIPTIONS.

I.

Etruscan: V·LEKNE· V · THAPIRNAL
Latin: O·LICINI C·F.   NIGRI.[1]

II.

Etruscan: PUP VELIMNA AU KAHATIAL
Latin: P· VOLUMNIUS A·F· VIOLENS CAFATIA NATUS.[2]

III.

Etruscan: ATH · UNATA·   VARNAL(IS)A
Latin: M· OTACILIUS· RUFUS · VARIA · NATUS.[3]

[1] Fabretti, No. 252.   [2] Ibid., No. 1,496.   [3] Ibid., No. 794.

IV.

Etruscan:

AELCHE PHULNI   AELCHES   KIARTHIALISA

Latin:

Q.   FOLNIUS A·F· . POM   FUSCUS [1]

V.

Etruscan: VL·ALPHNI·NUVI·KAINAL

Latin: C· ALFIUS·A·F·CAINNIA NATUS.[2]

VI.

Etruscan: KUINTE·SINU·   ARNTNAL

Latin: Q·   SENTIUS·L·F·ARRIA·NATUS.[3]

VII.

Etruscan: A· TITI·   A· VANIAL

Latin: A· TITIUS A F·   SCAE-CALIS.[4]

VIII.

Etruscan: V· KAZ:·   K·KLAN

Latin: C· CASSIUS·C·F·   SATURNINUS.[5]

IX.

Etruscan: ARTH·KIIRIZNA·   VARNALISLA

Latin: C·   CÆSIUS C·F·VARIA NAT.[6]

---

[1] Fabretti, No. 251. [2] Ibid., No. 792. [3] Ibid., No. 980.
[4] Ibid., No. 996.   [5] Ibid., No. 460.
[6] Ibid., No. 252. For convenience of reference I have

Before attempting a detailed analysis of these inscriptions it will be needful to compare the Etruscan with the Roman system of nomenclature, and to note the points of agreement and the points of difference. We shall then be able to identify with certainty the correspondent names, and so to select for further examination the cases in which a Latin name is a translation, and not a mere transliteration, of the corresponding Etruscan word.

The Roman system of nomenclature is well known. A Roman bore two, three, or four names. These were:—

1. The PRÆNOMEN, or 'personal name.'

2. The NOMEN, or 'surname,' which was derived from the name of the *gens* to which the person belonged. It usually ended in -*ius*, an old genitive form, having a patronymic force.

appended to each inscription a Roman numeral, and I have added the numbers by which they are noted in Fabretti's work. The Latin words have respectively been placed beneath the Etruscan words to which they apparently correspond, but the order of the words has in no case been changed. Doubtful letters are enclosed in brackets. In No. IV. I have for clearness separated the first three words, which in the inscription are run together without divisions.

3. The COGNOMEN, usually derived from some personal or family peculiarity.

4. The AGNOMEN, often derived from the name of the mother.

Thus in the case of Marcus Porcius Cato Salonianus, Marcus is the *praenomen*, Porcius the *nomen*, Cato the *cognomen*, while Salonianus is an *agnomen*, which was derived from the name of his mother Salonia.

It must be remembered that the records of the Etruscan tombs extend over several centuries, and naturally the system of nomenclature is much more simple at the beginning than at the end of this period. The bilingual inscriptions belong to the time when the Etruscan language was giving place to Latin, and they therefore exhibit the system of nomenclature in its most elaborate form, and partake to some extent of peculiarities introduced from the Roman system.

In these late Etruscan epitaphs we usually find four names, which occur in the following order:—

1. The PRAENOMEN, or personal name
2. The NOMEN, or family name.

3. The prænomen of the father, which thus forms a substitute for a PATRONYMIC.

4. The MATRONYMIC, being the name of the mother, with the suffix -*al*.

In the case of married women the place of the patronymic is often taken by the husband's name with the suffix -*isa*.

We may now compare the Etruscan with the Roman system, so far as the bilinguals enable us to do so.

1. The Prænomen. Here the correspondence is close. The Latin prænomen is in every case either a transliteration or a translation of the Etruscan prænomen. Thus in No. I. the Etruscan prænomen VELE) is translated by the Latin prænomen c(a)us), and in No. II. the Etruscan prænomen PUP(LE) is transliterated into the Latin prænomen P(UBLIUS).

2. The Nomen. Here also there is a close correspondence. The Etruscan nomen is transliterated, not translated, the suffix -*ius*, which characterises a Roman nomen, being appended. Thus in No. I. LEKNE becomes LICINIUS, and in No. II. VELIMNA becomes VOLUMNIUS.

3. The Patronymic. This is usually represented in the Etruscan by the initial or first syllable of the father's name, and in the Latin by the initial of the father's name and the letter F. It is worthy of note that in two cases, Nos. VI. and IX., the paternal descent is recorded in the Latin version, but omitted from the Etruscan. The introduction of a patronymic is of late date in Etruscan epitaphs, and was probably due to Roman influence or example.

4. The Cognomen. There is no instance of an Etruscan cognomen. In No. IV. the Latin POM. appears to be a cognomen formed by a translation of the Etruscan patronymic AELCHES.

5. The Matronymic. We have seen that the paternal descent is in two instances omitted from the Etruscan record, but carefully recorded in the Latin version. In like manner the maternal descent is in three instances omitted from the Latin version, but recorded in the Etruscan. The ethnological import of this difference has already been insisted on. There is no true Latin matronymic, but in four cases the Etruscan matronymic is translated by means of the Latin word *natus*. Thus in No. II. the Etruscan matronymic KAHATIAL is translated CAFATIA NATUS

6. *The Agnomen.* There is no instance of an Etruscan agnomen. In six instances the Latin version presents us with an agnomen, which has no direct equivalent in the corresponding Etruscan epitaph.

Paradoxical as it may seem, the most valuable portions of these inscriptions are those in which the Etruscan does not correspond to the Latin version. The points of difference are more instructive than the points of agreement. Now the chief distinction between a Latin and an Etruscan epitaph is that the Etruscan contains a matronymic and no agnomen, while the Latin contains an agnomen and no matronymic. Moreover, the place which the matronymic occupies in the Etruscan epitaph is invariably filled by the agnomen in the Latin version.

The relation between the agnomen and the matronymic will be seen at a glance, if we arrange in columns of correspondence the names in the five bilingual inscriptions in which the Latin version contains an agnomen.

Thus we have :—

		praenomen	nomen	patronymic	matronymic	agnomen
I.	Etruscan	V.	Lekno	V.	Thapirnal	(none)
	Latin	C.	Licini	C.F.	(none)	Nigri
II.	Etruscan	Pup.	Velimna	Au.	Kahatial	(none)
	Latin	P.	Volumnius	A.F.	Cafatia natus	Violens
VII.	Etruscan	A.	Titl	A.	Vanial	(none)
	Latin	A.	Titius	A.F.	(none)	Scæ. calis
III.	Etruscan	Ath.	Unata	(none)	Varnalisa	(none)
	Latin	M.	Otacilius	(none)	Varia natus	Rufus
IV.	Etruscan	Aelche	Phulni	Aelches	Kiarthialisa	(none)
	Latin	Q.	Folnius	A.F.	(none)	Fuscus

Since the Latin agnomen thus supplies the place of the Etruscan matronymic, it seems probable that they are in some way connected. Now a Latin agnomen, being ordinarily formed from the name of the mother, is the nearest approach to a matronymic which the Latin usage permitted. It is, therefore, in accordance with probability to suppose that the Latin agnomina Niger, Violens, Scæ. calis, Rufus, Fuscus, and Saturninus were derived by translation or reflexion from the Etruscan names borne by the mothers of these persons.

The bilinguals supply us with the following equivalents:—

TRANSLATED MATRONYMICS.

	Etruscan Matronymic	Latin Translation	Derived Latin Agnomen
I.	THAPIRNAL	(none)	NIGER
II.	KAHATIAL	CAFATIA NATUS	VIOLENS
III.	VARNALISA	VARIA NATUS	RUFUS
IV.	KIARTHIALISA	(none)	FUSCUS
V.	KAINAL	CAINNIA NATUS	(none)
VI.	ARNTNAL	ARRIA NATUS	(none)
VII.	VANIAL	(none)	SCAE. CALIS
VIII.	(none)	(none)	SATURNINUS
IX.	VARNALISLA	VARIA NAT.	(none)

Hence we obtain Latin translations of five Etruscan female names:

	Etruscan	Latin
I.	THAPIRI	NIGRA
II.	KAHATI	VIOLENS
III.	VARI	RUFA
IV.	KIARTHI	FUSCA
VII.	VANI	SCAE. CALIS

We have now to ascertain whether these five words are to be found in the Ugric languages, and whether they bear the meanings which are thus indicated by the Latin agnomina.

KAHATI, 'violent.' In Inscription No. II. the Latin agnomen VIOLENS is derived from the Etruscan matronymic KAHATIAL; therefore the Etruscan female name KAHATI must have meant 'violent.' The same word, bearing the same sense, runs through every branch of the Ugric stock—Turkic, Finnic, Mongolic, Tungusic, and Samojedic.

The Tungusic *kata*, the Burjüt (Mongolic) *kutu*, the Koibal (Turkic) *katex*, and the Samojedic *kartaga*, all mean 'fierce,' 'rough,' 'tough,' 'hard.' The Tungusic *kat-aram* and the Burjüt *kat-ernam* mean to 'galop.' In Ostiak *kat-tem* means to 'snatch' or 'seize.' In Tungus the word *kad-af*, applied to horses, means 'self-willed,' 'obstinate,' and in Yenissei *kat-lbeden* means 'swift,' 'mettlesome.'

In Hungarian *ked* means 'temper,' 'spirit,' and *hati* means he 'rushes in,' or 'enters by force.' 'Strength,' 'force,' is *kuvvet* in Osmanli, *kat'-uga* in Tschuktsch Tatar, and *zutche* in Burjüt. In Nogai and Qumuq Tatar a 'storm' is *kati-jel*, and in Tobolsk Tatar it is *katti-il*. Since *jel* and *il* mean 'wind,' *kati-jel* must mean 'violent wind,' and *kati* must mean 'violent.'

VARI, 'red.' In Inscription No. III. the Latin agnomen RUFUS is derived from the Etruscan matronymic VAR·NALISA, and therefore the Etruscan female name VARI must have meant 'red,' the lady being so named either from her ruddy cheeks or her red hair.

We have already met with this root *var*, meaning 'red,' which runs through the whole of the Ugric languages. Thus 'red' is *veres* in Hungarian, *veyry* in Ostiak, *veyr* in Wogul, and *werrew* in Esth. In Suomi *weri* is 'blood,' in Turkish *rer-d* is a 'rose,' and *jer-en* is 'fox colour.' In Mandschu *giru* is to 'blush,' while 'red-haired' is *zer-de* in Burjät, and *zar-da* in Tungus. The laws of letter-change enable us also to identify the Samojedic *narra*, the Turkish *kysel*, and the Lesghian *baar-af*, words which all mean 'red.'[1]

KIARTHI, 'swarthy.' In Inscription No. IV. the Latin agnomen FUSCUS is derived from the Etruscan

[1] See p. 137 *supra*; Schott, *Alt. Spr.*, p. 66.

matronymic KIARTHI-ALISA. Therefore the Etruscan word KIARTHI must have meant 'dark' or 'swarthy.' The word KIAR-THI probably contains two roots. In the whole of the twenty-two Turkic languages *kara*, *gara*, or *chara*, means 'black,' and in Mongolic 'black' is *kara* or *xara*. The second root is apparently an abraded form of the Turkic *tere*, *teri*, or *deri*, the Wogul *toul*, and the Lapp *tuolje*, all of which mean 'skin.' The Etruscan word KIAR-THI would therefore mean 'dark skinned' or 'swarthy,' a fair equivalent of the Latin *fusca*.

THAPIRI, 'black.' In Inscription No. I. the Latin agnomen NIGER is derived from the Etruscan matronymic THAPIR-NAL. Therefore the Etruscan name THAPIRI must have meant 'black'—probably black-haired rather than black-skinned. This word, although the vestiges of it in the Ugric languages are somewhat faint, is of special interest, inasmuch as the laws of Mongolic grammar enable us to show that it is simply the intensitive form of the preceding word. If KIARI meant 'dark' (fusca), THAPIRI would mean 'very dark' (nigra). Mongolic intensitives are formed by prefixing to the word the letter *p*, preceded by a reduplication of the first syllable. Thus in two Burjät dialects *kara* and *xara* mean 'black.' Hence are formed the intensitives *kap-kara* and *xap-xara*, 'quite black.'[1] The Etruscan THAPIRA, *niger*, would thus be an abraded form of *kap-kara*, *xap-xara*, *zap-zara*, or *thap-thara*, *k*, *x*, *z*, and *th* being interchangeable. The vowel change in the second syllable is interesting as an instance of the harmonic permutation of vowels which is so characteristic of the Ugric languages, the Etruscan specially following the peculiar Hungarian law. The Mongolic *xapxara* and the Etruscan *thapiri* taken together enable us to explain several anomalous Ugric words which mean 'black,' such as the Lapp *zioppad*, the Tungusic *sachrin* and *tschakarin*, and the Samojedic *sagar*, *tsaga*, and *piride*.

VANI. In Inscription No. VII. the Latin agnomen SCAE . CALIS is derived from the Etruscan matronymic VANIAL. In this case no very satisfactory explanation can be given, owing to the difficulty of determining the significance of the Latin agnomen, which possibly refers to some unknown augural rule. SCAE . CALIS

[1] Castrén, *Burjätischen Sprachlehre*, p. 21.

seems to denote a sinister, unlucky, or dangerous path. All that can be said is that the Ugric analogies of the Etruscan VANI mean 'dangerous,' 'rotten,' 'ready to perish' (see p. 102, *supra*).

In Inscription No. VIII. we have another agnomen, SATURNINUS, but as the corresponding matronymic is not given, it would be fruitless to discuss it.

Excluding from consideration the two last cases, in which materials are deficient, it may, I think, be alleged that the four names KAHATI, VARI, KIARTHI, and THAPIRI, yield by themselves an argument as to the affinities of the Etruscan language which closely approaches to a demonstration. The mathematical chances against any mere fortuitous coincidence of sound and meaning in these four words are quite overwhelming.

In addition to the agnomina reflected from the matronymics, we have in one instance a Latin cognomen which is apparently reflected or translated from the patronymic, and therefore equivalent to it in meaning. Inscription No IV. runs thus:

Etruscan: AELCHE PHULNI AELCHES KIARTHIALISA
Latin: Q. FOLNIUS A.F. POM. FUSCUS.

Here A.F. (Aelchi Filius) represents the Etruscan patronymic AELCHES, while POM. (Pomerius) seems to be a cognomen reflected from it. The praenomen AELCHE is also translated by Q., which stands for Quinctius or Quintus. We have therefore two translations of Aelche, namely Quinctius and Pomerius, which ought to be synonymous. Lord Crawford has suggested that the name Quinctius is analogous to Lentulus, Fabius, and some other Roman names, and means 'quince-apple.' In support of this view he affirms that a coin of the Quinctia gens bears a device which appears to be intended for a small round fruit. If this etymology be correct, QUINCTIUS and POMERIUS, the two translations of the Etruscan AELCHE, would be nearly synonymous, and AELCHE ought to mean a 'quince-apple.' The word AEL-CHE seems to contain two roots. The first is seen in the Turkish *el-ma*, the Hungarian *al-ma*, 'apple,' the Esthonian *willi*, 'fruit,' and in *ul-amos*, 'fruit,' one of the five Lycian words which have come down to us. The second root may be referred to the Thushi *chil*, 'fruit,' or the Georgian *khili*, 'apple.'

The word AEL-CHE might therefore mean 'quince-apple' or 'apple fruit.'[1]

In three of the bilinguals the Etruscan prænomen is transliterated in the Latin version, but in the other six cases it appears to have been translated. We have the following equivalent prænomina:

	No. I.	No. III.	No. IV.	No. V.	No. VIII.	No. IX.
Etruscan:	V.	ATH.	AELCHE.	VL.	V.	ARTH.
Latin:	C.	M.	Q.	C.	C.	C.

Hence we see that the common Latin name CAIUS is thrice taken as the equivalent of the common Etruscan name VELE (Nos. I., V., VIII.), and once as the equivalent of the Etruscan name ARTH. Also ATH, a very common Etruscan name, is translated by MARCUS (No. III.).

The Etruscan name ATH, or AT as it is sometimes written, is of great interest. It was borne by the Emperor Salvius Otho, who was of ancient Etruscan lineage, belonging, we are told, to the *principes Etruriæ*.[2] It may be also identified with the name

---

[1] See Crawford, *Etruscan Inscriptions*, p. 68; Ellis, *Armenian Origin of Etruscans*, p. 50; Ellis, *Asiatic Affinities of Old Italians*, p. 20.

[2] Müller, *Die Etrusker*, vol. i. p. 419.

Etc, which was borne by the chieftain of the fourth of the seven Magyar tribes at the time of their settlement in Hungary. It seems also to form the first portion of the name of Oth-man, the great Turkic sultan from whom the Otto-man empire and the Os-manli language take their name.

There can be little doubt as to the meaning of the name Ath, At, or Otho. It means 'horse,' 'horseman,' or 'cavalier.' In twenty-two of the Turkic languages *at* means a 'horse,' and the root can be also traced in the Mongolic, Tungusic, Samojedic, Finnic, and Caucasic stocks.

The Latin name Marcus, which is employed as the translation of the Etruscan Ath, may be explained by reference to a wide-spread Aryan word which means 'horse.' We have the Sanskrit *mrga*, the 'chase,' 'hunting,' the Keltic *marc*, 'horse,' the old High German *march*, 'horse,' and the English *mare*. The word is not classical Latin, but its existence in Low Latin is indicated by the French word *maréchal*, a 'groom' or 'farrier,' the source of the English *marshal*.

The name CAIUS is used in the bilinguals as the equivalent of two Etruscan names, VELE and ARTH.

Two plausible derivations of the name Caius or Cajus might have presented themselves to a Roman. It might have been referred to the Latin word *caja*, which according to Isidore and Fulgentius meant a 'cudgel;' or it might have been explained by reference to the ancient custom by which in Roman marriage festivals the bridegroom and bride were designated as Caius and Caia, equivalent to 'man and wife,' or 'baron and femme.'[1] The name Caius may therefore have been taken to mean either a 'husband' or a 'cudgel.' The Etruscan name Arth, which is one equivalent of Caius, may be referred to the Turkic *ar*, *er*, *ir*, 'husband,' 'man,' and the Mongolic *ere*. The Etruscan Vela, the other equivalent of Caius, may be explained by the Yenisseian *ful* and *pul*, which mean the 'shaft' or 'handle' of an axe, a root which is seen also in *ful-ben*, a 'stick.' In Mordwin *päl* is a 'post' or 'stake,' and the root may be traced in Wogul, Olonets, Hungarian, Samojed, and other Ugric languages.

[1] This usage seems to be non-Aryan. Compare the Egyptian *ka*, 'husband,' 'male,' the Basque *gizon*, 'man,' the Turkic *kisi*, 'man,' and the Turkic relative pronoun *ki*.

CHAPTER IX.

FORMS OF DEDICATION.

The Dowries of the Dead—Inscribed Lares—Suthina, an 'offering'—The verb substantive—Kana, a 'statue'—Phleres, a 'gift'—The Etruscan verb—Turke, 'he placed it'—The pronoun—The participle—Words denoting fabrication—Alpan, a 'tribute'—The double-faced girl—The Lares of children—Ken, 'this'—The Orator—Kver—The parting of Admetus and Alcestis.

ETRUSCAN inscriptions divide themselves into two classes. The first class consists of the mortuary records, which have been discussed in the last three chapters; the second class comprises inscriptions of dedication or donation, which are engraved on statues, lamps, dishes, and other works of art.

Inscriptions on such objects, when written in Latin or Greek, are denominated 'votive inscriptions,' since they usually are found to record the dedication of the object to some deity, in fulfilment of a vow. But this name is not applicable to the corresponding class of Etruscan inscriptions. There exists a fundamental difference as to the nature and motive of the gift; a difference which must be constantly and carefully kept in view if we would hope to arrive successfully at an interpretation. The treasures of Etruscan art which bear inscriptions of dedication do not seem to have been placed in any temple, to have been dedicated to any deity, or to have been given in satisfaction of any vow. They were not offerings in honour of the gods, they were gifts for the uses of the dead.

It is, as we have seen, the characteristic habitude of Turanian nations to make the tomb the treasure house, and not the temple. The gods needed no gifts, but the wants of the ancestral spirits had to be dutifully supplied. The Turanian creed was Animistic. This creed taught that in the ghost-world the spirits of the departed are served by the spirits of those utensils and ornaments which they have used in life. It thus became the pious duty of the survivors to place in the tomb, and to dedicate to the perpetual service of the deceased, the most precious treasures which they possessed. These constitute the costly objects which the

Etruscan tombs have yielded in such profusion, and which now crowd the shelves of our museums.

The inscriptions which are frequently engraved upon these gifts will be found, as a rule, to record a presentation of the object to the ghostly owner. One of them, for instance, may be translated thus: *I am a gift to the ghost of* . . . . The inscription itself will be given and commented on hereafter.

Utensils and objects of art, such as cups, dishes, lamps, armour, vases, gems, seals, and jewellery, form, however, the smallest class of the inscribed objects which have thus been dedicated to the ancestral spirits. Far more numerous are the inscribed LARES, which are little portrait statues of the deceased. We have already seen how the Ostiaks, Samojeds, Mongols, and other pagan Ugric races are still in the habit of making little images to represent the dead. These images are kept in the house for a year or two after the decease, and are treated with the same honour and respect which were paid in his lifetime to the person whom they represent.[1] At the end of a regulated period the

See pp. 124, 125, *supra*.

images are deposited in the tomb, where they are annually visited by the survivors.

This, or something like this, was also the Etruscan practice. From them the usage descended to the Romans. Every Roman family had its LARARIUM, a chamber which contained the images of ancestors. The Etruscan tombs have yielded vast numbers of these little portrait statues, which occasionally bear dedicatory or commemorative inscriptions. Such is the nature of the greater portion of the records which will be discussed in the present chapter.

It must be acknowledged that the inscriptions on these dedicated objects are, as a rule, more difficult of interpretation than the mortuary records. We have less to guide us in our interpretation, the possible limitations of meaning are less narrow, while the Ugric analogies are certain to be more obscure, since the words employed are not of the same primary importance, and the same universal diffusion as the terms which denote age or kinship.

Much, therefore, that will be put forward in this chapter is of a character more or less conjectural, and I do not expect in every case to carry my readers with me in the interpretations which I shall advance. Indeed, if it were not for the certainty that I should be accused of having shirked the discussion of these inscriptions, I would gladly have confined my labours to the easier and more certain ground of the mortuary records. But although I can hardly hope, in this chapter, materially to strengthen the argument in favour of the Ugric affinities of the Etruscan race, I trust I may be able to show that the inscriptions of dedication cannot be held to be incapable of explanation from Ugric sources. There is another reason why these inscriptions cannot be neglected. They supply us with the elements of Etruscan grammar, a knowledge of which is of supreme philological importance, besides being a necessary preliminary to any attempt at the interpretation of the longer records.

In investigating these inscriptions of dedication I shall begin with the shortest and simplest forms, and from them work up to those of a more complicated character.

SUTHINA.—This word is found engraved on a great variety of objects which have been discovered in tombs. It is usually unaccompanied by any other words. Thus a statue, a brass boss, a mirror, and several brass dishes have been found which bear this word as their sole inscription. Occasionally, however, the word is preceded by a proper name. Thus, on a brass dish we find the words

LARTH · METIES · SUTHINA,

and on another dish,

ARTH KEKNA SUTHINA.[1]

It is open to question whether the name in these cases is that of the donor or the donee. The inscriptions may signify that the object was a SUTHINA presented to the spirit of Larth Meties, or of Arth Kekna, or these persons may have presented a SUTHINA to the spirits of unnamed relatives.

The meaning of the word SUTHINA has already been indicated.[2] It has been shown that the Ugric root *sut* denotes 'burning,' and that the Etruscan word SUTHI was used to designate a 'place for

---

[1] Fabretti, Nos. 2,095, 602 bis, 2,604.
[2] See pp. 140, 215, *supra*.

ashes,' or a 'tomb.' In Finnic grammar the desinence *na* signifies 'belonging to.' Therefore, SUTHINA would mean something connected with sacrifice, or with cremation, or something belonging to a tomb. At the present day the Chinese and other Turanian nations burn the objects which are offered for the use of the deceased, in the belief that the spirit of the object will be thus made available for the uses of the spirit of the departed. Chinese frugality has even gone so far as to substitute a cremation of paper representations of the objects offered, the articles themselves being retained for the use of the survivors. In the Etruscan inscriptions the usage of the word SUTHINA plainly shows that it must have denoted an 'offering,' while the etymology indicates that it originally meant either a 'burnt offering' or simply a 'sepulchral offering.'

MI.—A large number of Etruscan inscriptions begin with this word. In no instance does it occur except at the beginning of a sentence. It has been generally admitted that it cannot be anything else than the first person singular of the verb substantive, and that it must be equivalent in meaning to the

276   DEDICATIONS.

Latin *sum*. For instance, on the statue of a priestess making a libation we read:

MI : THAN(A)S,[1]

which evidently means, *I am Thanas*. There is also an inscription on a tomb at Saluzzo which runs:

MI SUTHI LARTHIAL MUTHIKUS [2]

I am (the) tomb (of) Larthial Muthikus.

Both the Finnic and the Turkic languages bear such unmistakable witness to the correctness of this interpretation of MI, that it would be a superfluous labour to go into the evidence at length. The citation of one or two analogies will suffice. Such are the Tataric *min*, the Turkish *im*, or the Ziriauian *em*, all of which signify 'I am.'

KANA.—Inscriptions on portrait statues repeatedly begin with the words MI : KANA, followed by a proper name. Since the word KANA never occurs except in inscriptions on statues, there has been a very general agreement among Etruscan students that it necessarily means 'statue.' Thus there was

---

[1] Fabretti, No. 2,007.
[2] Ibid. No. 42.

found at Volterra a marble statue of a woman carrying a child. On her arm is engraved an inscription which apparently refers to the child:

MI : KANA : LARTHIAS : VANL : VELCHINEI : SE'K] [1]

I am (the) likeness (of the) daughter (of) Larthius Vanl Velchinei.

Again, on a portrait statue found near Florence is inscribed:

MIKANALARTHIAL
NUMTHRALLAUKIN
NUIU [2]

I am (the) statue (of) Larthial Numthral Laukin [?].

Assuming the Etruscan word KANA to mean a 'statue' or 'effigy,' some of the Ugric analogies are very striking. In Yenissei-Ostiak *kinse* means an 'image' or 'idol.' The approximation is still closer in Samojed, where *kane* means 'face' or 'visage.'[3] The letters *h* and *k* being interchangeable[4] we easily identify the Samojedic *kane* with the word *hane*, the name by which the Tunguses designate

[1] Fabretti, No. 349.
[2] Ibid. No. 264.
[3] Castrén, *Wörterverzeich. Samoj. Spr.* p. 114.
[4] Schott, *Altaische Spr.* p. 57.

their sacred images or idols. The Ugric languages abound with related words. Several have been already enumerated.[1] We may add to the list the Finnish *kuwa*, the Lapp *kow*, and the Hungarian *kep*, which all mean an 'image.' We have also the Mongolic *kep*, and the Turkic *kip*, a 'shape' or 'form.'[2]

PHLERES.—This is a word which frequently occurs in inscriptions on dedicated offerings, more especially on small moveable objects. It has been universally held by Etruscan students that it must mean a 'gift.' We also meet with an alternative form PHIERES, from which the *l* has disappeared. When Etruscan words begin with two consonants, we find that one of them tends to be elided, as in the case of the words TLENACHEIS and LENACHE, which will presently be discussed. We need, therefore, feel no hesitation in identifying the words PHLERES and PHIERES as forms of the same word. In searching for Ugric analogies the second of these forms is that which we should exclusively expect to find, since the

---

[1] See pp. 108, 110, *supra*.
[2] Schott, *Altaische Spr.* p. 113.

modern Ugric languages do not tolerate initial double consonants. Bearing this rule in mind, we may recognise the Etruscan PHLERES or PHIERES in the Osmanli *verish*, which means a 'giving,' a 'selling,' an 'offer.' In the same language *vera* means a 'giving up,' a 'surrendering;' and *ver-mek* (root *ver*) means 'to give.' In the Turkic languages of Siberia *wer*, *ber*, or *bir* signifies to 'give,' in Mongol *bari* is to 'give' or to 'receive,' in Hungarian *ber* means a 'payment' or 'reward,' in Finn *wero* means a 'delivery,' a 'giving up,' and in Lapp *wiär-to* is to 'offer.'[1]

The root of the Etruscan PHLERES is PHLER, meaning to 'give.' The suffix -ES, as we shall presently discover, is a participial sign. We may therefore translate PHLERES as an 'offering,' a 'thing given,' a 'gift.'

Mention has already been made of the most noteworthy of the inscriptions in which this word occurs. It is engraved on a small bronze LAR, or portrait statue, which is now in the museum at Florence. The letters are not very legible, and the inscription

---

[1] See Schott, *Altaische Spr.* p. 140.

has not hitherto been deciphered, but Fabretti has engraved a rubbing, which reads:

MI : PHIERES : HIN(I)THEA(L). . . .[1]

I am a gift to the ghost of . . . .

Sometimes we have a contracted form of the word. Thus two small cups of black glazed pottery, which were found in a tomb at Volterra, are respectively inscribed:

MI · PH · ULUI

and MI · PH · ULUIAL[2]

These two cups were evidently 'offerings' for the respective uses of the spirits of a mother, ULUI, and her child, ULUIAL.

On a small bronze statue, or LAR, there is engraved the single word:

PHLEZRU.[3]

This form is unique. It is, however, pretty certain that it must be a verb. We have seen that in the Tatar languages the third person singular of

---

[1] Fabretti, plate xxiii. No. 267. See p. 103, *supra*.
[2] Ibid. Nos. 353, 354.
[3] Ibid. No. 1,929.

the verb ends in *e* or *u*. We have already met with the Etruscan forms LEIN·E, *vicit*; LUP·U, *obiit*; KERIN·U, *fecit*; and TULAR·U, *sepelit*, and we shall presently come to ALPN·U, *tribuit*. Therefore, since PHLERES means *donum*, we may take PHLEZRU to be *donavit*.

In dealing with the longer forms of dedication it may be taken for granted that each of them will almost certainly contain a verb, and it is highly probable that this verb will be in the third person singular. Taking the two standard forms LEIN·E and LUP·U as our guides, the detection of the verbs becomes a very simple matter. In every one of the longer inscriptions of dedication we find, either in the middle or at the close of the sentence, a word with the suffix ·E or ·U. If we assume that this is the verb, it will in every case be found to furnish a convenient key by means of which the inscription may be interpreted.

The principal verbs thus indicated are TURKE, TENINE, TEKE, THEKE, LENACHE, ERSKE, ALPNU, and KERINU. An inspection of this list makes it probable that *k* or *n* served in Etruscan as a sign of the preterite, as is the case in several Finnic, Turkic, and Mongolic languages.[1]

TURKE.—Of the verbs just enumerated, the most common is TURKE, which occurs in about a dozen inscriptions. TURKE is the normal form, but we also meet with the more or less devocalised forms TURUKE, THRKE, and TRKE. The analogy of Latin inscriptions of dedication makes it probable that this frequently recurring word will mean *dedit, posuit, dedicavit, fecit,* or something of the kind. It is plain, however, that it cannot mean *fecit,* since, in one instance, it is found between two proper names without any other words. Thus, on the handle of a mirror we find the inscription:

VILIA ALSINAI TURKE VERSENAS KAIIA[2]

Vilia Alsinai and Versenas Kaiia are both common female names. The purport of the inscription must be that one of these persons either 'gave' or 'offered' the mirror to (the spirit of) the other. It would seem, therefore, that TURKE means either *dedit* or *posuit.*

---

[1] See Wiedemann, *Tscherem. Gram.* p. 135; Castrén, *Koibal. Spr.* p. 35; Castrén, *Burjät. Spr.* p. 39.

[2] Fabretti, No. 2,180.

The Ugric analogies leave no doubt whatever as to which of these two meanings we should select. Throughout the whole of the Turkic languages we find a series of words denoting things that stand up, which are derived from the wide-spread root *tur*, which means to 'stand.' Thus we have the Turkic imperative *tur*, 'stand!' *tur-a*, a 'tent'—hence a 'house' or 'town'—*tur-ak*, a 'rake' or 'comb,' *tur-na*, a 'crane' or 'stork,' and the verb *dur-mak*, to 'stand' or 'stand up.' Also in Samojed we find *tur-ku*, a 'finger,' and *tur*, the 'hair on the body.'

It is difficult to find a precise English equivalent for TURKE. The literal translation would seem to be 'he stood it,' or 'he stuck it up,' but we shall not be far wrong if we translate 'he offered,' 'deposited,' 'presented,' or 'placed it.'

A few instances of the usage of the word TURKE may make the signification more clear, and at the same time yield us some additional words.

On a little bronze statue or LAR, now in the Vatican, these words are engraved:

IN TURKE: VEL: SVEITUS [1]

[1] Fabretti, No. 2,614 *ter*.

which apparently mean *me posuit Velus Sceitus*. The Ugric analogies make it almost certain that IN means 'me.' The Hungarian *en*, 'I,' is an almost identical form, and we have also the Turkish *beni*, the Tatar *mene*, and the Samojedic *man*, which mean 'me.'

It is impossible at present to affirm with any certainty what was the corresponding Etruscan word for 'I.' It may possibly have been MA, a word which occurs three times in the inscriptions. We have two *cippi*, which are respectively inscribed:

and
    MI · MA · LARIS · SUPLU
    I MI : MA : VELUS RUTLENIS AVLESLA.[1]

Where these *cippi* were found is not recorded. If they were intended for sepulchral uses the word MA will almost certainly mean 'I,' a meaning which would accord with the Ugric analogies. 'I' is *ma* in Ostiak, *me* in Zirianian, and *man*, *ma*, or *m* in Samojed, similar forms being traceable through the other Ugric languages.[2] If, however, as seems more

---

[1] Fabretti, Nos. 351, 352.
[2] See Castrén, *Ostiak. Spr.* p. 36; Castrén, *Samoj. Gram.*

probable, these *cippi* were originally placed not as gravestones but as landmarks, we must explain them by means of the Finnic word *ma*, 'earth,' 'land,'[1] and read *I am the land of Laris Suplu;* and *I am the land of Velus Rutlenis Avlesla.* The third inscription is on a golden fibula, and runs:

MIMAMERSE[L]ARTESI.[2]

Unfortunately, this inscription does not decide the question, owing to the words being undivided. If we divide MI MA MERSE LARTESI, we must take MA to mean 'I.' But if, as seems more probable, we should read MI MAMERSE LARTESI, it follows that MAMERSE would be a proper name. To decide the question we must await the discovery of an additional inscription which contains the word MA.

On a round *basso reliero* plate of bronze, which apparently formed the cover of a dish, is engraved:

MI · SUTHILVELTHURITHURA : TURKE : AU : VETHURI PHNISKIAL.[3]

pp. 210, 344–351; Wiedemann, *Tscher. Gr.* p. 133; Wiedemann, *Syr. Gr.* p. 42.

[1] See p. 121, *supra*.
[2] Fabretti, No. 2,184.
[3] Ibid. No. 2,603.

The letter *l* is the sign of the passive in the Tatar languages,[1] and SUTHIL may be taken to mean 'a thing offered.' The word THURA is probably a substantive containing the same root as the verb TUR-KE, and may be translated 'a deposit,' the phrase THURA TURKE being parallel to the common Latin form *dono dedit*. The inscription, therefore, signifies:

I am an offering which Velthuri deposited as a deposit for Ande Velthuri Phniskial.

On a bronze LAR, which is now in the Museum at Florence, is written:

LARKE : LEKN:E) TURKE PHLERESUTHURLAN VEITHI.[2]

The agglutinated word PHLERESUTHURLAN seems to be compounded of PHLERES, a 'gift,' and a word THURLAN, which probably contains the same root as the words THURA and TUR-KE. The *l*, as before, would be the sign of the passive, and the suffix -AN is probably a sign of one of the participles.

In numerous Ugric languages—Turkic, Mongolic, and Finnic—the participle ends in *han, ban, pan,*

---

[1] See Kasem-Beg, *Türk. Tatar. Gram.* p. 85.
[2] Fabretti, No. 255.

van, *gan*, or *an*. We shall hereafter meet with Etruscan forms in -VAN, -PAN, and -AN, which can hardly be anything but participles. We may therefore render the inscription thus:

Larke Lekne deposited (this) deposited-gift for (the spirit of) Veithi.

In the word ZILACHN-THAS we have already met with another Etruscan participle.[1] The usage in the inscriptions and the Ugric analogies alike indicate this as a participial form. In Koibal Tatar the sign of the present participle is the suffix *-as*, *-bas*, *-pas*, or *-mas*. In Burjät it is *-si*. In Zirianian the participle ends in *-ys*, and in Turkish we have forms in *-mis*, *-mys*, *-ez*, *-az*, and *-iu*.[2]

The suffixes denoting this participle in Etruscan seem to be -THAS, -AS, and -EIS. The first of these forms appears in the inscription on a bronze LAR found at Clusium. It reads:

UTNI ɪ THUPHULTHASA TURKE.[3]

---

[1] See p. 209, *supra*.
[2] Castrén, *Koibal. Spr.* p. 43; Wiedemann, *Syr. Gr.* p. 69; Kasem-Beg, *Türk. Tat. Gr.* pp. 126, 132.
[3] Fabretti, No. 804.

The word THUPHULTHASA appears also in the forms THUPH-ULTHAS, THUPH-LTHIKLA and THAP-NA. Taking the *l* as the sign of the passive, the root seems to be THUPH or THAP. In the Ugric languages we usually find the unaspirated forms of letters which are aspirated in Etruscan, so that THUPH would be the phonetic equivalent of *tup* or *dub*. We may therefore with some probability explain this difficult word by reference to the Yenissei-Ostiak verb *dib-bet*, ' to make,' the root of which is *dib*; so the inscription UTNI : THUPHULTHASA TURKE would mean,

Utni deposited (this) fabricated (lar).

The word THAPNA is found in the inscription on the celebrated bronze candelabrum from Cortona, which is justly regarded as the masterpiece of the Etruscan bronze-workers. The inscription runs :[1]

```
THAPNA : LUSNI[: T]
INSKVIL : ATHLI[K]
SALTHN
```

A fracture in the right hand corner has partially

---

[1] Fabretti, No. 1,050; Dennis, *Etruria*, vol. ii. p. 443; Ellis, *Armenian Origin of the Etruscans*, p. 125.

destroyed two letters. The word THAP-NA, which exhibits the common Finnic desinence -na, appears to be derived from the same root as THUPH-LTHAS, and may be taken to mean a 'fabric.'

It seems probable that the next word LUSNI might mean 'light' or 'flame.' It is not, however, by any means certain that it can be claimed as a Turanian word. The difficulty of identifying it is increased by the phonetic variations which usually occur in the Ugric analogues of Etruscan words containing the letters *l* and *s*. In favour of the Aryan affinities of the word is the Erse *luisne*, 'flame'; and the old Latin *lucna*, *lucina*, and *luna*. On the other hand, we have the evidence of an Etruscan mirror, on which Diana is called LOSNA, a word which may be the archaic form of *luna*. In Tungus *luna* means 'brimstone;' while the Samojedic *leju*, 'flame,' and *loires*, 'to burn,' are phonetically equivalent to LUS, the root of LUS-NI.

The word SALTHN is unique. As it can hardly be strained into any connection with *suthina*, I am inclined to explain it by means of the Koibal *sal-*

erben (root *sal*), which means to 'leave,' to lay a thing down,' and to translate SALTHN a 'deposit.'

The word ATHLI(K) is unique. It may possibly be a proper name.

The third word is probably to be read TINSKVIL, a word which is of frequent occurrence. Like SUTHINA it frequently appears on dedicated gifts, unaccompanied by any other words. But there are two peculiarities in its usage. It has only been found on objects exhumed at or near Cortona, and it appears, without exception, on fabrics of bronze or brass. Thus, on the celebrated bronze chimæra, on the bronze griffon now at Leyden, on a bronze dog, and on a bronze pedestal, the word TINSKVIL forms the sole inscription.[1] The definite usage of the word appears to indicate some sort of reference to the material. The second syllable of the word probably contains a root which appears in many Ugric words relating to metallurgy. Thus in Turkish *kal* denotes the 'action of melting metals,' *kal-eb* is a 'mould' for casting, *kal-etmek* is to 'melt' or 'refine,' *kal-je* is a 'refiner,' *kil-ij* is a 'sword,' *ki-aghi* the 'edge of

[1] Fabretti, Nos. 468, 1,047.

a cutting instrument,' and *kyul-unk*, a 'stone-cutter's pick.'

The meaning of the first syllable is less certain. Probably it is connected with an Etruscan verb TEN-INE, which means *posuit*,[1] so that TINSKVIL would denote a 'metallurgic offering.'[2]

A second instance of the use of the word THUPHLTHAS is found in an inscription on a bronze lamp, which runs:

A · VELS [·] KUS · THUPLTHAS · ALPAN · TURKE[3]

Before we can translate this inscription, we must discover the meaning of ALPAN, which is a frequent word in dedications. We meet with the three forms ALPAN, ALPNAS, and ALPNU. We may regard the two last as devocalised forms equivalent to ALPAN-AS and ALPAN-U, which would be, respectively, the participle and the third person singular of the verb, while ALPAN

---

[1] See p. 303, *infra*.
[2] Possibly TIN may mean 'sand' or 'clay,' following the analogy of the Turkish *tin*, the Ostiak-Samojed *tu*, and Koibal *tir*. In this case TINSKVIL would mean 'cast in sand,' or a 'bronze casting.' We may also note as possible explanations that the Tatar *ten* means 'like,' 'resembling,' and in Samojed *tin* is a 'tomb.'
[3] Fabretti, No. 1,054.

would be a substantive from which the verb was formed. The word seems originally to have signified 'from below,' denoting something coming from or belonging to an inferior. This primitive sense can be traced in Hungarian, Samojed, Mordwin, Karelian, Koibal, and other Ugric languages. Hence the word came to mean a 'tribute' or 'tax,' something rendered by an inferior to a superior. This secondary meaning attaches to the Kot-Yenissei *alpan*, which signifies a 'tribute.' The Mongolic *alban* has the same meaning, and so has *alman*, the Samojedic form of the word.[1]

It is open to question whether we should assign to the Etruscan word the primary or the secondary Ugric sense. Carefully comparing all the cases in which it occurs in the inscriptions, it is, I think, less easy to translate it 'humbly, or 'suppliant' than to render it a 'tribute.' Possibly *munus* or *debitum* may be the best equivalent. Taking this sense the inscription may be translated:

A. *Velskus deposited (this) fabricated tribute.*

[1] See Castrén, *Jen. Ost. Spr.* p. 197; *Wört. Samoj.* p. 178.

The form ALPNAS occurs on a bronze LAR, which is inscribed:

TITE : ALPNAS : TURKE AISERAS : THUPHLTHIKLA : TRUTVEKIE[1]

I am unable to explain the suffix *ikla*. The word TRUTVEKIE occurs here only. In a bilingual inscription which may or may not be in Etruscan, the word TRUTNUT is represented in the Latin version by HARUSPEX. AISER means 'gods' or 'spirits,' and AISERAS would be 'his gods.' ALPNAS means either 'making a tribute' or 'his tribute.' I will not attempt a translation, but the general meaning of the inscription seems to be that, by augural direction, Tite presented the fabric as a tribute to the spirits.

The form ALPNU occurs twice. It is found on a mirror,[2] and also in the inscription on a small bronze statue of a man (a LAR), now in the British Museum. We read:

KANVATE
SALVANSL
LETHANEI·ALPNU
EKN·TURKE LARTHI [3]

[1] Fabretti, No. 2,603, *bis*. [2] Ibid. No. 2,412.
[3] Ibid. No. 2,582, *bis*.

Here ALPNU seems to be a verb formed from ALPAN. As from PHLERES, *donum*, we get PHLESRU, *donavit*, so from ALPAN, *tributum*, we should have ALPNU, *tribuit*. KANA is a statue, and KAN-VATE may be 'this statue';[1] EKN may be either 'it' or 'here.'[2] SELVANSL, as we shall presently see, conveys the notion of badness or unworthiness. The meaning of the inscription seems to be:

Lethanei contributed this unworthy statue. She deposited (it) here for Larthi.

In various inscriptions we find the words SELVAN, SELVANSL, SELANSL, SANSL, and SL. They seem to be related words, and may be conveniently considered together.

In Yenissei *sel* means 'bad,' 'wicked,'[3] and -*van* in Hungarian is the sign of the participle present. The final *l* may denote the passive. It would therefore seem that the meaning in these words is the unworthiness either of the giver or the gift. The forms SANSL and SL may be only contracted forms of

---

[1] See pp. 137, 277.　　[2] See pp. 213, 301.
[3] Castrén, *Jen. Spr.* p. 252.

SELVANSL. If they are independent words we might explain them by reference to the Samojedic *sini*, and the Turkish *zanu*, which both mean 'knee,'[1] and translate 'suppliant.'

The word SL occurs in the inscription on a bronze statue, or LAR, of a child holding a bird. We read:

LARTHIA: ATEINEI ı PHLERES : PUANTRN SL ; TURKE [1]

Larthia Ateinei is the name of a woman. Assuming PUIA to be 'child,' the Ugric analogies indicate that PUA-NT-R-N would mean 'to her children.'[2] We may therefore translate:

Larthia Ateinei unworthily offered (this) gift to (the spirits of) her children.

There are few monuments of Etruscan art which are more curious than two small inscribed bronzes which were found in 1847, concealed in the niche of an ancient wall at Cortona. The two figures are almost facsimiles of each other. Each represents a nude girl, two-headed, one of the faces looking for-

[1] Fabretti, No. 1,055, *bis*.
[2] In numerous Turkic languages *n* is the sign of the dative case, and *r* of the plural. In Samojed *nd* is a suffix denoting 'her.'

wards, the other backwards. These bronzes do not seem to have been LARES, but may possibly have been offerings of atonement for acts of deceit or immodesty. The inscriptions are respectively:

1. V · KVINTI · ARNTIAS · KULPIANSI ALPAN · TURKE
2. V · KVINTI · ARNTIAS · SELAN SL TEZ · ALPAN TURKE [1]

In the first inscription KUL·PIAN·SI is the only doubtful word. The two last syllables may be respectively signs of the pronoun and the participle, and the root may, as before,[2] denote a bronze fabric. The first inscription may be translated:

V. Kvinti Arntias deposited as-a-tribute a-casting-of-her-figure.

In the second inscription the difficult word, TEZ, may possibly receive an explanation either from the Turkic *tis*, a 'knee,' or *dush*, 'pollution.' The meaning seems to be:

V. Kvinti Arntias, an unworthy penitent, deposited (this) tribute.

The word TEZ is probably unique, though we

[1] Fabretti, Nos. 1,051, 1,052.   [2] See p. 290, *supra.*

have something like it in the inscription on a LAR, representing a youth. It reads:

TSTURKERANUTHALPHIA TAVI· SELVAN [1]

This must be divided thus:

TS TURKE RANUTHAL PHIA TAVI SELVAN

Here the word TS may be merely a contraction of Tites, one of the commonest of proper names. RANUTHAL is certainly a proper name. TAVI occurs here only, and I am unable to explain it. All the other words are already familiar to us.

The terms KLENSI and KLEN KECHA, which occur repeatedly in dedications, may be regarded either as substantives or as adverbs. Since KLAN means 'son,' KLENSI might be either 'his son,' or possibly 'like a son,' and hence might signify 'filially,' 'dutifully,' 'piously.' The analogies indicate that the root meaning of KECHA is 'little.' The Avar *koka*, the Turkish *kuchuk*, and the Hungarian *kis*, all mean 'little.' Therefore KLEN KECHA may be either 'a little son,' or possibly 'dutifully and humbly.'

We have already come across the word KLENSI

[1] Fabretti, No. 78.

in an inscription at the entrance to a tomb at Vulci :

EKA : SUTHIK : VELUS : EZPUS : KLENSI : KERINU [1]

This may be translated :

Here-is-a (tomb) which Velus Ezpus piously made.

Or it may be :

Here (is the) tomb (of) Velus Ezpus. His-son made (it).

We shall again meet with the word KLENSI in the inscription on the 'Orator.'

A good illustration of the usage of the phrase KLEN KECHA may be found in the well-known inscription on a small statue of Apollo crowned with laurel, which is now at Paris. Three letters are doubtful, but the most probable reading seems to be :

MI : PHLERES : (EP)UL (: A)PE : ARITIMI
PHASTI RUIPHRIM : TAKE : KLEN : KECHA [2]

It is not known whether the statue was a sepul-

---

[1] Fabretti, No. 2,163; see p. 148, *supra*.

[2] Fabretti, No. 2,613. Compare Lanzi, vol. ii. p. 525; Ellis, *Asiatic Affinities*, p. 80 Ellis, *Armenian Origin*, p. 116.

chral or a votive offering. Assuming it to have been found in a tomb, I should translate:

I am Apollo, brother of Artemis, a gift (which) Phasti Ruiphrim deposited for (the spirit of) her little son.

The statue may, however, have been a votive gift to Artemis, in which case we might read:

I am a gift to Apollo's sister Artemis. Phasti Ruiphrim deposited it dutifully and humbly.

The phrase KLEN KECHA occurs also in the inscription on the statue of a boy, a LAN, now in the Museum at Leyden. It runs:

VELIAS · PHANAKNAL · THUPHLTHAS
ALPAN · LENACHE · KLEN · KECHA · TUTHINES · TLENACHEIS [1]

The word TUTHINES, as in other instances, may be regarded as equivalent to SUTHINES. The words LENACHE and TLENACHEIS seem to contain the same root. The Ugric analogies are found chiefly in the Yenisseian languages, which give us *len*, 'work,' *lon*, 'industrious,' and *lanat*, the 'arm with the hand.' Probably LENACHE is equivalent to *fecit*, and TLENA-

[1] Fabretti, No. 1,055.

CHEIS is the participle. The other words have been already explained; and the meaning of the inscription seems to be:

Velias Phanaknal wrought this fabricated tribute as his wrought offering for (the spirit of his) little child.

Over the chief figure in the tomb of the Pompeys is written:

LARIS : PUMPUS ARNTHAL : KLAN KECHASE [1]

I do not see how to connect KLAN KECHASE with the phrase KLEN KECHA. Probably KEKASE is a verb, equivalent to *obiit*. This is indicated by the Turkish analogues *chik-mak*, 'to depart,' and *chikish*, 'departure.'

KEN, KEHEN, ANKEN, EKN. At the bottom of the niche for corpses in the tomb of the Matuna family is written:

ANKEN · SUTHI · KURICHUNTHE
MATUNAS LARISALISA [2]

The word ANKEN means either 'here' or 'this.' We have already met with KEHEN (p. 217), and

[1] Fabretti, Nos. 2,279, 2,280.   [2] Ibid. No. 2,600.

in the inscription on the 'Orator' we shall meet with KEN, both of which words seem to mean 'this.' The Ugric analogies are numerous and definite. In Burjät *ken*, and in Koibal and Karagass *kem*, mean 'who' or 'he who.' The word, deprived of its initial consonant, appears in the Turkish *in*, 'this.' In Yenissei we have *kina*, 'these,' *kin*, 'here,' and *kan*, 'there.' We have also the Yenisseian forms *uncan*, 'there,' and *incan*, 'hence.'[1]

The word KURICHUNTHE seems to be a verb. The first syllable means 'made' in Etruscan, and for the latter part we may compare the Yenesseian *xont*, 'ashes,' and translate the inscription :

This-here tomb Matanas Larisalisa made-for-ashes.

One of the mortuary inscriptions runs :

LARTH KEISINIS VELUS KLAN KIZI ZILACHNKE [2]

The word KIZI seems to mean a 'body' or corpse. We may compare the Turkish *kischi*, a 'man,' the Basque *gizon*, a 'man,' the Turkish *jessed*, a 'body,' the Armenian *ges*, a 'corpse,' the

[1] Castrén, *Jen. Spr.* pp. 103, 150 ; *Koib. Spr.* p. 23.
[2] Fabretti, No. 2,339.

Yenissei *kei*, a 'corpse,' and the Yenissei-Ostiak *kus*, an 'idol,' the 'image' of a god. The inscription may be translated:

The body which-is-coffined (is) *Larth Keisinis Velus Klan.*

I have brought forward this inscription in order to explain the word CHISELIKS, which occurs in the inscription on the statue of the 'Orator.' CHISELIK must mean the 'effigy' or 'likeness' of a deceased person, and seems to be formed from KIZI by the addition of *lik*, a suffix which is ordinarily used in Turkic languages to form substantives denoting the abstract function or quality of a thing.[1] Therefore if KIZI means 'body,' CHISELIKS would denote 'his effigy.'

Probably there is no work of Etruscan art which is better known than the celebrated bronze statue called the 'Orator,' which is now in the Uffizi at Florence. Inscribed upon it is the longest and most important of all the inscriptions of dedication. The interpretation of this record may be considered

[1] Thus *ak-lik*, 'whiteness,' is formed from *ak*, 'white,' and *gurmek-lik*, 'sight,' from *gurmek*, to 'see.' Kasem-Beg, *Türk. Tatar. Gram.* p. 41. From *ata*, 'father,' comes *ata-lik*, 'one who stands in the place of a father.'

a sort of test of the adequacy of any proposed solution of the Etruscan riddle.

The inscription is in three lines, and reads as follows:

AULESI · METELLIS · VE · VESIAL · KLENSI
KEN · PLERES TEKE · SANSL · TENINE
TUTHINES CHISIELIKS [1]

We are now familiar with all the words in this inscription except two, TEKE and TENINE. These we at once recognise as verbs.

The meaning of TENINE is *posuit*; it is almost synonymous with TURKE. The Ugric analogies are unmistakable. In Burjät *ten-am* and *ten-ap* mean 'I lay,' 'put,' or 'place;' in Koibal *tenan-erben* is to 'rest,' or 'repose;' in Samojed *tan-nam* and *tan-nau* mean to 'bring;' and in Tungus *taw-um* means to 'place.'

With regard to TEKE there are two possible meanings indicated by the Ugric analogies—to 'present,' and to 'make.' It is worthy of note that we have also two Etruscan forms, TEKE and THEKE, which seem respectively to bear these two

[1] Fabretti, No. 1,922.

meanings. The Ugric analogies are as follows. To 'give' is *taka* in Mordwin, and *adok* in Hungarian. In Turkish *tak-dim* is a 'presentation,' *tak-dimmet* is to 'present,' *tok-met* to 'pour out,' and *tak-disset* to 'consecrate.'

On the other hand to 'make' is *teka* in Finn, and *tak-ket* in Lapp, while in Turkish *takim* means 'tools,' and *tak-met* means to 'fix' or 'fasten.'

As to the interpretation of the inscription, only one ambiguity remains. It is obviously a LAR, but it is not certain whether it was presented by the son, or by the widow of the deceased. If by the widow, the first four words would be the name of the donor, and KLENSI must be translated 'piously' (see p. 297). I am inclined, however, to think that it was presented by the son, and should therefore translate:

AULESI METELLIS VE VESIAL KLENSI TEKE
To Aulesi Metellis Ve Vesial his-son presents

KEN PLERES SANSL TENINE TUTHINES
this gift. Unworthy, he-deposited (as) his-offering

CHISELIKS
this-effigy.

The word THEKE, *fecit*,[1] occurs in a record inscribed on the door-post of a tomb at Perugia.

ARNTHLARTHVELIMNAS
ARVEALTHUSIUR
SUTHIAKILTHEKE.[2]

This must be divided thus:—ARNTH : LARTH : VELIMNAS : ARVEAL : THUSIUR : SUTHI AKIL : THEKE.

We may take SUTHI AKIL to mean a 'tomb for ashes,' or a 'tomb for the dead.'[3] The word THUSIUR is unique. It is obviously a plural form. The Ugric analogies indicate as the meaning, the 'inner chambers,' or 'those things that are within.'[4] The inscription probably means:

Arnth Larth Velimnas Arveal made the-chambers-within for-a-sepulchre.

On a statue of an armed man, found at Ravenna, we read:

THUKERHERMENASTURUKE[5]

This should be divided:

THUKER : HERMENAS : TURUKE

---

[1] See p. 304, *supra*.   [2] Fabretti, No. 1,487.
[3] See p. 99, *supra*.
[4] Compare the Samojed *suse*, *tons* and *tura*, Durjāt *dotor*, Tungus *do*, and Yenissei *tuosa* and *tosal*.
[5] Fabretti, No. 49.

The statue seems to be a LAB deposited by Hermenas[a], the widow of the person represented. TURUKE gives us the archaic form of TURKE, and THUKER may be derived from the same root as TEKE (p. 303). We may therefore translate;

A gift (which) Hermenas deposited.

KVER.—This word, which occurs in several inscriptions, is of doubtful meaning. Since the Etruscan surname Kvelne is Latinised Ciluius, we see that KVER is phonetically equivalent to *ker* or *kir*. The Hungarian *ker-ve*, 'beseeching,' makes it possible that KVER may mean 'suppliant,' but it seems more probable that the root is either the same as that of TINS·KVIL, or of the verb KER·INU, *fecit*. If so, KVER might mean a fabric. On a bronze mirror we find the inscription:

IT)ITEKALE : AZIAL : TURKE MALSTRIA KIVIER

Malstria deposited (this) fabric for Tite Kale Azial.

The word KVER occurs also in an inscription on a brass LAR, which reads:

[1] Fabretti, No. 2,582.

PHLERES TLENAKES KVER[1]
The gift of a wrought fabric.

On another bronze LAR, which represents a boy holding a bird, we have:

PHLERSZEKSANSLKVER[2]

The words must obviously be divided thus:

PHLERS ZEK SANSL KVER

The word ZEK is unique. It may be equivalent to TEKE, *dedit,* or it may possibly be explained by means of the Hungarian *csök*, a 'forfeit,' or the Turkish *adak*, a 'vow' or 'oath.' The meaning may be:

The bounden gift of an unworthy fabric.

or:

An unworthy person gave this fabric as a gift.

The word SEMNA occurs twice, and in each case on a statue which seems to be that of a priestess holding a dish.[3] It is possibly related to the word *shaman,* which denotes a sorcerer or priest throughout the Siberian region.

---

[1] Fabretti, No. 2,599. [2] Ibid. No. 1,030.
[3] Ibid. Nos. 456, 458.

Among the host of painted vases which have been discovered in the Etruscan tombs there is none which is better known, or is of greater interest, than a vase from Vulci, on which is depicted the parting of Admetus and Alcestis.¹ The well-known legend informs us that the Fates had decreed that Admetus must die, but that his life might be spared if one of his nearest relatives would consent to become his substitute. When the hour arrived, his wife Alcestis came forward, and devoted herself to death to save her husband.

The vase represents the parting embrace between ATMITE (Admetus) and ALKSTI (Alcestis). On either side stand the two hideous demons of the grave;² one of them, evidently meant for CHARUN, is preparing to strike down Alcestis with his uplifted hammer; the other brandishes two serpents, as an indication of the remorseful tortures which await Admetus. In the space between Charun and Alcestis runs this inscription:

EKA : ERSKE : NAK : ACHRUM : PHLERTHRKE

[1] Figured by Dennis, *Etruria*, vol. ii. frontispiece, and by Birch, *Ancient Pottery*, vol. ii. p. 218. Cf. Braun, in *Bull. di Corrisp. Arch.* 1847, pp. 81–88.
[2] See p. 116, *supra*.

We have seen that ᴇᴋᴀ means 'here'; ᴘʜʟᴇʀᴇꜱ is a 'gift' or 'offering;' and ᴛʜʀᴀᴋᴇ is equivalent to *posuit*. The vase is of late date, and we need not therefore be surprised to find that the Greek word ᴀᴄʜʀᴜᴍ (Acheron) is used to denote the unseen world. We learn from Festus that ᴀʀꜱᴇ was an Etruscan verb equivalent to the Latin *averte*. The Ugric analogies of this word will be adduced in the next chapter; it may here suffice to note that the preterite of this verb would be *arske*,[1] and we may therefore translate ᴇʀꜱᴋᴇ, she 'averted,' or, she 'turned aside.' This is the only inscription in which the word ɴᴀᴋ occurs, but its Ugric analogies are unmistakeable. In Hungarian *nak* means 'to,' in Ostiak *nok* means 'up to,' in Samojed *na* means 'towards,' in Albanian *nga* and *ngakka* means 'to,' and in Thushi *nagw* means 'to.' This preposition *nak* may be regarded as the source of the Etruscan and Finnic desinence -*na*, which Weske has shown to be the source of the case endings in the Finnic languages.[2]

---

[1] See pp. 331, 281.
[2] Weske, *Vergleich. Gram.* passim.

The legend apparently contains two verbs, and would therefore consist of two clauses. It is doubtful whether the words NAK ACHRUM belong to the first clause, or to the second. If to the first, we may translate, EKA : ERSKE : NAK : ACHRUM : PHLERTHRKE

Here she-turned-away to Hades. She-offered-herself-as-a-gift

In the other case the meaning would be:
Here she-turned-away (the doom). To Hades she-offered-a-gift.

The inscriptions of dedication have now been placed before the reader.

I think that the meanings assigned to the words SUTHINA, MI, KANA, PHLERES, IN, KEN, TURKE, ALPAN, TEKE, TENINE, CHISELIKS, THAPNA, ERSKE, NAK, and LENACHE, may be taken as tolerably certain. The words as to which I have the greatest doubt are TINSKVIL, MA, KVER, SANSL, KULPIANSI, and TEZ.

I do not claim for the versions which I have offered any higher merit than that of being probable approximations to the meaning. But tentative though they may be, I trust that they may suffice to show the general character of the inscribed objects, and to prove that they must be regarded as gifts made to the spirits of the dead, rather than offerings to the Gods, as has been heretofore supposed. Apart, therefore, from their philological importance, these inscriptions have a definite value from an ethnological point of view. They show the distinctively Turanian character of the Etruscan belief as to the condition of the dead, and they establish a singular agreement as to sepulchral practices between the Etruscans and their Siberian kinsmen.

CHAPTER X.

THE ANCIENT VOCABULARIES.

Etruscan words preserved by the Grammarians — Needful cautions — Keltic words set down as Etruscan — Genuine Etruscan words — Names of animals and plants: horse, goat, hawk, falcon, ape, burrus, vine, poplar — Arms and clothing: belt, helmet, toga, shirt, veil — Personal functions: prince, dancer, piper, profligate — Miscellaneous words: mantissa, favissa, fanum, Tages, atrium, tepus, fala, arse verse — Latin words derived from Turanian sources: arbiter, caler, ager, circus, securis, sagitta.

Our knowledge of Etruscan words is derived mainly from the records in the tombs. The materials which they supply are abundant in quantity, and unimpeachable as to quality.

These epitaphs and dedications furnish the larger and better portion of our Etruscan glossary. To the words thus obtained may be added a few Latin words, non-Aryan in type, which seem to have been borrowed from the Etruscans, although no ancient writer expressly asserts this to have been the case. We have also a score or so of reputed Etruscan words which have been handed down to us by the ancient grammarians, chiefly by Hesychius, Festus, Varro, Servius, and Isidore.

It is, however, needful to remember that the words thus conserved must be regarded with the utmost caution. They are subject to manifold sources of error which do not affect the inscriptions, or even the naturalised Latin words. Not to speak of the errors which have arisen from the carelessness of transcribers, and the corruption of manuscripts, allowances must be made for the misapprehensions and the defective knowledge of the writers, as well as for their inability to apprehend and to express correctly the strange sounds of a foreign and unknown idiom.

It would seem that in several cases the grammarians, without due inquiry, have put down as Etruscan, words which they found current in northern Italy, and which they knew to be foreign to the Latin language. Some of these words prove to be Etruscan, but others seem to be either Keltic, Sabine, Umbrian, or Pelasgic. On the other hand there is reason to believe that some words which they have classed as Sabine or Keltic, are really of a genuine Etruscan character.

Among the reputed Etruscan words which appear to belong either to the conquered Aryan substratum of Etruria, or to the Senones and other Keltic tribes whose occupation of the valley of the Po cut into two parts the primitive Rasennic realm, the following may be specially enumerated.

1. DRUNA, 'sovereignty.' Hesychius calls this an Etruscan word. It may be probably referred to the Erse *dron*, 'right.'

2. LENA, a 'woollen garment.' Festus is doubtful whether the word is really Etruscan. It seems to be the Gaelic *leine*, a 'shirt,' or the Greek χλαῖνα.

3. GAPUS, a 'chariot,' was an Etruscan word, according to Hesychius. It may possibly be from the same root as the Etruscan *cap-ra* and *capys*,[1] but is more probably to be referred to the Gaelic *cap*, a 'cart.'

4. LANISTA, a 'gladiator,' was an Etruscan word according to Isidore. The first element seems to be the Erse *lann*, a 'sword,' and the second may be the

[1] See p. 317, *infra*.

word HISTER, a 'player' or 'actor.' Livy says that *hister* was an Etruscan word. It seems, however, to belong to the Aryan root from which the English *jester* is derived.

5. ANTAI, the 'winds,' ANDAS, the 'north wind,' and ANTAR, an 'eagle,' are said by Hesychius to have been Etruscan words. I can find no trace of them in any Turanian language. They seem to be Aryan words, related to the Latin *ventus*, the Greek ἄνεμος, and the Teutonic *wind*. Mr. Robert Ellis has pointed out that the same relation may exist between *andas* and *antar* as between *aquilo* and *aquila*.

6. GINIS, a 'crane,' attributed by Hesychius to the Etruscans, seems to be an Aryan word, from the same root as the Greek χήν.

There are two words doubtfully assigned to the Etruscans, on which I can throw no light. They are NANUS, a 'wanderer,' and VORSUS, 'one hundred feet square.'

All the other words,[1] twenty-three in all, which

---

[1] I exclude *apluda* and *stroppus*, since they are not expressly asserted to have been Etruscan by any ancient writer. The second is undoubtedly Aryan.

are attributed by ancient writers to Etruscan sources, can be satisfactorily explained by means of the Ugric languages.

Four of these words have been already explained in the preceding pages. They are:

> ÆSAR, 'gods,' p. 144.
> AUSEL, the 'dawn,' p. 143.
> CAMILLUS, a 'messenger,' p. 150.
> AGALLETORA, a 'boy,' p. 239.

The rest may be now briefly passed in review.

DAMNUS, according to Hesychius, was the Etruscan for a 'horse.' As to the Ugric affinities of this word there can be no shade of doubt. In Finn *tamma* is a 'mare'; a 'horse' is *tamp* in Lapp, and *tund* in Samojed; and *adun* is a 'troop of horses' in Burjät. The word seems to be allied to the Basque *zam-aria* a 'packhorse,' the Albanian *samaros*, a 'beast of burden,' and the Mandschu *temen*, a 'camel.'[1]

CAPRA, a 'she-goat,' was an Etruscan word ac-

---

[1] See Ellis, *Asiatic Affinities*, p. 59; Ellis, *Ethnography of Italy*, p. 51.

cording to Hesychius. In Lapp *habra* means a goat.' The root is seen in the Lapp *kapa* and Finn *kipa*, to 'jump' or 'skip,' and the Turkish *capuk*, 'swiftly.'[1]

ARACOS meant a 'hawk' in Etruscan, according to Hesychius. In Kuibal and other Turkic languages *karakus* means an 'eagle,' the last syllable *kus* meaning 'bird' in Kirghiz and other Turkic languages. In Ostiak *kurak* is an 'eagle.' The first part of the word is either the Turkic *kara*, 'black,' the Ostiak *sarag*, 'swift,' or perhaps the Tschazischi *karak*, Tschjulim *ura*, Finn *waras*, a 'robber' or 'thief.'

CAPYS, according to Servius, meant a 'falcon.' An Etruscan painting, representing some human-headed birds, bears the unexplained legend KAPE MUKATHESA. From Bishop Agricola's enumeration of the deities of the ancient Finns we gather that they had an object of worship which bore the name KAPEIS. He says:

Prædaque fit Kapeis, non vigilante Jove.

The second syllable of the Etruscan word CAPYS

[1] Schott, *Altai. Spr.* p. 112.

may be the Turkic *kus*, 'bird,' which we have found in the word ARACOS, and the first syllable may be the root of CAPRA.[1] We have also the Ude *kappesun*, and the Turkic *kap, jap, japysch*, to 'snatch,' 'seize by force,' as well as the Hungarian *kap*, 'to get possession of.'[2] CAPYS would therefore be a 'bird of prey.'

ARIMI, according to Strabo and Hesychius, meant 'apes.' Naturally no word for 'ape' is found in the Siberian vocabularies. Possibly ARIMI meant 'little men.' In the Turkic and Mongolic languages *ar* or *er* is a 'man,' and 'little' is *hene* in Yenissei.

BURRUS, Hesychius says, was the Etruscan equivalent of κάνθαρος, a word which means a 'beetle,' and also a 'drinking cup with handles.' Festus tells us that BUBRA was a name applied by the Italian peasants to a red-nosed heifer, and he adds that a red-nosed drunkard was called BURRUS. The sharp bend or crook at the bottom of a plough was called BURIS. All these words can be explained by means of the Turkic *burun*, a 'nose.' The Avar *baaran*,

---

[1] See p. 317, *supra*.   [2] Schott, *Altai. Spr.* pp. 53, 67.

'red,' would explain BURRA and BURRUS, but not BURIS.

ATAISON, according to Hesychius, meant in Etruscan a 'climbing vine.' The two Turkish words *ot*, 'plant,' and *uzum*, 'grape,' sufficiently explain this word as the 'grape-plant.'

No tenable Aryan etymology of POPULUS, the 'poplar tree,' has as yet been suggested. The poplar has been for ages planted in Lombardy as a support for the vine, and the tree may therefore have been deemed sacred to Phuphluns, the Etruscan Bacchus. The Etruscan *ph* loses its aspiration in Latin, a change which is exhibited in the name of the city of Populonia, which is usually supposed to have taken its name from Phuphluns.

BALTEUS, a soldier's 'sword belt,' was, according to Varro, an Etruscan word. In Yenissei and Samojed *baltu* means an 'axe.' A 'girdle' is *bel* in Koibal and Karagass Tatar, and *behe* in Burjät. Both roots run through all the Turkic languages. The resemblance to the Teutonic *belt* is very remarkable, but I will not attempt to account for it.

CASSIS, a 'helmet,' was an Etruscan word according to Isidore. The ancient forms *cassila* and *cassida* point to a primitive form *cassilda*. We have the Turkic *sas, tzas, tschatsch*, 'hair,' and the Tungus *olda*, a 'covering,' a 'roof,' whence comes the Tungus *gula*, a 'tent.'

TOGA. The national Roman garb was adopted from the Etruscans. It is therefore probable that its name may also have been of Etruscan origin. The Tatars still wear an outer garment of similar character. The name can be traced in several Ugric languages. The Hungarian *tu*, a 'needle,' gives the root of many Ugric words which mean to 'sew' or 'stitch.' In Kasan Tatar, from *tik-mak*, to 'stitch,' is derived *tiku* a 'garment,' literally, 'that which is stitched.'[1] This word may be identified with the Samojedic *toho, tohe*, a 'shirt,' and the Mongolic *goje*, a 'garment.'

The form TEBENNA or TEHENNA is probably a 'man's garment.' It will be shown in the next chapter that the Etruscan suffix *-henna* denoted a 'man.'

PANNUS has been claimed as an Aryan word, but

[1] Kasem-Beg, *Türk. Tatar. Gram*. p. 49.

the resemblance to the Samojedic *pany*, a 'woman's overcoat,' is too close to be easily accidental. That this word is radically Ugric is shown by the fact that to 'spin' is *panau* in Samojed, *banam* in Lapp, *pun-tem* in Ostiak, *pun-on* in Finn, and *fon* in Hungarian.

VELUM, a 'sail,' also the 'veil' or 'curtain' of a tent, may also be an Etruscan word. The root seems to exist in the word *voilock*, which is the name given by Tatar tribes to the felted sheets of wool and camel's hair of which their tents are constructed.[1]

LUCUMO, the name given by Latin writers to the Etruscan nobles, is a word of such importance that it cannot be cursorily dismissed. We learn from Servius that it denoted strictly the twelve chiefs of the twelve Etruscan tribes: *Tuscia duodecim lucumones habuit, id est reges.* The word must be divested of its Latin garb before its etymology becomes manifest. Now in the mortuary inscriptions of the Etruscan tombs we find the form LAUKANE, as well as LAUKANESA, which denotes the wife of a LAUKANE. This seems to be the source of the Latin

[1] See Atkinson, *Siberia*, p. 285.

proper name Lucanus. We may therefore take *laukan* or *lukan* as the radical form. The two roots of this word, *lu*, great, and *kan*, prince, are both found in the most ancient monuments of Turkic speech which have come down to us. According to the Chinese annals of the dynasty of Shang (B.C. 1700–1200), the word *kan* meant a 'prince' in the speech of the Huns. The word is evidently related to the Chinese *kiun*, a 'prince.' In Koibal and Karagass Tatar *kan* means a 'prince,' probably one of the blood royal, from *kan*, 'blood.' In Osmanli the word *khan* is used to denote the sultan, and *khan-edan* means a 'noble family.' It is curious to note that the change from *n* to *m*, which appears in the Latin form Lucu*m*o, appears also in old English writers, who speak of the GREAT CHAM of Tartary, a phrase which precisely translates the Etruscan title LU-CUMO. In Osmanli *ulu* means 'great.' We have the less abraded form *ulug*, 'great,' in Karagass Tatar. In this language 'great prince' would be *ulug-kan*, a word which, if devocalised according to the Etruscan usage, would give us the exact Rasennic form *lukan*. The same devocalised form which we see in *lu-kan* existed also among the ancient Huns, who, according to the Chinese historians, called their chiefs *lu-li*, a title equivalent to 'great man.'

The most notable of Etruscan personal names is TAR-QUIN. In the equivalent form Tar-khan, the Etruscan name repeatedly appears in the heroic legends of the Siberian tribes. Thus the chieftain who headed the Yakuts, a Turkic tribe, in their migration from the region of Lake Baikal to the lower Lena, bore the name Depsi Tarkhan-tegin.[1]

LUDUS, LUDIO. Appian and other writers assert that the LUDI and LUDIONES of the Romans were introduced from Etruria. The name is therefore probably also of Etruscan derivation. It may be affirmed that no satisfactory Aryan etymology has ever been suggested. The word, however, still survives among the Ugric nations. The Roman LUDI were at first sacred dances which accompanied the celebration of certain public sacrifices. In their origin they were as definitely religious observances as were the Greek dramatic representations. Now

[1] Tite and Ath, two very common Etruscan names, may be recognized in the earliest Magyar legends.

among the Wotiaks, a pagan tribe of Finnic blood who dwell on the western slope of the Ural, the word *lud* is still used as the designation of the holy places set apart for sacrifices.[1]

SUBULO, according to Festus and Varro, was an Etruscan word denoting a 'flute-player,' *tibicen*. The mural paintings show that these flute-players were always boys, and they show also that the Etruscan flute, constructed of two reeds, was of the same v form as the flute represented in the Egyptian tombs.

The word SUB-ULO contains two roots. The second is obviously the Turkic *oulou*, ' boy,' a word which has been already identified with the Coptic *alou*, ' boy.' The other root is seen in the Coptic *sub*, a ' reed,' and the old Egyptian *sb* or *sba*, a ' flute.' We have also the Turkish *chib-uk*, a ' pipe,' the Rhæto-Romansch *schiblot*, a 'flute,' and the Dacian *seba*.

The frequent interchange of *s* and *t* makes it

---

[1] Castrén, *Finn. Mythol.* p. 215. We have already seen (p. 124, *supra*) that an Etruscan *l* answers to *j* in Samojed. Therefore the Samojedic *jead-andm*, to ' dance,' is phonetically equivalent to *ludo*. The Etruscan form is LAUTN. See p. 327, *infra*.

possible to explain from the same root the word TUBA
a 'trumpet.' Roman tradition assigned an Etruscan
origin to this instrument. The Latin TIBIA may be
explained from the same source.

The LITUUS, or crooked staff used by the augurs,
was undoubtedly an Etruscan word. The laws of
letter change[1] enable us to identify it with the
Samojedic *nidea*, a 'crook.'

NEPOS, according to Festus, meant in Etruscan a
luxurious or extravagant person, *luxuriosus*. This
is one of the Etruscan words which have been
retained in the Albanian language, which gives us
nepes, a 'glutton.'

MANTISSA, Festus says, was an Etruscan word
meaning a 'makeweight,' a piece of meat thrown
into the scales to turn the balance. The Yenissei,
which has preserved so many Etruscan words, has
retained this. In the Kot-Yenissei language we find
the exact word *mintus*, still signifying 'a little,' 'a
bit.'[2]

FAVISSA denoted an excavation used as the cistern

---

[1] Schott, *Alt. Spr.* pp. 120, 121.
[2] Castrén, *Jen. Spr.* p. 227.

or cellar of a temple. Müller and Donaldson are of opinion that it was an Etruscan word, though this is implied, rather than expressly asserted, by Festus. A sufficient etymology may be obtained from the Yenis-sei-Samojed *fubu*, which means an excavated grave.

FANUM originally meant, not a temple, but simply a 'sacred place.' This word seems to have been the common property of the Turanian races of Italy. The annual assemblage of the Etruscan tribes was held at a place which Latin writers call Fanum Voltumnæ. The Sabines assembled at Fanum Lucinæ, and the Vulsci at Fanum Artenæ. The Fanum Voltumnæ was not a temple, but has been identified with the vast cemetery now called Castel d'Asso.

It has been already shown that the most sacred places, the true temples of the Etruscans, were their tombs. Like other Ugric peoples, they were wont to celebrate the annual funeral feast, and to worship the ancestral spirits, in the guest-chamber of the family tomb. Now in the two largest of these temple-tombs, inscriptions have been found which contain the word PHANU, used apparently as a designation of this chamber. In the tomb of the Pompeys at Tarquinii, the great central pillar exhibits a long inscription, which commences:

EITH : PHANU : SATHEK : LAUTN PUMPUS : SKUNU. . . .[1]

The long inscription over the great arch of the San Manno tomb at Perugia contains a similar phrase: . . ETH : PHANU : LAUTN. .

The word LAUTN denotes the 'funeral feast,' and ETH or EITH may be explained by means of the Yenissei-Ostiak *uts, utes*, 'close by.'[2]

The word PHANU apparently designates the antechamber or the temple-tomb itself. We have already seen that the Etruscan word VAN·TH meant 'death,' and that the Yenisseian *fenan* means ashes.[3]

It would seem that the Etruscan word PHANU meant originally a sepulchral chamber, secondarily a sacred place of assemblage, and hence in later Roman usage a temple, a 'fane.'

TAGES. According to the Etruscan tradition,[4] the laws and institutes of the Rasenna were divinely

[1] Fabretti, No. 2,279.   [2] Castrén, *Jen. Spr.* p. 165.
[3] Ibid. p. 225. See p. 101, *supra*; and p. 324, *note*.
[4] Cicero, *De Divinatione*, l. ii. § 50.

imparted to them by TAGES, a *genius* who arose out of the earth, and disappeared as soon as he had fulfilled his mission. The name TAGES seems to be simply the law 'giver,' from the Etruscan TEKE, *dedit*, a word whose Ugric affinities have been already traced.[1]

ITUS, according to Varro, was an Etruscan word equivalent to the Latin *idus*, the division of the month. Divested of its Latin guise, the word may perhaps be referred to the Mongolic root *otol*, to 'divide' or 'cut.'

IDULIS, according to Festus, denoted the sheep which was sacrificed to Jupiter on the Ides of every month. The word can be explained from Aryan sources, but a sufficient Ugric etymology may be extracted from the Samojedic *ular*, a 'sheep,' taken in conjunction with the Etruscan *it-us*.

ATR, a 'day.' Quinquatrus meant the fifth day after the Ides. We have also the words triatrus, sexatrus, septimatrus, and decimatrus, meaning respectively the third, sixth, seventh, and tenth days

[1] See p. 303, *supra*.

after the Ides. We learn from Varro and Festus
that these terms were of Etruscan origin. If we
abstract the Latin elements of these words we see
that the root ATR must have meant 'day.' The
Ugric analogies are sufficiently plain. In Burjüt,
a Mongolic language, *öder* and *ödur* mean 'day.'
This seems to be the same word as the Tungus *tyr-ga*,
a 'day.'[1]

ATRIUM. That the word *atr* meant day, is
indicated by another Latin word, ATRIUM, which,
according to Varro, was derived from the Etruscans.
The atrium of a Roman house was the common hall,
roofed in only at the sides, and therefore partly open
to the day, apparently a survival of the large hooped
aperture at the top of a Tatar tent.[2]

FALANDUM, according to Festus, was an Etruscan
word which meant the 'sky.' From Hesychius and
Festus we also learn that FALÆ meant 'mountains,'

---

[1] In other languages we have the common change of *r* to *l*, as in the Samojed *tel*, Wogul *katal*, Ostiak *chatl*, Koibal *djiala*, which all mean a 'day.'

[2] With *atrium* we may compare the old Egyptian *atr*, a 'chamber,' and the Turkish *oda*, a 'room.'

and that they were so called from their 'height,' *ab altitudine*.

These two ancient Ugric words enable us to explain the connection between a large number of modern Ugric words which mean 'sky,' 'high,' and 'mountain.' Thus we have :

Etruscan	F	A	L	E				mountains.
Samojed	F	I	L	OI	O			high.
Ostiak	P	E	L					mountain.
Andi	P	I	L					mountain.
Mokscha	P		A	N	D	A		mountain.
Mordwin	P		A	N	D	O		mountain.
Mongol	B	O	L		D	E	X	mountain.
Ostiak	P	Y	L	N		A		high.
Permian	W	Y	L	N		A		high.
Lapp	P	A	L	WA				cloud.
Mokscha	W	A		N	D	A		mountain.
Tscheremis	P	I	L	PU	N	D	A SH	sky.
Etruscan	F	A	L	A	N	D	U M	sky.

TEPÆ, according to Varro, was the Pelasgic and Sabine word for 'hills.' There can be little doubt as to the Turanian character of this word. In Nogai Tatar and other Turkic languages *tepe* is a 'hill.' We have also the Finnic *typä*, and the Mongolic *dobo*, a 'hill.' The TIBER is probably the 'hill water,' the suffix being the Turanian root *ur*, water.

ARSEVERSE meant *averte ignem*. Festus, explaining this expression, says that in Etruscan ARSE meant *averte*, and VERSE meant *ignem*. It is hardly worth while to spend much time over the phrase, since it is by no means certain that it is really Etruscan, both of the words being explicable from Aryan sources.

If, however, the phrase be indeed Etruscan, the following explanation may be offered.

An inscription given in the last chapter[1] shows that the Etruscan word ERSKE meant 'she turned away.' The present tense of this verb would be ERSE, a form explicable by means of the Turkish adverb *asre*, 'on the other side,' 'behind,' or the Samojed verb *fursi-em*, 'I turn back.'[2]

The word VERSE may be referred to the Ostiak *wyrte*, and the Hungarian *veres*, which mean 'red,' or the Samojedic *por-uan* and *par-adm*, which mean to 'burn.'

A considerable number of Latin words continue to baffle the resources of Aryan philology. Many

[1] See p. 309, *supra*.
[2] Compare the Koibal *erak* 'away,' the Tungus *nsli*, and the Yenissei *uske* 'back again,' the Yenissei *ar* 'away,' and *erai* 'out,' and the Albanian *err* 'to keep off.'

of them will, I believe, prove to be Turanian, belonging either to the Finnic aborigines of Italy, or to their Rasennic conquerors.

It is to be hoped that some competent scholar may, before long, undertake the investigation of the non-Aryan elements of the Latin language. There can be little doubt that a rich harvest awaits the labourer in this almost untrodden field. Meanwhile it will not, I trust, be deemed an impertinence if I submit for consideration a few ears which I have gleaned by the wayside.

ARBITER, an umpire, a judge.

ARBITRIUM, a judgment, a decision, an arbitrary sentence.

No Aryan etymology has been found for these words. Uncultured races are prone to seek a decision of difficult questions by casting lots, or by some similar process of divination. This has been especially the case with the Turanians. The invention of dice is attributed to the Etruscans, and dice have frequently been found in their tombs. Excluding from consideration the Latin suffixes, the root of ARBI-TER and ARBI-TRIUM is seen to be *arbi*, which may be identified with the Finnish *arpi*, which means a 'lot,' a 'divining rod,' or other instrument of divination. We have also the Finnish *arpa-mies*, a 'caster of lots,' an 'arbiter,' and *arpe-len*, to 'decide by lot,' to 'divine.'

CELER.—The legend states that Romulus had a body guard of 300 patrician horsemen, called CELERES. The first syllable may be referred to the Wotiak *zäl*, *tschel*; Tatar, *jel-tak*, *jel-tam*, or *djel-dam*, 'quick.' The suffix is capable of explanation both from Aryan and Ugric sources.

AGER.—The Ugric root, *ker*, denotes a field or enclosure. A 'field' is *aker* in Lapp, *kyra* in Ostiak, *kyr* in Turkoman and Bashkir, and *akjer* in Kusnezk Tatar. It is difficult to believe that there is no connection between these Ugric words and the Latin words *ager*, *curia*, *circus*, and *circenses*, particularly when we remember that the Roman *curia* and *circus* date from the period of the Etruscan domination in Rome.

SECURIS, an axe. There is no accepted Aryan

[1] See Wedgwood, in *Philological Transactions* for 1856, p. 166.

etymology of this word, but it receives an easy explanation from Turanian sources. We recognize the second element of the word in the Sabine *curis*, a 'spear.' So the *Quirites* were probably the 'spearmen.' The *cardo* denoted originally the sacred 'spear' with which the augur marked out the four points of the compass. All these words seem to be survivals from a primitive stone age. The Turanian root, *ker*, means a 'stone' as well as a 'field.' A 'stone' is *kera* in Tschetschenz, and *kewi* in Finn. Hence are derived a large number of Ugric words denoting weapons, which, before the introduction of metal, would be made of stone. Thus in Finn *kerwys* is an 'axe,' and *kaira* a 'borer' or 'piercer;' and in Samojedic dialects, *char, har*, and *kura*, mean a 'knife.'

The first syllable of SECURIS is capable of a similar explanation. In it we may recognise a wide-spread Turanian root, related to *seco* and *saxum*, which is used to denote a great variety of cutting or piercing weapons. This root seems also to be a survival from the stone age, and to be ultimately traceable to the Chinese word *sah* or *shih*, a stone. Thus, in Abase, a 'sword' is *sa*, and in Tscherkes a 'knife' is *seh*. An 'axe' is *suka* in Tungus, *suxe* in Mongol, *suga* in Karngass Tatar, and *tuk* in Yenissei-Ostiak. An 'arrow' is *zawa* in Tungus, *bzey* in Tscherkes, and *sogam* in Yenissei.

I do not know of any word more curious and more suggestive than SAGITTA, an 'arrow.' The history of this word forms the first chapter in the History of Civilisation. The invention of the arrow has probably had as much influence on human history as the invention of gunpowder. There is hardly any word which is more widely diffused. It can be traced in numerous Aryan, Semitic, and Turanian languages. It exists in Arabic, Sanskrit, Welsh, and Latin. The primitive meaning of SAGITTA is the 'bow-stone.' The first syllable may be referred to the Turanian root *sah*, a 'sharp stone,' which we have found in *securis*. The second part of the word means a 'bow' in the Turanian languages. A 'bow' is *xyt* and *kyet* in Yenissei-Ostiak, *chis* in Abase, *jogot* in Ostiak, and *seoger* in Samojed. The Samojed *johota*, an 'arrow,' is phonetically identical with the Latin *sagitta*.

It would be easy to add a long list of Latin words which can be explained without difficulty from Ugric sources. Such are Luceres, Tities, Arvales, lucar, as, apex, calceus, flamen, cliens, urbs, pilum, cervus, pomus, columba, pulex, nares (Wotiak, *nyr*, 'nose'), porcus (Finn, *porsas*, a 'pig'), faba (Finn, *papu*, 'beans,' Hungarian, *bab*), carex (Finn, *kara*, 'sedge'), manus, 'good,' manis, 'little.' The foregoing instances may, however, suffice to indicate the probable extent and importance of the Turanian element in the Latin language.[1]

[1] See Mr. Wedgewood's papers in the *Philological Transactions* for 1856.

CHAPTER XI.

NAMES.

The Names of the Etruscan Nation—Rasenna, the 'men of the nation' —Tursenna, the 'men of the tents'—The Tiber and the Arno— Soracte—Names of cities.

THE names of nations, rivers, mountains, and cities, are among the most enduring monuments of ancient races. If it had not been for the fortunate preservation of the inscribed records of the Etruscan tombs, it would have been necessary to rely on the analysis of the local names of Etruria as the chief evidence of the ethnic affinities of the Etruscans. It would be easy to prove the Ugric character of these names, but in the hope that this additional evidence will be deemed superfluous, I shall deal very briefly with the subject, noticing only some half-dozen names which possess a special interest or importance.

Beyond all comparison the most important of Etruscan names are the names which were borne by the Etruscan nation. Dionysius informs us that they called themselves the RASENNA. The Greeks and Romans designated them by a name which we receive from ancient authors in the forms Turrhēnoi, Tursēnoi, Tursci, Tusci, and Etrusci, variations which may be regarded as Aryan corruptions of an original name TURSENNA or TURHENNA.[1]

RASENNA and TURSENNA, the two designations of the Etruscan tribes, exhibit the same suffix, *senna*, *henna*, or *enna*. It will, in the first place, be necessary to discover the meaning of this suffix.

I have shown elsewhere [2] that ancient names were in their origin common names rather than proper names. Ancient river-names as a rule mean simply 'The River' or 'The Water'; ancient mountain-names mean 'The Mountain' or 'The Height.' So also it is almost universally the case that primitive names of tribes and nations signify simply 'The Men,' 'The People,' or 'The Tribe.'

No proposed etymology of the names RASENNA and TURSENNA will therefore be altogether satisfactory

---

[1] See p. 23, *supra*.
[2] *Words and Places*, chapters iv. and ix.

unless it conform to this general law. The common element in the two names RASENNA and TURSENNA ought therefore to mean 'people.'

Widely spread throughout the Ugric area we find a word which takes the forms *sena, kena, ena,* or *aina.* This word denotes a 'man' or 'person'— *homo.*

Thus a 'man' is *sin* in Tschuwash, a 'soul' is *sünä* in Koibal, *sunesi* in Burjät, and *aina* in Sajanian Tatar.

In the Aino language *ainu* means a 'man.' In Tscheremis *en* means 'people,' 'nation.' In Mandschu *enen* means 'posterity.' In Finn a 'man' is *innimene*, and in Samojed it is *ennetsche.*

In the Turkic languages the root *en,* meaning 'person,' is to be traced in the personal pronouns *men* 'I,' *sen* 'thou,' *kini* 'he;' forms which may be represented as 'I-man,' 'Thou-man,' and 'He-man.' The relative pronoun 'he who' is *ken* or *kem* in all the Turkic and Mongolic languages. The same ancient root is seen in the Turkic *er-in* 'husband,' and *kat-in* 'wife,' literally 'male-person' and 'female person.'[1] Another indication that *sen* was the primitive Turkic word for 'man' is found in the curious Turkoman tradition that the progenitors of their race were Szön Khan and Eszen Ili.[1] This tradition has been handed down for upwards of three thousand years, as we shall see when in the next chapter we examine the important legend of TSENA, the mythic ancestor of the Turks, which has been preserved by the ancient Chinese historians.[2]

This root *sen* enters largely into the ancient Siberian tribe-names. According to the Chinese annalists, the empire of the Tukiu (Turks) was, long before the Christian era, preceded by that of the Jeu-sen or Tseu-sen, and this again by that of the Sien-pi. The same root appears as a suffix in the names of the Alani, the Roxalani, the Cumani, the Huns, the Ussuni, and other ancient nations of Ugric blood.

Still more worthy of note is the name of the Assan, a still existing Yenisseian tribe, who are now dwindled down to the inhabitants of a single village.

[1] See Vambéry, *Travels*, p. 325.
[2] See p. 374, *infra*.

Their language, which is represented by the Kot grammar and vocabulary of Castrén, is a most archaic and anomalous form of Ugric speech, and comes nearer to the Etruscan than any other existing language.

There seems to be a strong probability that in the ASSAN of the Yenissei we may recognise that portion of the RASENNA who were left in possession of their ancestral pasturages by their more adventurous kinsmen who moved westwards in that career of conquest which finally placed them on Italian soil.

The Etruscan word for 'man' would assuredly enter largely into the names of persons. Now the personal names of the Etruscans exhibit one striking peculiarity which has repeatedly been noticed. This characteristic feature of their system of nomenclature is the employment of the suffix *enna*, which we find in the well-known names of Porsenna, Vibenna, Spurinna, Perpenna, Cæcina, and Mæcenas (Mekenna).

All these arguments point to one inevitable conclusion: that the names RASENNA and TURSENNA were analogous in their formation to such names as

Englishmen, Irishmen, or Frenchmen, and that the suffix *enna* or *senna* signified 'men' in the Etruscan language.

The first syllable in the name RASENNA is not difficult to identify. It means the 'nation' or the 'people.'

The Esths call themselves RAHWAS, the 'people'; they call their country MA-RAHWAS,[1] the land of the people, and the name of their chief city, REVAL, is a corruption of RAHWA-LA, the 'place of the people.'

But as a rule the Ugric languages avoid an initial *r*,[2] and hence we usually meet with the form *las* instead of *ras*. Thus the Finns call themselves Suome-laiset, the 'Fen-people,' and the Karelians call themselves Kiria-laiset, or the 'Hill-people.' The name of the Lesghi is derived in the same way from the Lesghic *les*, a man.[3] The Samojedic dialects give us the two very instructive equivalent forms *lize* and *kasa*, which both signify 'a man.' We

[1] Müller, *Ugrische Volkstamm*, vol. i. p. 22.
[2] See p. 205, *supra*.
[3] The names of the Lycians, the Ligures, the Leleges, and a host of Turanian nations, are in all probability derived from this root.

have here exhibited the transition from the Finnic to the Turkic form.¹ The Turkic *kis*, 'man,' 'person,' which again is identical with the Basque *gizon*, 'man,' enables us to explain the names of the Kirghiz, the Karagass, the Tscherkes (Circassians), and many other tribe-names.

The name of the RASENNA would therefore follow the analogy of a host of Ugric ethnic names, and would signify the 'men of the nation,' or, as we should say, 'our fellow-countrymen.'

The meaning of the first syllable in the name TURSENNA or TURHENNA is no less plain.

The nomad tribes of Siberia ordinarily designate themselves by what we may call tent-names—names derived from the size, colour, or some distinguishing feature of their tents. There are three Siberian words which mean a 'tent'—*ordu*, *mat*, and *tura*; and these three words enter largely into the composition of Siberian tribe-names. The Turkic and Mongolic *ordu*, a tent, is the same word as the English *horde* and the Samojedic *yourt*, and is the usual word now employed in the designation of the various Kirghiz

¹ See Schott, *Alt. Spr.*, pp. 63, 119.

and Turkoman 'hordes.' We have the famous Syra Orda, or 'Golden Horde,' the Kokorda, or 'blue tents,' and the Akorda, or 'white tents.'[1]

Similarly from the Samojedic *mat*, a 'tent,' we derive the ancient tribe-names of the Sarmatæ, Jaxamatæ, Charnmatæ, Thisamatæ, and Agamatæ, as well as the existing names of the Motors, the Yomuts, and the Lamuts.

The Turkic root *tur* means, as we have seen, to 'stand.'[2] From this root we have in Kot, Koibal, Karagass, Samojed, Mongol, and other Siberian languages, the derivative *tura*, which meant originally a 'tent,' but which has come, in the language of the settled tribes, to mean either 'chamber,' 'house,' or 'village.'

This, the most ancient of the words for 'tent,' must be regarded as the source of the ethnic names TURK, TURKOMAN, TATAR, and TURANIAN, which were all originally applied to nomad tribes living in tents. The Hut-urns from Albano[3] prove that the TURSENNA

---

[1] See Müller, *Der Ugr. Volkstamm*, vol. i. pp. 563, 566.
[2] See p. 293, *supra*.
[3] See p. 44, *supra*.

at the time of their arrival in Italy, were dwellers in tents, and we may therefore with the greatest probability explain their name as signifying THE MEN OF THE TENTS.

The names of the Etruscan nation have been treated in some detail. A few specimens of the bulky evidence afforded by other Etruscan names must here suffice.

The most significant local names are those of rivers, mountains, and cities.

Etruria had two great rivers, the Arno and the Tiber. The name of the TIBER has already been explained.[1] The word ARNO means the 'channel,' or the 'water-course.' Vambéry informs us that the natural water channels which irrigate the plain of Khiva are still called *arna*.[2]

The most conspicuous natural feature in the Tuscan land is the towering peak of SORACTE, a grey limestone crag rising in isolated grandeur from the plain, and clad in winter and early spring with a snowy mantle.

[1] See p. 330, *supra*.
[2] Vambéry, *Travels*, p. 339.

The last syllable of the name Sorac-te is the word *tagh, ta, tu, tai, di,* or *tau,* which means 'mountain' in a host of Ugric languages,[1] and forms the suffix in most of the Siberian mountain names, such as the Al-tai, the Ac-tou,[2] and the Ektagh.

The former part of the name may be explained by means of the Tschuwash *schorak,* 'white.'[3] In Tschuwash *schoraktu* would mean 'white mountain.' The word *schorak* means literally 'snow-white,' as is seen by comparing the Samojed *ser, sira,* 'snow,' and the Turkic *ak,* 'white.'

There is no more characteristic feature in the names of Etruscan cities than the perpetual recurrence of the prefix VEL or VOL. We have, for instance, the names of VELATURI (Volaterræ, Volterra), VOLCI (Vulci), VELSUNA (Volsinii, Vulsinii, Bolsena), VELSINA (Felsina, Bologna), VOLTUMNÆ, VULTURNUM, VELITRÆ, VELIMNAS, and FALERII.

The Greek form of this prefix is Οὐολ, as in Οὐόλκοι or Οὐολσίνιοι. This is phonetically the same

---
[1] Castrén, *Jen. Ost. Spr.* p. 233; *Koib. Spr.* p. 136; *Samoj. Wört.* p. 143; Klaproth, *Sprachatlas,* xxvii.
[2] Atkinson, *Siberia,* p. 565.
[3] Müller, *Ugr. Volkst.* vol. i. p. 331.

as the word *aoul* or *aul* which is universally employed by the Kirghiz, the Yomuts, and other Tatar nomads, to designate the encampment of the tribe; it denotes strictly the space occupied by the whole of the yourts. Among the tribes who have given up their nomad habits the word has come to mean a 'village' or 'town.' Thus in Tscheremis *ula* or *ola* means a 'town.' In Osmanli the word appears in two differentiated forms, *awlu* meaning a 'court,' and *eyl* or *il* denoting a nomad tribe, a nation, a country. For instance, the well-known province of BUMELIA, is Rum-eyli, the land or nation of the Romans.[1]

This root is usually exhibited as a prefix in Etruscan city names. We also find it as the medial syllable in the name of VET-UL-ONIA, the 'water-town,'[2] and as the suffix in the name of AG-YLLA, or 'old town.'[3]

---

[1] The root is one of the most widely diffused among Turanian words, being the source of the suffix *ilia*, so common in ancient Iberian town names, and explains ELIS, ILIUM, and a host of ancient Turanian town names.

[2] Finnic *veden*, 'water.' An oar is the symbol on the coins of Vetulonia.

[3] Agylla was the oldest Etruscan city. Virgil, bred in the Etruscan Mantua, speaks of it as *urzo fundata vetusto*. The

The suffix in the name of VETUL-ONIA is very common in Etruscan town names. It is seen in the names of Clavenna, Chiavenna, Ravenna, Capena, Velsina, Velsuna, and Capua. It may possibly be the same as the suffix of the name Rasenna, but is more probably, I think, to be referred to the Finnic *huone*, Tscherkes *unneh*, Turkic *in*, Coptic *onh*, Wogul *ion*, related words which all signify a 'house' or 'dwelling,' but which originally meant a 'cave.'

prefix is explained by the Hungarian *agg*, 'old.' The name was afterwards changed to CÆRE, the 'town.' In Wotiak and Ziriapian *kar* is a 'town.'

CHAPTER XII

THE EPILOGUE.

Conclusions—The Etruscans were not Aryans, or Semites, or Armenians, but Turanians — They were not Euskaric, or Egyptic, or Leuphic, but Ugric—Summary of the Arguments—Difficulties in the way of any more definite solution — Classification of the Ugric Nations—The European and the Asiatic branches of the Ugric stem —Existence of two elements in the Etruscan people, one European, one Asiatic—The conquest was effected by an Asiatic horde—Philological considerations pointing to the Yeniseian languages—Legends and traditions connecting the Etruscans with Siberia—Tradition as to the Huns—Siberian origin of the myth of Romulus—The wolf-race—The Asena and the Rasenna—Larentia—Rape of the Sabines—The path of migration—Turan and Tyrrhene—Rhasena—Persian and Kourd tradition—The Aryan epics.

It now becomes possible to define with more precision than heretofore the exact ethnological affinities of the Etruscans.

That the Etruscans were neither Aryans nor Semites, may, I think, be accepted as a certain and absolute conclusion. Their social institutions and their religious beliefs are of a character so entirely un-Aryan and un-Semitic, as by themselves to be almost decisive. In favour of the Aryan hypothesis the strongest argument that can be adduced is the argument of mere geographical proximity, which has already[1] been shown to be the feeblest of all ethnological arguments. The representation on Etruscan vases of subjects taken from the cycle of Greek myth proves nothing, since such subjects do not appear in the earlier works of Etruscan art, and their introduction has universally been regarded as a sure token of late date. An examination of the Etruscan creed shows clearly its fundamental independence of the Hellenic inheritance of Aryan myth.

Still more formidable are the philological difficulties which stand in the way of either an Aryan or Semitic solution of the problem.

It may, I think, be affirmed that there is not a single Aryan or Semitic language which has not, in its turn, been brought forward as supplying the required key. But the most violent etymological artifices, employed with the utmost ingenuity and unscrupulousness for more than a hundred years, have conspicuously failed to connect the Etruscan

[1] See p. 68, *supra*.

language with any Aryan or Semitic form of speech. It is true that half-a-dozen Etruscan words have been successfully explained from the resources of the Armenian, the Albanian, and the Rhæto-Romansch languages. These languages are Aryan as regards their grammatical structure, but they have incorporated a large number of Turanian words. Therefore the acknowledged fact that the only Aryan languages which contain any Etruscan words are languages whose vocabulary is largely Turanian, must be held to be an argument which makes for, rather than against, the Turanian affinities of the Etruscans.

If then it be acknowledged, as it must be, that the Etruscans were neither Aryans nor Semites, we arrive, by a process of elimination, at the conclusion that they could only have been Turanians.

Directly we examine this, the only remaining possibility, we find that it satisfies every ethnologic test that can be devised. The characteristics of the Etruscan tombs, of the Etruscan customs, and of the Etruscan creed, alike confirm the conclusion that a positive result has at last been attained. This, then, is our first absolute conclusion. There can hardly be a doubt that the Etruscans belonged to the Turanian family.

If we attempt to proceed further, and to define more narrowly the place occupied by the Etruscans among the Turanian nations, the considerations by which we must be guided are mainly philologic rather than ethnographic. There is no branch of the Turanian stock with which the Etruscans have not much in common. On every side we meet with tokens of relationship. A connection, more or less defined, can be traced with the Sinitic, the Euskaric, the Dravidic, the Caucasic, the Egyptic, and the Altaic stems. To which of these can they be affiliated?

Though the Euskaric and Rasennic vocabularies possess many words in common, there are wide differences in grammatical structure. Moreover, the numerals, which form the easiest, and at the same time the most certain of ethnologic tests, are found to have diverged so widely as to furnish a decisive argument against any very close affinity of race.

The three Turanian stems which occupy the south-east of Asia, the Sinitic, the Dravidic, and the

Malayic, may also be summarily set aside. The linguistic resemblances are only of a faint and general character.

In favour of an Egyptic solution something more may be urged. It must be confessed that with one or two exceptions the numerals are wholly different, and the other linguistic agreements are scarcely closer than in the case of the Euskarians. But a far stronger argument may be drawn from the substantial identity of certain sepulchral usages, and from the striking resemblances which are shown by many of the artistic remains. We have in Etruria and in Egypt the same two types of sepulchre; the cave-tomb and the pyramid-tomb were employed by both nations. In either case we meet with the scarabæus, the sphinx, the lotus ornament, the converging door-jambs; and, especially in the earlier Etruscan designs, there is a singular agreement in the modes of drawing and colouring the human figure. Some of these resemblances are very striking; but they are superficial rather than real. They can all be explained on the hypothesis that the early Etruscan artists were trained in the Egyptian school of art, and that a considerable commercial intercourse existed between the two civilised Turanian races which bordered on the Mediterranean Sea.

In the case of the Egyptians the philological argument must be held to be conclusive. The Egyptian language is well known to us—the Etruscan bears to it no closer relation than that of a distant cousinship.

All the possible solutions of the problem are now exhausted except two. These are the Caucasic or Lesghic, and the Ugric or Altaic. I think it may be affirmed that the choice lies between these two. In many points these two stocks approach each other very closely, as closely perhaps as Welsh and Latin, or even as Sclavonic and Teutonic. Both of them approach the Etruscan more closely than is the case with any other languages. The Caucasic solution would best agree with that universal tradition of the ancient world which brought the Etruscans from Asia Minor, and would conform itself to any residuum of historic fact which may possibly be conserved in the Iliad and the Æneid. I do not affirm that a Caucasic solution of the Etruscan problem is impossible. The linguistic agreement is probably close enough to make it possible to interpret the Etruscan records with no other aid than that afforded by the various Lesghic and Abkhasic dialects.

I can only say that in every possible instance I have carefully compared the Etruscan vocabulary and the grammatical forms of the Etruscan language with those of the Ugric languages on the one hand, and of the Caucasic languages on the other, and that the result of this comparison is that the approximation to the Ugric forms is beyond question the more close. The relationship between the Etruscan and the Ugric languages seems to be a relationship in the direct line, analogous to that between Latin and French; while the resemblance between the Etruscan and the Caucasic languages is indirect, something like that which subsists between Latin and Albanian.

By a process of exhaustion or elimination we are therefore brought to the conclusion that the Ugric or Altaic branch of the Turanian stock is the only one to which the Etruscans can be directly affiliated.

Every indication points to this as the necessary

solution of the problem. The anthropological evidence is strongly in its favour. The mythological coincidences are, I think, impossible to explain on any other hypothesis. The modes of burial, the dedication of lares, the indications of primitive polyandria, the laws of inheritance, the form of government, supply arguments which separately are of no inconsiderable force, but whose cumulative weight becomes almost overwhelming.

Last in order, but first in importance, comes the linguistic evidence, to which so large a portion of this book has been devoted.

Jacob Grimm has laid down the philological axiom that there are three characteristic tokens of the primordial affinities of language—*drei Kennzeichen der Urverwandschaft*—the numerals, the personal pronouns, and certain forms of the verb substantive. These three, the surest tests of linguistic affinity which we possess, have been shown to agree in their indication that the Etruscan was a Ugric form of speech. Next in philological importance are the words which denote kinship. Fortunately there is no class of Etruscan words which is better known than these important words, and they are all, without exception, definitely and unmistakably Ugric in their character. The grammatical inflexions bear evidence no less decisive. The case endings in -*na*, the plural in -*ar*, the third person singular of the verb in -*e* and -*u*, the two participles in -*an* and -*as*, are all distinctively Ugric forms.

There are six characteristic notes which distinguish the Ugric or Altaic languages.[1] They are:

1. Agglutination instead of Inflexion.
2. The use of Post-positions instead of Prepositions.
3. The Harmonic Permutation of Vowels.
4. The personal declension of Nouns.
5. The large number of similarly sounding words.
6. The avoidance of double initial consonants.

It has been shown in the preceding pages that these six notes likewise characterise the Etruscan language.

This, then, is our second absolute conclusion. The

---

[1] See Castrén, *Ethnologische Vorlesungen*, pp. 17, 18.

Etruscans belonged to the Ugric or Altaic branch of the Turanian family.

To advance further than this, and definitively to connect the Etruscans with any one of the five divisions of the Ugric stock, is perhaps not altogether impossible, though every onward step in the enquiry is beset with increasing difficulty.

The cause of these difficulties is manifest. The Etruscan was not a literary language. The speech represented by the inscriptions was obviously in an unfixed condition. In the same tomb, nay, even in the same inscription, we find perplexing variations in the formation of the letters; and the powers of the letters are so uncertain that the same name is not uniformly spelt in the same way. We have, for instance, in the same inscription, such variations as Lart and Larth, or Arnt and Arnth. The punctuation is also most irregular; and the words are constantly undivided, or divided wrongly. There is no system in the abbreviations; vowels are thrown out or retained in a haphazard and unreasonable fashion. It is evident, in short, that the Etruscan language was the language of a people without literary culture.

As respects the Ugric languages the difficulties are as great or greater. We can only expect to find the scantiest remains of the primitive vocabulary among nomad tribes of hunting and fishing savages which have, for thirty centuries, been isolated in the wilds of Siberia. The language of races without a literature, and without much mutual intercourse, is exposed to an immense amount of phonetic corruption, and of linguistic decay and regeneration. It is only within comparatively recent times that any of the Ugric dialects have arrived at the dignity of a literary language, possessing a fixed grammar and vocabulary; and, unfortunately, the three languages which have made this step in linguistic progress have been largely corrupted by foreign influences. The Osmanli abounds with words and constructions derived from Arabic and Persian sources; the Magyar has absorbed numerous Sclavonic elements; and the Finnish languages of the Baltic have been extensively Teutonized. The Ugric student is therefore in perpetual danger of being misled by these foreign elements.

Under these circumstances the absence of any very close correspondence between the Etruscan and the Ugric languages would not be a legitimate cause for surprise. The marvel is, not that the resemblances are so faint, but that after so many centuries have elapsed it should remain so definite and unmistakable as in the preceding chapters it has been shown to be.

These considerations will make plain how formidable are the uncertainties and difficulties which beset any further prosecution of the inquiry as to the affinities of the Etruscans. The difficulties are indeed great, but not altogether insuperable.

Referring to the ethnological table given on p. 29, it will be seen that there are five great branches of the Ugric stem: the Finnic, the Samojedic, the Turkic, the Mongolic, and the Tungusic. To these I believe it will be found necessary to add a sixth, the Yenissic, which would occupy a place intermediate between the Samojedic and the Turkic stocks.

In the endeavour to ascertain to which of these stocks the Etruscan approached most closely, it is necessary to remember that the separation of the Etruscans from the Ugric stem took place, at the lowest estimate, some 3,000 years ago. At that period the differentiation of the five Ugric stocks must have been far less pronounced than it is now. At all events the linguistic divergencies between Finns and Samojeds on the one hand, and between Turks, Mongols, and Tunguses, on the other, could hardly have been very great.

It may, however, be assumed as certain that at the period when the Etruscan migration took place there were in existence two well-marked branches of the Ugric stem. These may be designated as the Western, or European branch, and the Eastern or Asiatic.

Now it is difficult to avoid the recognition of two distinct elements in the Etruscan mythology and the Etruscan language. One of these manifestly approximates to the European, the other to the Asiatic branch of the Ugric stock. We learn from Livy, himself a native of the Etruscan region, that in

Etruria the speech of the towns differed distinctly from that of the country districts. If, then, there were two races in Etruria, the inhabitants of the country villages must be deemed to belong to the aboriginal population, while the dwellers in the towns would represent the later conquerors.

Any aboriginal pre-Aryan population of Greece or Italy must almost of necessity have been Finnic. If not Finnic it could only have been Euskaric, and there is no indication that this was the case. I have therefore throughout this book ventured to call this aboriginal element in the population of Italy the FINNIC SUBSTRATUM, leaving in abeyance the question whether, as seems probable, it comprised the Pelasgi, or whether it consisted only of the Sabines, Marsi, Ligures, Siculi, and other hill tribes whose names bear witness to their distinctly Finnic origin. With regard to the Sabines the case seems to be tolerably clear. The Sabine words and names which have come down to us seem to be, with hardly an exception, of a Finnic type.[1] Thus NUMA, who in Roman myth stands as the representative of the Sabine element in

---

[1] See pp. 143, 147, 326, 330, 334, *supra*.

the population of Rome, bears a distinctively Finnic name, while the word SABINE is itself phonetically equivalent to SABME, the national appellation of the Lapps.

The Turanian words which have been incorporated into Latin, and those elements of Turanian mythology which became naturalised in the Roman system, seem to belong almost exclusively to the European branch of the Ugric stock, in other words to the Finnic Substratum of Italy.

But while fully recognising this aboriginal Turanian element, it is, on the other hand, equally impossible to ignore the existence in the Etruscan language and mythology of an element which is distinctively ASIATIC in its character, that is, Tataric, rather than Finnic. This element is discerned with the greatest clearness in the monumental, as distinguished from the literary remains of the Etruscan people. It appears conspicuously in the mythology of the mirrors, in the inscriptions on the lares, and in the mortuary records in the tombs. On the other hand this Asiatic element does not, as a rule, appear in those Turanian words and worships which were assimilated by the Romans. Now the epitaphs, the mirrors and the lares, have been exhumed almost exclusively from those vast cemeteries which surrounded the twelve great Etruscan cities; they have been obtained, with few exceptions, by rifling the tombs of wealthy and noble families, and are evidently the memorials of the upper class of ruling nobles who were the lineal descendants of the conquerors.[1]

Our conclusion therefore is this—the conquered class belonged to the European or Finnic branch of the Ugric stem; while the conquerors belonged to the Asiatic or Tataric branch.

These two elements would readily amalgamate. The differences of language would not probably be greater than those which in the tenth century distinguished the Old-English of Wessex from the Scandinavian speech of Lincoln.

If this reasoning be correct, there is only one question which remains to be answered. Is it possible approximately to determine the locality of the Asiatic region from which the invading Tatar

[1] See p. 17, *supra*.

horde set forth? The evidence, such as it is, is of two kinds. We have the witness of language, and the witness of legend.

There can, I think, be little doubt as to where we are to seek for the least altered vestiges of the speech of the invaders. The languages of the Yenissei, namely the Kot-Yenissei, and the so-called Yenissei-Ostiak, exhibit the most archaic forms of Ugric speech now in existence. These languages have, in the preceding pages, again and again furnished explanations of Etruscan words and forms which have either wholly disappeared from the other Ugric languages, or can only be recognised in altered guise by means of the laws which regulate phonetic change. Moreover these Yenisseian tribes retained, only fifty years ago, that ancient ethnic designation of ASSAN or ASSENA, which may probably be regarded as identical with the name RASENNA, which the Etruscan nation applied to themselves.

Foremost, then, in nearness to the speech of the Etruscan conquerors, as represented by the monuments of the tombs, I place the Yenisseian languages. Next in sequence come the dialects of the Ostiaks, the Woguls, the Yukahiri, the Tschuwashes, the Wotiaks, the Uigurs, the Magyars, and the Ugrian tribes which form the ethnic link between the Finnic and the Turkic stocks.

The philological considerations which connect the Etruscan race with the Siberian steppe—more especially with the region of Lake Baikal and the upper waters of the River Yenissei, are supplemented by certain traditions which are not without their weight.

The rule of the Etruscan augurs that the north-eastern quarter was more sacred than the rest, and that this was the region inhabited by the greatest of the Gods, may indicate a tradition that the home from which the nation migrated lay to the north-east.

But a much more definite tradition is indicated by an inscription on an Etruscan mirror which is now in the Museum of the Louvre at Paris. On this mirror is engraved a design representing the fabrication of the Trojan horse.[1] The horse is

[1] Fabretti, No. 2,492, and p. 1,343. The woodcut is taken from Gerhard, *Etruskische Spiegel*, plate ccxxxv.

labelled PEKSE, which seems to be only a transliteration of the Greek PEGASUS. The artificer who holds the uplifted hammer in his hand must, according to the legend, be Epeius. In the design he is labelled

THE TROJAN HORSE.

ETULE, which evidently means the 'Ætolian.' The progress of the work is superintended by SETHLANS (Vulcan). So far this mirror is remarkable only as showing the powerful influences of Greek legend on

EPILOGUE.

Etruscan art. But the mirror has another label, which can only be explained by means of the primæval traditions of the Rasenna as to their early home. On the further side of the horse, away from the spectator, is the door by which the Greeks were to enter. This door is represented as set open on its hinge, and it bears the unmistakable label HUINS. This word must denote the occupants of the interior of the horse, and has hitherto been dismissed by the commentators as an unintelligible equivalent of DANAIOI. It would appear therefore that in the Etruscan language the word HUINS meant ' warriors ' or ' enemies.' Now from the Chinese historians we learn that at a period not far remote from that at which the Rasenna are supposed to have made their appearance in Italy, there were two cognate but hostile hordes of nomads who roamed along the northern frontier of the Chinese empire. One of these hordes was the ASENA, who subsequently acquired the name of Turks, or, in Chinese orthography, *Tukiu*. The other horde was the fierce race of HUNS, or, as the name is spelt in Chinese, *Hiong-nu*. The ASENA migrated westward, and, as I believe, are to be identified with the RASENNA, who, about the same period, established themselves in Italy. It is not unreasonable to suppose that the name of the fierce and warlike horde of the HUNS, to whose hostility we may ascribe the westward migration of the Asena, should have lingered in the speech of the weaker nation as the designation of ' warriors ' or ' foes.' At all events, the mirror is an unimpeachable witness that some such signification was attached in the language of the Rasenna to the word HUINS.[1]

Another piece of evidence which is even more curious than the foregoing may also be derived from the Chinese annals. These ancient records have preserved the eponymic legend as to their origin which, three thousand years ago, was current among the Siberian ASENA or TURKS. Strange to say, this legend is in almost every detail identical with the eponymic legend which professed to account for the origin of the great city which the Etruscans founded on the Tiber.

[1] The final *s* in Huins is probably the Etruscan definite article. See p. 110, *supra*.

EPILOGUE.

According to the Chinese historians the forefathers of the Turkic race belonged to a Hunnic horde which was well nigh exterminated by its enemies. The sole survivor was a boy, ten years of age, who, with the loss of his hands and feet, succeeded in escaping the massacre which befel his kindred by crawling into a morass. There he was found by a she-wolf, who suckled and fostered him in a cave. Taking the name of his foster-mother, the boy was called TSENA, from the Mongolic *schino* or *tschino*, a 'wolf.' When he had grown up to manhood he took his foster-mother to wife. She bore to him ten cubs, who grew up to be mighty warriors. Having captured wives from a neighbouring tribe, they became fathers of the race of the Asena, whose banner was adorned with the heads of wolves. This horde afterwards became known as the Tukiu or Turks, a name which is accounted for by another legend, which it is needless to repeat.[1]

It is not difficult to discover the genesis of the

[1] See Castrén, *Ethnol. Vorles.* p. 60; Klaproth, *Asia Polyglotta*, p. 264.

legend. It has been already shown that the ancient Ugric word *sena* meant a 'man.'¹ The analogy of a host of ancient tribe-names leaves little doubt that the Asena simply called themselves 'the men.' This obvious etymology of the name having in lapse of time become obscured by linguistic changes, the word *schino*, a 'wolf,' was assumed to be the true source of the national appellation, and the myth came into existence as a means of accounting for the name of the nation which proudly called itself the 'Wolf-race,' and bore the wolves' heads as its *totem*.²

This singular myth of the eponymus of the Asena is identical with the myth of the eponymus of Rome. In its origin Rome was an Etruscan city, and the legend of the eponymic founder of the Rasennic nation would naturally be transferred, with the necessary change of name, to the eponymic

¹ See p. 339, *supra*.
² In like manner a host of Aryan legends have arisen from the similarity between the words λύκος, 'wolf,' and λευκός, 'white.' We may thus account, for example, for the mythologic legends of the wolf-destroyer which have clustered round the name of the Lycian Apollo, who, etymologically, is only the light-giving sun. See *Words and Places*, chap. xv.

founder of the Roman city. Nor is there any reason to suppose that the overthrow of the rule of the Etruscans by their Latin subjects would efface the memory of the ancient Rasennic legend.

The Siberian and the Italian myths correspond with singular closeness. In the Roman, as in the Siberian legend, we have the MORASS in which the boy is found, we have the SHE-WOLF who finds him, and also the CAVE in which she fosters him. In the Roman legend, after a certain period ACCA LARENTIA takes the place of the she-wolf as the foster-mother of Romulus, and she becomes the mother of twelve sons, of whom Romulus is represented either as the brother or the father. Now since Acca Larentia was also called LUPA, the 'she-wolf,' we may identify her with the she-wolf who is represented as the bride as well as the foster-mother of the boy in the Siberian legend. Moreover the Ugric character of the name Acca Larentia is indisputable; she is the 'mother of the mighty ones;'[1] the mythic ancestress of the twelve khans of the twelve tribes of the Rasenna.

[1] See p. 124, *supra*; Castrén, *Finn. Mythol.* pp. 30, 34, 142, 178.

THE MYTH OF ROMULUS.

But while the Roman version of the legend accounts for the tribal division of the Etruscans, it is worthy of note that in the Siberian version the wolf-wife of Tsena becomes the ancestress of the TEN chiefs of the ten tribes of the Asena. The division of the Ramnes, the tribe of Romulus, into ten curiæ or sub-tribes, seems to be a survival of this earlier tenfold tribal division.

The rape of the Sabine women is another element in the Roman myth which may be plainly traced in the Siberian legend, and this itself may be a tradition referring to the primitive Turanian custom of exogamy.

It is hardly necessary to point out that clustered round the Roman legend are certain features borrowed from the great cycle of Aryan myth, and which may be recognised in the myth of Pelias and Neleus, as well as in that of the Dioscuri.

There is perhaps no more remarkable instance of the persistency with which myths are handed down among illiterate races than the fact that the Tatar hordes of Siberia have preserved to this day, by oral tradition, recognisable vestiges of the eponymic myth which was committed to paper by the Chinese annalists three thousand years ago. In its modern form we find it coupled with a significant addition, which connects it still more unmistakably with the Roman myth. The Turkomans assert that the progenitors of their race were Szön Khan and Eszen Ili.[1] It is obvious that Szön and Eszen are only differentiated forms of the eponymus of the Asena, just as Romulus and Remus are two forms of the eponymus of Rome. But the noteworthy feature of this tradition is that in the Turkoman ILI we may recognise the name of ILIA, who, according to the Roman tradition, was the mother of Romulus.[2]

The progress of the Seljuk Turks from the Kirghiz steppe to the Bosphorus occupied four or five centuries. It is therefore possible that a considerable period of time may have been needed for the successive stages in the migration of the Rasenna from the Yenissei to the Arno. As to the route

[1] See p. 325, *supra*.
[2] The mythical genealogy of Romulus consists exclusively of Ugric names. Such are Æneas and Anchises, Ascanius and Iulus. The two last may be compared with Szön Khan and Eszen Ili. Ilium and Pergamus are also Turanian words.

THE RASENNA ON THE CASPIAN.

which was taken nothing very definite can be said. It would seem, however, that a halt of long duration took place in the neighbourhood of the Caspian, since in this region we find several concurrent indications of a powerful race bearing the names Rasenna or Turrhenna.

The name TURAN, by which the Persians knew the Ugric nomads on their frontier, is the source of the modern ethnic term TURANIAN. I have already ventured to suggest the possible identity of this name with that of the Italian TURRHENOI.[1]

In the land of Turan, not far from the head waters of the Tigris, was an important city, which bore the name of Rhesæna or Resen. Without laying any undue stress on mere similarity of names, which is so often misleading, it must be confessed that the correspondence of the names Rasenna and Rhesæna is too remarkable to be altogether overlooked. This city of Rhesæna has been identified with the city which Xenophon calls LARISSA, and it is worthy of note that the name Larissa is also

---

[1] See p. 23, *supra*.

applied by Dionysius to the Etruscan city of Vulturnum (Capua).

The ethnic names of marauding frontier tribes are not unfrequently used by neighbouring races to denote thief or robber. Thus, from the name of the Ugrians is derived the Tatar word *ugry*, a 'thief.'[1] Now in the language of the Kourds, an Aryan race inhabiting the mountainous frontier of Persia, and contiguous to the land of Turan, the word for 'robber' is *rakhsen*. Also in Persian a 'robber' is *razen*. These designations can at once be accounted for if we suppose that at some remote period a marauding nation which bore the name Rasenna pitched its tents in the Turkoman steppe.

It is possible that some distorted traditions of the Rasennic migration may be embedded in the two great Aryan epics. Underlying the Homeric poems we may recognise as the residuum of historic fact, that after a protracted struggle the Aryan race subjugated the Turanians of Western Asia. The Æneid brings a portion of the vanquished race to

[1] The English word *ogre* is from the same source. See *Words and Places*, chap. xvi.

Italy, and connects it with Romulus, the representative of the Etruscan element in the population of Rome. Virgil doubtless found current in his Etruscan birthplace some such tradition, which would harmonise with that concurrent belief of the ancient world which derived the Etruscans from Western Asia.

In the preceding pages I have endeavoured to keep one object constantly in view. By my success or failure in attaining the object, I desire that my labours should be judged. Leaving to others the systematic interpretation of the Etruscan records, I have endeavoured to make everything subordinate to the task of establishing the ethnic affinities of the Etruscan people. It would have been easy, following the example of my predecessors, to have propounded conjectural versions of all the longer inscriptions. No one could have proved that such renderings were wrong, or that they were right. I have taken the opposite course, confining myself as far as possible to the analysis of words and phrases as to the meaning of which there exists some independent indication. A test is thus furnished of the reasonableness of the interpretations proposed, and of the adequacy of the Ugric hypothesis which has been propounded.

Lastly, it will, I trust, be remembered that the argument is a cumulative argument. A single coincidence, or several, may be set aside as accidental; but when we find scores, nay hundreds, of minute correspondences in customs, creeds, vocabulary and grammar, such an explanation becomes no longer possible. A cumulative argument is a chain with many parallel links;—the strength of such a chain is not measured by the weakness of the weakest of the links, but by the united strength of all those that are without a flaw.

GLOSSARY of ETRUSCAN WORDS.

NOTE.—There were only eighteen letters in the Etruscan Alphabet. The letters B, D, O, and O, are wanting. To avoid confusion, I have adopted what may be called the established system of transliteration, and have represented the θ by TH, the φ by PH, the χ by CH, and the Digamma by v. I believe it would have been better to have represented θ by D, χ by X, φ by V, and the Digamma by F. The four Roman letters D, X, V, and F, would then represent the four Etruscan letters out of which they were developed.

AEL

A

AELCHE, *a quince-apple*, 265
ESAR, *Gods*, 144, 293, 316
AGALLETORA, *young son*, 233, 316
AGER, *field*, 333
AGYLLA, *old town*, 347
AISERAS, *the spirits, his Gods*, 293
AITAS, *Hades*, 105
AKIL, *ashes*, 305
·AL, *mother's child*, 110, 220–224, 229
·ALK, *grandchild*, 228
ALPAN, *a tribute*, 291
ALPNAS, *making-a-tribute*, 291, 293
ALPNU, *tribuit*, 281, 291, 293
·AN, *participial sign*, 286
ANKEN, *this*, 300
antar, antai, andas, 315
APE, *sister*, 227, 208
apluda, *chaff*, 315
·AR, *plural suffix*, 145

BUR

ABACOS, *a hawk*, 317
ARBITER, *an umpire*, 332
ARIMI, *apes*, 318
ARITIMI, *Artemis*, 228
ARKE, *husband*, 191, 245
ARNO, *a channel*, 345
ARSEVERSE, *averte ignem*, 309, 331
ARTH, *husband*, 268
·AS, *participial sign*, 287
ASA, *dame*, 221
AT, ATH, *horseman*, 267
ATAISON, *a vine*, 319
ATHLIK, *a councillor ?* 288
ATE, *day*, 329
ATRIUM, *court*, 329
AUSEL, *the dawn*, 143, 316
AVIL. *age*, 196, 205, 208
AVILS. *his age*, 170, 204
ACHRUM, *Acheron*, 309

B (See P)

BALTEUS, *sword-belt*, 319
BURBUS, *red-nosed*, 318

GLOSSARY.

C (See K; CH, see X)

CEBE, *town*, 318
CAMILLUS, *messenger*, 150, 316
CAPRA, *goat*, 316
CAPYS, *falcon*, 317
CARDO, *spear*, 334
CAREX, *sedge*, 336
CASSIS, *helmet*, 319
CELER, *quick*, 333
CLIENS, 230
CORIS, 333
CURIS, *spear*, 334

D (See TH)

DAMNUS, *horse*, 316
druna, *sovereignty*, 314

E

-E, sign of third person singular, 281
EKA, *here*, 148, 212, 213, 300, 309
EKASUTH, *Here is a tomb*, 212
EKN, *it, or here*, 294, 304
-ENNA, *person, homo*, 339, 341
EPURE, *Apollo*, 206, 297, 298
ERSKE, *she turned away*, 281, 309
ETH, EITH, *here*, 327
-ESA, *dame*, 236
ETERA, *young*, 191, 231–234

F (See V and PH)

FABA, *a bean*, 336
FALE, *mountains*, 320
FALANDUM, *the sky*, 320
FANUM, *a sacred place*, 326
FATISSA, *an excavation*, 325

G (See C and K)

gapus, *a chariot*, 314
GENIUS, *the guardian spirit*, 126
ginis, *a crane*, 315

H

HEL, *son*, 222, 232
HINTHIAL, *ghost*, 103–110, 129, 210, 260
hister, *an actor*, 315
HUINS, *Huns*, 76, 368
HUTH, *six*, 192, 165–167

I

IDULIS, *a sheep*, 328
IN, *me*, 283, 284
IPE, *sister*, 227
-ISA, *dame*, 220, 236, 242–244
-ISLA, *head-wife*, 245
ITUS, *Ides*, 328

K (See C)

-K-, sign of præterite, 281
KAHATI, *violent*, 260
KANA, *a statue*, 108, 276, 294
KANVATE, *this statue*, 294
KAPE, *birds?* 317
KEALCHL, *forty*, 176, 182
KECHA, *little*, 297, 298
KECHASE, *obiit*, 300
KEHEN, *this*, 217, 300
KEN, *this*, 300
KERINU, *fecit*, 148, 298, 306
KI, *two*, 167–169, 191
KIARTHI, *swarthy*, 261, 262
KIEMZATHRM, *eighty*, 176, 185–188
KIS, *second*, 176, 178
KIZI, *a corpse*, 301
KLAN, *son*, 228–234

GLOSSARY.

KLA

KLANIU, *stepson?* 239
KLENAR, *children*, 191, 234
KLENARASI, *his children*, 234
KLENSI, *his son*, 148, 297, 304
KULMU, *The Grave*, 93–100
KULPIANSI, *the casting*, 296
KURICHUNTHE, *made-for-ashes*, 301
KVER, *a fabric*, 306

L

·L·, sign of passive, 286
kona, *a cloak*, 314
lanista, *a gladiator*, 314
LAR, LARTH, *Lord*, 123
LARTHI, *lady*, 123
LARES, *The mighty ones*, 122, 124, 221
LARTH, 122
LASA, *fate*, 118
LAUKANE, *prince*, 321
LAUKANESA, *princess*, 321
LAUTN, *for sacred games*, 227
LEINE, *rival*, 199–202, 281
LEMURES, *ancestral spirits*, 120, 125
LENACHE, *fecit*, 281, 299
·LIK, *substantival suffix*, 302
LITUUS, *a crook*, 325
LUCUMO, *great prince*, 84, 321
LUDIO, *a dancer*, 323
LUDUS, *a dance*, 323
LUPU, *obiit*, 196, 202, 281
LUSNI, LOSNA, *flame, light*, 280

M

MANES, MANIA, MANTUS, *underground*, 120–121
MANIM, *I myself*, 191
MA, *land*, 121, 284
MA, *I?* 281
MACH, *one*, 160–162, 176

PU

MACHS, *first*, 179
MALAVISCH, *prosperity?* 106, 128
MANTISSA, *a makeweight*, 325
MEALCHL, *twenty*, 176, 182
MEALCHLSK, *twentieth*, 176, 182
MEAN, *The guardian of the dead*, 119
MENVRA, *Minerva, the dawn*, 135–138
MI, *I am*, 275, 277, 280, 284
MUNTHUCH, *eye-sight*, 128, 129
MUVALCHL, *thirty*, 176, 182

N

·N·, sign of the preterite, 281
·NA, *of*, 275, 277, 289, 309
NAK, *to*, 309
·NAL, *mother's child*, 280, 284
NANUS, *a wanderer*, 313
NAPER, *numeral adjunct*, 192
NATHUM, *The Pursuer*, 111, 113
NEPOS, *luxurious*, 325
NESL, *fore-wall?* 216
NETHUNS, *Neptune, the Sun God*, 138
NUSTRICH, *a dragon?* 113

P (See PH, F, and V)

PANXUS, *a shirt*, 320
PARCHIS, *ancestor?* 191
PENATES, *household spirits*, 127
POPULUS, *the poplar tree*, 319
PORCUS, *pig*, 336
PUANTRN, *to her children*, 285
PUIA, *a maiden*, 226, 284, 335
PUIAM, PUIUS, PU, 176, 226

GLOSSARY.

Q (See K)

QUIRITES, *the spearmen,* 314

R

RAS, a numeral adjunct, 193
RASENNA, *countrymen,* 29, 338–343
RIL, *years,* 191, 196, 199, 205–208

S

-S, *dame,* 236
-S, definite article, 110, 269
-S, ordinal suffix, 179
-S, possessive pronoun, 204, 226, 304
SA, *four,* 172–174
SAGITTA, *an arrow,* 335
SALTHN, *a deposit,* 289
SANSL, SELANSL, SL, *unworthy,* 293–298, 304, 307
SAS, *fourth,* 176, 179
SECH, SEK, SAK, *daughter,* 176, 234, 235, 247
SECURIS, *an axe,* 314
SEMNA, *priestess,* 307
SEMPH, *seventeen?* 185
SESPHALCHL, *ninety,* 176, 185
SESPH, *fourteen?* 183, 185
SETHLANS, *The Fire God,* 140, 214
SIANS, *guests,* 217
SNENATH, *health,* 128
SORACTE, *white mountain,* 345
SUBULO, *flute-player,* 324
SUTNA, *ashes,* 215
SURTES, SURTI, *widow,* 245–247
SUTHIL, *offered,* 286
SUTHINA, *an offering,* 215, 274, 275
SUTHI, *a tomb,* 146, 212, 214, 300, 305

T

TAGES, *lawgiver,* 327
TARQUIN, 79
TEBENNA, TEBENNA, *a man's garment,* 320
TEKE, *dedit,* 291, 303
TENE, numeral adjunct, 193
TENINE, *posuit,* 291, 281, 303
TEPH, *hills,* 330
TEZ, *suppliant?* 296
TIDER, *hill water,* 330
TINA, *Heaven,* 132, 133
TINSKVIL, *a bronze offering,* 290
TIVRS, *tenth,* 176, 184
TLENACHEIS, TLENACHES, *fabricated,* 290, 307
TOOL, *a garment,* 320
TRKE, see TURKE, 300
TRU'AL, *son of Troy,* 110
TRUTVEKIE, *augural?* 293
TUBA, *a trumpet,* 325
TULAR, *tombs,* 211
TULARU, *he buries,* 211
TURAN, *heaven (Venus),* 129, 134
TURKE, *posuit,* 281–283, 286
TURMUKAS, 106
TURSENNA, *men of the tents,* 23, 343, 344
TUSURTHI, *married,* 241, 245
TUTHINES, *his offering,* 299, 303

TH (See D)

THALNA, *Juno, day,* 142
THANA, *Diana,* 133
THAPIRI, *black,* 262
THAPNA, *a fabric,* 288
-THAS, a participial sign, 287
THEKE, *fecit,* 303, 305
THESAN, *Aurora, sunrise,* 139, 141

GLOSSARY.

THR

THRKE, *pomit*, 282, 309
THU, *five*, 160–169
THUI, *conditur*, 209–211
THUKER, *a gift*, 306
THUNESI, *nine*, 172
THUPHULTHASA, *fabricated*, 283–291
THURA, *a deposit*, 286
THURLAN, *deposited*, 296
THURMS, *Hermes*, 105, 149
THUSIUR, *inner chambers*, 305

U

-U, sign of third person singular, 203, 281
-UL, *father's child*, 229, 222, 229
ULSSI, *his wife*, 245, 191
USIL, *the sun*, 208, 139, 142

V (See PH and F)

VANI, *unlucky*, 263
VANTH, *Death*, 95, 100–103
VARI, *red*, 261
VEL, VOL, *town*, 346
VELE, *a club*, 266, 268

ZIP

VELCM, *a veil*, 321
VERSE, *fire*, 331
VETULONIA, *water town*, 347
VIPNA, *a mirror*, 120
VORSUS, 315

PH

PHANU, *a sacred place, fane*, 327
PHLERES, PHIERES, *a gift*, 278–280, 298, 309
PHLEZRU, *donavit*, 281
PHUPHLUNS, *the Sun God*, 141

CH or X

CHARU, *Charon*, 116, 117, 308
CHISELIKS, *his effigy*, 302

Z

ZAL, *three*, 191, 170–172
ZEK, *vowed ?* 307
ZILACH, *a sarcophagus*, 208, 209
ZILACHNUKE, ZILACHNTHAS, ZILATH, 209, 301
ZIPNA. See VIPNA

INDEX.

ACHILLEUS, 101-103
  Admetus and Alcestis, 303
Age, formulæ denoting, 195-200
Ager, 147, 333
Aggintimation, 5, 217
Agnomen, 234, 237
Agylla, 317
Alans, 76
Albanians, 20, 331
Allophyllians, 23
Altaic languages, 26
Amenti, 128
Anaïtis, 133
Ancestors, worship of, 48, 50
Animals, names of, 267, 316
Animism, 28, 279
Anthropology, 31
Anubis, 140
Aphusa family, 95
Arbiter, arbitrium, 232
Architecture, 33
Arimer, 186
Armenians, 351
Arno, river, 315
Art, Egyptian, 32; Etruscan, 32, 63
Article, 110, 137, 204, 362
Aryan races, 31, 66, 68; colonisation, 69; deities, 130, 135, 141, 146, 148; legends, 138, 271, 376
Asens, 365, 368-371
Assan, 340
Athena, 135
Atrium, 329
Attila, 75
Augury, 53
Avars, 74

BABER, 73
  Belham, Sir W., 3
Bilingual Inscriptions, 156, 201, 230, 236, 249-269
Birds, names of, 317
Black, 262

Boy, 222, 223
Bronzes, 289-291
Bulgars, 76
Burial, 34-52, 92-100, 191-217, 270, 326

CAIUS and Caia, 208
  Camel, 151
Capcis, 317
Camillus, 160, 318
Candelabrum of Cortona, 289
Capra, 316
Capua, 16, 275
Capys, 317
Cave tombs, 11, 42, 46, 50, 52
Celer, 323
Ceres, 147
Charon, 116
Cheekbones, 62
Children, 191, 220-235, 260, 291, 292
Chronology, 14
Cities, names of, 316
Cliens, 230
Clytemnestra, 111
Cognomen, 258
Colours, 261-263
Crawford, Lord, 3, 189, 286
Cumanians, 74

DARIUS, 79
  Daughter, 276, 224
Dawn, the, 132-137
Death, 102
Dedications, 262
Deities, Aryan, 130; Etruscan, 66-154, 328; Semitic, 131, 135
Diana, 133
Dice of Toscanella, 137
Digits, 160-174
Dionysius, 12, 16, 22
Djermes, 124
Donaldson, Dr., 2, 152

INDEX.

EGY

EGYPTIAN art, 52; tombs, 89; mythology, 50, 97, 122, 135, 140, 253
Eighty, 167
Eldest son, 231
Ellis, Mr., 3, 216
Æneid, 8, 178
Epitaphs, 176, 191-262
Esquimaux, 65
Ethnologic methods, 31
Etruscans, their name, 11, 33; affinities, 16, 349; country, 16; migrations, 17, 18, 23, 374; art, 62, 85, 253; tombs, 46-49, 92, 121; customs, 12, 11, 52; mythology, 86-131; language, 3, 18, 352, 365
Endiarics, 19, 78, 131
Exogamy, 55-59

FANUM, 126
 Feronia, 140
Finger, 160, 161
Finns, 27, 71; mythology of, 122, 124, 139, 147, 217; settlements of, in Italy, 12, 20, 23, 77, 362
Fire gods, 140
Five, 162-165
Forty, 182, 183
Four, 172-174

GALLERY graves, 45
 Garments, 220
Genealogical tables, 210, 213
Genius, 126
Gerund, 203
Ghosts, 109
Ghouls, 92
Gifts to the dead, 278-280
Girl, 227
Government, Etruscan, 36
Grammar, Etruscan, 3, 248, 285; agglutination, 217, 257; declension, 197, 204, 211, 216, 275, 294, 309; gerund, 203; participle, 272, 289, 297; passive, 256; plural, 111, 211, 224, 295; pronouns, 234, 301; ordinal suffix, 178, 179; suffix of nui, 229, 231, 275; inn, 226, 242, 244; verb, 241, 271, 274; 309, 321; verb substantive, 275; vocabularies, 312
Grondsbild, 228
Griffons, 22

LYD

HAIR, colour of, 21, 282
 Hand, 161, 162
Heavenly powers, 133
Helen, 149
Herini family, 240
Hermes, 149
Herodotus, 12, 43
Hills, names of, 329, 330, 345
Horlic, 213
Horse, 267
Hungarians, 28, 71, 77, 82
Huns, 70, 73, 80, 368
Husband, 215, 293
Hut urns, 42, 344

ILIUM, 317
 Inscriptions, character of, 248; bilingual, 249, 268; on vases, 11, 303; on mirrors, 189, 142, 282, 293, 306; in tombs, 18, 143, 176, 190-217, 237, 261, 294, 327; on statues, 227, 273, 276, 307
Intensitives, 282
Isis, 61, 97
Isolated races, 68, 71

JAPAN, 139
 Jinns, 104, 126
Juno, 125, 142
Jannnes, 127

KALEVALA, 6, 8, 21, 98, 97, 98, 111, 124, 139, 141
Kalma, 97
Kalmuks, 68
Kekri, 147
Kettle words, 144, 213
Khan, 322
Kinship, words denoting, 213-246
Kirghiz Tatars, 61, 70

LANDMARKS, 285
 Lares, 123; inscriptions on, 271-273, 277, 279, 286-288, 293-307
Larva, 122
Latin, Turanian words in, 120-127, 130, 160, 230, 268, 312-336, 362
Lightning, 132, 148, 151
Litmus, 325
Livy, 16, 20-21
Louies, 123
Lycians, 11, 63, 69; tombs of, 38
Lydians, 12, 11, 56; tombs of, 56

INDEX. 367

MAAHISET, 121, 129
   Mordwas. 111
Magi, 79
Magyars, 26, 76, 82
Manala, 122
Mandschus, 71
Manducus, 121
Marcus, 267
Marli, 19
Marriage customs, 65
Maral, 117
Maternal descent, 57-59
Matronymics, 58, 59, 221, 224, 235, 236
Medes, 79
Menander, 90
Mental type of Etruscans, 83
Mercury, 119
Metal work, 280-91
Migrations of Ugric nations, 72, 73
Minerva, 135
Minos, 122
Mirrors, 105, 139, 142, 282, 305
Mongols, 61, 62, 70, 73
Mother, 230-37
Mordstan, 164
Mundas, 121
Musical instruments, 321
Mythology, 6, 8, 86-151, 317, 325

NAMES, 237-319
   Natsgmi, 113
Nature worship, 89, 90-92
Necrology, 93
Neptune, 138
Niebuhr, 6, 16, 105, 200
Nogai Tatars, 74
Nomenclature, Roman system of, 253
Novensiles, 142
Numa, 8, 362
Names, 136
Numeral adjuncts, 193
Numerals, 8, 158-192

ODYSSEUS, 105
   Offerings in tombs, 121, 123, 262-311
One, 161
Orator, statue of, 302
Orcus, 100
Ordinal numbers, 179
Orestes. 111
Osmanli Turks, 18, 74, 82, 83, 267

Othman, 207
Otho, 208

PARTICIPLE, 279, 286-87
   Passive, 230, 291
Patroklos, 101-103
Patronymics, 222, 236, 267
Penates, 127
Pembedlos, 105
Perkunas, 117
Petruni family, 211, 213
Philology, comparative, 31
Physical type, 80
Picts, 32, 83, 230
Plants, 319
Plural, 145, 224, 225
Polyandria, 50, 59
Pomerium, 265
Pompeys, tomb of, 327
Populus, 319
Porsenna, 311
Praenomen, 251-266
Priesthood, Etruscan, 52
Procoens, 284, 301
Pyramids, 81

QUINCTIUS, 265
   Quirites, 331

RADIX of numeration, 177-181
   Rasenna, 11, 14, 16, 21, 42, 80, 81, 238, 241, 243, 350, 371
Red, 261
Religion of Turanians, 89, 91, 132
Rhaetians, 21
Roman history, 7, 15, 372
Roman nomenclature, 253
Romulus, 8, 272, 374
Rosetta Stone, 156

SABINES, 19, 143, 147, 326, 330, 331, 362, 361, 372
   Sagitta, 325
Samojeds, 62, 71
Sampo, 158
Saraiska, 124
Sammeyas, 149
Schlefner, 22
Serarius, 332
Semitic religion, 131, 135
Sethlans, 140
Sister, 227
Six, 165-167
Shadows, 100
Shah-nameh, 23

Shamans, 53. 146. 307
Sky gods, 131, 153
Soracte, 345
Sorcery, 53, 79
Soul, journey of, 115
Spectra, 106–108
Statues, 227, 278
Stanb, Dr., 21
Stone circles, 43 ; weapons, 334, 335
Stroppus, 315
Subulo, 321
Summanus, 146
Summary of numerals, 189
Summer, 206
Sun gods, 131, 139, 143, 153, 151
Suomi, 27

TABLE of Turanian family, 29
    Tarquin, 79, 323
Tatars, 73, 344
Teen, 188
Temple tombs, 49, 226
Ten, 184
Tent life, 14, 343–348
Three, 170–172
Thunder gods, 131, 143, 146, 154
Thuschi, 33
Tiber, 330, 345
Tibia, 325
Tifanati, 135
Time, division of, 326
Timur, 73
Tiresias, 108
Toga, 320
Tombs, antechamber of, 326 ; builders of, 25–27 ; Etruscan, 17, 40–52, 94 ; inscriptions in, 176–307 ; of the Herini, 238 ; of the Kvenle, 237 ; of the Lekse, 237 ; of the Petruni, 241 ; offerings in, 270. See *Burial*.
Tossanella, dice of, 157
Traditions as to the origin of the Etruscans, 9, 12, 310, 366–376
Tribal government, 79, 81
Tribe names, 147, 337–344
Tribute, 292
Trojan horse, 365

Tschengis Khan, 73
Tschermiss, 62
Tschud, 27
Tuba, 325
Tumuli, 41 46, 50, 51
Turanian, 34, 63, 344 ; definition of word, 25, 26, 375 ; table of family, 29 ; religion, 48, 53, 131, 152
Turks, 17, 60, 74, 82, 340, 344, 370
Turkish, Turkic, definition of words, 27
Tyrrhenoi, 11, 23, 375
Turannes and Turhenna, 23, 338, 344
Tuscans, 67
Two, 167–169
Two-headed girl, 296
Tyrrhenians, 24
Tzar, 124

UGRIC, meaning of word, 26 ; languages, 4, 29, 77, 357–355

VARUNA, 146
    Vela, 288
Velum, 321
Venus, 129, 134
Verbs, 281, 291, 294
Vesta, 146
Vetulonia, 347
Vigesimal system, 161, 163
Votive forms, 289

WAINAMOINEN, 135
    Weapons, 334
Widow, 216
Wife, 236, 237, 345
Winter, 207
Woguls, 62, 71, 77
Wolf-race, 371
Women, position of, 60

XANTHUS, 12, 13

YAKUTS, 70
    Yeniseian languages, 325, 365
Younger son, 232
Yourt, 42, 43, 343

www.ingramcontent.com/pod-product-compliance
Lightning Source LLC
Chambersburg PA
CBHW031412230426
43668CB00007B/286